Interreligious Reading After Vatican II: Comparative Theology and Receptive Ecumenism

Directions in Modern Theology Book Series

Born out of the journal *Modern Theology*, the Directions in Modern Theology book series provides issues focused on important theological topics and texts in current debate within that discipline, whilst looking at broader contemporary topics from a theological perspective. It analyses notions and thinkers, as well as examining a wide spectrum of 'modern' theological eras: from late Medieval through to the Enlightenment and up until the present 'postmodern' movements. Attracting distinguished theologians from a worldwide base, the book series develops what is a unique forum for international debate on theological concerns.

Titles in the series include:

Heaven on Earth? Theological Interpretation in Ecumenical Dialogue
Edited by Hans Boersma and Matthew Levering

Faith, Rationality and the Passions
Edited by Sarah Coakley

Re-thinking Dionysius the Areopagite
Edited by Sarah Coakley and Charles M. Stang

The Promise of Scriptural Reasoning
Edited by David Ford and C. C. Pecknold

Aquinas in Dialogue: Thomas for the Twenty-First Century
Edited by Jim Fodor and Frederick Christian Bauerschmidt

Re-thinking Gregory of Nyssa
Edited by Sarah Coakley

Theology and Eschatology at the Turn of the Millennium
Edited by L. Gregory Jones and James Buckley

Catholicism and Catholicity: Eucharistic Communities in Historical and Contemporary Perspectives
Edited by Sarah Beckwith, L. Gregory Jones and James J. Buckley

Theology and Scriptural Imagination: Directions in Modern Theology
Edited by L. Gregory Jones and James Buckley

Spirituality and Social Embodiment
Edited by L. Gregory Jones and James Buckley

Interreligious Reading After Vatican II: Scriptural Reasoning, Comparative Theology and Receptive Ecumenism

Edited by
David F. Ford and Frances Clemson

WILEY Blackwell

Published as Volume 29, Issue 4 of *Modern Theology*
© 2013 John Wiley & Sons Ltd

Blackwell Publishing was acquired by John Wiley & Sons in February 2007. Blackwell's publishing program has been merged with Wiley's global Scientific, Technical, and Medical business to form Wiley-Blackwell.

Registered Office
John Wiley & Sons Ltd, The Atrium, Southern Gate, Chichester, West Sussex, PO19 8SQ, UK

Editorial Offices
350 Main Street, Malden, MA 02148-5020, USA
9600 Garsington Road, Oxford, OX4 2DQ, UK
The Atrium, Southern Gate, Chichester, West Sussex, PO19 8SQ, UK

For details of our global editorial offices, for customer services, and for information about how to apply for permission to reuse the copyright material in this book please see our website at www.wiley.com/wiley-blackwell.

The rights of David F. Ford and Frances Clemson to be identified as the author(s) of this work / of the editorial material in this work has been asserted in accordance with the UK Copyright, Designs and Patents Act 1988.

Library of Congress Cataloging-in-Publication Data has been applied for.

ISBN 9781118716236
ISSN 0266 7177 (Print)
ISSN 1468 0025 (Online)

A catalogue record for this book is available from the British Library.

Cover design by Richard Boxall Design Associates.

Set in 10 on 12 pt Palantino by Toppan Best-set Premedia Limited

Printed in Singapore.

1   2013

Modern Theology

Volume 29 No. 4   October 2013

CONTENTS

Special issue
Interreligious Reading After Vatican II: Scriptural Reasoning,
Comparative Theology and Receptive Ecumenism
Guest Editors: David F. Ford and Frances Clemson

Articles

Unless otherwise indicated references to the documents of the Second
Vatican Council are from Norman P. Tanner, SJ (ed), *Decrees of the
Ecumenical Councils*, vol. II: *Trent to Vatican II* (London: Sheed & Ward
and Georgetown, WA: Georgetown University Press, 1990).

Abbreviations:

AG   *Ad Gentes*

DV   *Dei Verbum*

LG   *Lumen Gentium*

NA   *Nostra Aetate*

UR   *Unitatis Redintegratio*

Modern Theology 29:4 October 2013
ISSN 0266-7177 (Print)
ISSN 1468-0025 (Online)

DOI: 10.1111/moth.12058

INTRODUCTION—
INTERRELIGIOUS READING
AFTER VATICAN II:
SCRIPTURAL REASONING,
COMPARATIVE THEOLOGY AND
RECEPTIVE ECUMENISM

DAVID F. FORD

In the religious history of the twentieth century, ecumenical engagement among Christian churches, encounters of the world's religions with each other, and the Second Vatican Council of the Roman Catholic Church must each be considered of major importance. The essays which follow explore aspects of all three, approaching them through what Paul Murray calls "families of receptive theological learning". A key element in Vatican II itself was, as several essays make clear, *ressourcement* through rich theological thinking and scholarship, and its discussions and documents were shaped by appreciative reception of much that came from beyond its own tradition.

Scriptural Reasoning has been centred in groups studying Jewish, Christian and Muslim scriptures together, practising mutual hospitality around these texts. Since it began in the mid-nineteen-nineties Catholics have taken part in it alongside other Christians, so it has been a place of intra-Christian as well as inter-faith encounter, and it has also been influenced by Vatican II. Among the essays below, those by myself and Mike Higton include accounts that might help in introducing Scriptural Reasoning to those not familiar with it.

David F. Ford
Faculty of Divinity, University of Cambridge, West Road, Cambridge, CB3 9BS, UK
Email: dff1000@cam.ac.uk

Comparative Theology is a scholarly and theological practice in which individual thinkers engage in the study of Christian texts alongside those of another religious tradition, to date mainly Hinduism. Those new to it might begin with the opening pages of Francis Clooney's response to the essays in which, as the pioneer of Comparative Theology, he vividly gives an insider description of what it is about.

Receptive Ecumenism is also represented by its founder, Paul Murray, who gives perhaps the most succinct and comprehensive account of it so far in his essay. It is a form of Christian ecumenical engagement that emphasizes how different churches can learn from each other and so improve their own Christian understanding and practice. Murray's essay sketches a systematic theological rationale for Receptive Ecumenism and reflects on the inter-twined roots and mutual significance of Receptive Ecumenism, Comparative Theology and Scriptural Reasoning.

The essays are followed by responses from Francis Clooney (Christian), Maria Dakake (Muslim) and Peter Ochs (Jewish). Clooney offers a nuanced account of each essay, both summarizing and interrelating them, with a self-critical concern for the integrity and future of the practice he founded. Dakake comments on each from a Muslim perspective and as a participant in Scriptural Reasoning. Drawing on the Qur'anic image of a good word that is like a good tree, she reflects on the significance of tradition and commentary as being like the trunk of a tree, and responds to a range of issues raised by the essays. Ochs, co-founder both of Textual Reasoning (discussed in my essay) and of Scriptural Reasoning, does three things. First, he describes Scriptural Reasoning in relation to its institutional and historical settings, linking these to its "one and many" patterns. Second, he imaginatively extrapolates from what has been happening in many contexts in order to conceive a set of possibilities for Scriptural Reasoning in the future, both formational and reparative—a daring exercise that might serve as a framework for the creative development of Scriptural Reasoning theory and practice. This culminates in the image of "hearth-to-hearth", where gathering round the fire of scripture represents both homely warmth and incendiary danger. Third, he draws out elements in each of the essays that resonate with his vision.

Conceptualities

The concluding responses might appropriately first be read alongside this introduction, in order to gather a set of categories, issues and judgements that can helpfully be borne in mind and tested while reading the other contributions, and then reread in conclusion.

Indeed, in reading both the essays and the responses I suspect that one of the things readers might find particularly valuable is the conceptual tools that are given for thinking about the topics discussed. These are too numerous to mention, but time and again I have been struck by the categories, terms and frameworks (sometimes inextricable from particular theological substance, as in Michael Barnes' essay, sometimes nearer to logical generality, as in Nicholas Adams') which we are offered, and with which it is fruitful to think further, whatever our response to the positions they help to formulate here. This is most obviously the case with the essays of Barnes, Anna Bonta Moreland, Murray, Higton and Adams, but each of the others also makes a contribution. In the case of my own essay, the effect is sought by the retrieval of five seminal, and to some degree paradigmatic, events in the history of Scriptural Reasoning in combination with Vatican II's concepts of *ressourcement, aggiornamento* and *conversazione* and the "five deepenings" associated with Scriptural Reasoning.

Theology

While the essays are all thoroughly theological, there are several points at which their theological substance becomes clearest.

The most comprehensive theological framework is proposed by Murray in twenty-seven bullet points summarizing Receptive Ecumenism. I see this as a distilled wisdom in the spirit of Vatican II, uniting *ressourcement, aggiornamento* and *conversazione*. It exemplifies the principle of multiple deepenings, because this in-depth theology of Catholic Christian ecumenism could also be a guide and inspiration for analogous in-depth theologies both of ecumenism in other Christian traditions and of Christian inter-faith theology. Each of the bullet points is worth thinking through from those standpoints too—together they would make a well-rounded family of theologies.

Barnes goes to the theological heart of Vatican II through *Dei Verbum* and other Council documents. This is the "dialogue of salvation" that God has with all humankind and that "seeks always the broadest bounds of God's providential action in the world".[1] This capacious vision of the Church participating in God's universal purposes is the horizon within which there is the double movement of *ressourcement* and "the generosity of a never-ending *colloquium* with the wider world".[2] This is a learning church, and

> wherever the church finds itself caught up in God's dialogue of love, interrogating and being interrogated by the Word, whether in the liturgy itself or in the engagements with the wider world which prayer inspires, the Holy Spirit is present, leading the church into all the truth.[3]

Barnes' theology of the Spirit and of "seeds of the Word" means that "interreligious dialogue is not a matter of looking for some analogous 'message' in

---

[1] Barnes, p. 24.
[2] *Ibid.*, p. 31.
[3] *Ibid.*, p. 28.

other places but of working with other communities in order to *learn together* something of the gracious and surprising ways of the Divine Other."[4] Barnes' own monograph on interreligious learning is a most perceptive Christian exploration of the theology and practice of that sort of dialogue which combines deep rooting in one tradition with radical openness towards others.[5] Perhaps the greatest threat to this generous vision and associated practices came, as Tracy Sayuki Tiemeier describes, with the promulgation of *Dominus Iesus* in 2000 (see also the discussion of it in my essay).

Kevin Hughes takes us deeper into the historical roots and theological implications of Barnes' capacious vision. His own participation in the three-year project at the Center of Theological Inquiry at Princeton (described in my essay) has contributed to his account of the rich connections between Scriptural Reasoning and Vatican II. In particular the recovery of the multiple senses of scripture by Daniélou, de Lubac and others enables a greater appreciation of rabbinic interpretation that has been influential in Textual Reasoning and Scriptural Reasoning:

Like the Christian discourse of the "fourfold sense" . . . rabbinic discourse presumes that the scriptural word is semantically saturated, and so multiple senses within the broader context of a tradition of inquiry and argument do not call the authority of the scriptural word into question. On the contrary, this tradition supports and affirms the rich resources of revelation . . .[6]

Recovery of "the Christian interpretive tradition *in the presence of Abrahamic fellowship* offers the discipline of encounter with others, so that it becomes more than a recovery, becoming instead a re-invigoration and re-imagination of the deep wisdom of our own tradition".[7] It also enables self-criticism on such matters as supersessionism.

David Dault sees Scriptural Reasoning on its Christian side as Protestant in its origins, perhaps more Protestant than it was in fact, given both Catholic and especially Anglican participation.[8] But his main point is in line with the ethos of Scriptural Reasoning regarding multiple deepenings: Catholic reasoning (including interpretation of scripture) cannot be seen as simply "Christian", but is distinctive in several ways, above all in the roles of tradition and the Magisterium of the church; therefore it needs to be cultivated

---

[4] *Ibid.*, p. 30.
[5] Michael Barnes SJ, *Interreligious Learning: Dialogue, Spirituality and the Christian Imagination* (Cambridge: Cambridge University Press, 2012).
[6] Hughes, p. 43.
[7] *Ibid.*, p. 55.
[8] In what might be taken as a companion to the present volume, the Anglican dimension of Scriptural Reasoning is dealt with by several contributors in a special issue of the *Journal of Anglican Studies* (forthcoming, November 2013).

in depth for it to enrich both the church and inter-faith engagement in worthwhile ways. He gives illuminating examples from his own Memphis diocese of what Catholic reasoning looks like in local practice.

Higton's essay parallels Murray's in its systematic scope: he is concerned with the roles doctrine plays in Christianity, and how these relate to both Comparative Theology and Scriptural Reasoning. His key question about the latter is one that has often bothered me during almost twenty years practising Scriptural Reasoning: "is there a way in which doctrinal questions can appropriately be addressed in Scriptural Reasoning, where both the agenda and the modes of conversation by which it is pursued are subject to constant negotiation between participants from multiple traditions?"[9] His answer is that "for Christian readers, Scriptural Reasoning is an inter-faith discipline within a Christian discipline of devout reading".[10] This reading (conceived along the lines developed by Paul Griffiths) is at the heart of Christian doctrine. Further:

> If Christian doctrine is construed in this way, the question of its relation to Scriptural Reasoning can be transformed. Instead of asking whether it is possible, without inhibiting the flow of Scriptural Reasoning practice, to bring Christian doctrine into it, one can ask whether it is possible for the practice of Scriptural Reasoning to become, for its Christian participants, part of their discipline of Christian doctrinal reading.[11]

As I reflect on my own theological work, that accurately describes the main role Scriptural Reasoning has played. It also poses challenges both to Christian traditions and to Jewish and Muslim traditions. Higton's own collaborative work with the Quaker theologian Rachel Muers is one of the most constructive and provocative responses to his own challenges.[12]

Moreland actually does what many of the other contributors talk about, by tackling a specific instance of inter-faith engagement: Christian theology trying to make sense of the prophethood of Muhammad. She approaches it through analogical thinking, and Clooney notes that Moreland's argument "invites us into a comparative theological experiment (by studying Qur'anic texts on prophet and prophecy)" and that it opens up

> the prospect of a case for Scriptural Reasoning (by reading the Christian texts Moreland cites with Jewish and Muslim counterparts, along with prophetic texts of their choosing), and even Receptive Ecumenism (by

---

[9] Higton, p. 121.
[10] *Ibid.*, p. 122.
[11] *Ibid.*, p. 130.
[12] Mike Higton and Rachel Muers, *The Text in Play: Experiments in Reading Scripture* (Eugene, OR: Cascade, 2012).

then bringing fresh insights back to Christian theological conversations on prophecy, in and beyond and after Biblical sources).[13]

Overall, Moreland does what Adams recommends, dealing with a binary opposition in a triadic way that can lead into new and fruitful investigations. This "shaping of thought" allows for what Adams calls "long-term disagreement".[14] He notes that Scriptural Reasoning and Receptive Ecumenism are not primarily about aiming at agreement: "They are practices which make deep reasonings public, and which foster understanding and collegiality in the face of enduring differences."[15] His three "grades" of long-term disagreement—claims, conflicts and obscurities—helpfully differentiate between levels of theological competence. The third is especially promising.

> Each tradition also has its blind spots: those areas of expression where language is stretched to breaking point, zones of experimentation, paradox and wilful self-contradiction. These are found in the mystical traditions, in negative theology, in the more speculative regions of philosophy, in the areas of theology that, in those traditions who practise or have practised censorship, are considered too dangerous for popular teaching. Areas of obscurity show up where experience contradicts the deep grammars, and where mutating social forms stimulate descriptions that extend beyond the reach of settled categories . . . Theological debates over political forms, sexual practices, and medical interventions are often marked by conflicts between deep grammars and new words, and by categories being stretched and shrunk as they are pressed into unfamiliar use. The third grade of engagement is reached when a member of one tradition is able to identify and rehearse the obscurities that mark another tradition.[16]

This, as he notes, is as yet "a largely untapped potential" of Scriptural Reasoning and Receptive Ecumenism.[17] Yet Comparative Theology is leading the way, as seen in what Clooney describes himself attempting in his forthcoming book.

Collegiality and Friendship

I recognize well Tracy Sayuki Tiemeier's description of

> the back and forth flow of the group. Dialogue, even when "successful" (whatever that means), is often tedious, boring, circuitous, meandering,

---

[13] Clooney, p. 186.
[14] Adams, p. 169.
[15] *Ibid.*, p. 169.
[16] *Ibid.*, p. 170.
[17] *Ibid.*, p. 188.

and frustrating. Actual conversations cannot be scripted or clearly structured. The ebb and flow of a dialogue moves forward, backward, sideways, and every which way in between. Particularly for those persons
looking to "accomplish something", dialogue is bound to be an exercise
in madness.[18]

Though she does not directly connect this with what she says about friendship, I do see the two going together. "I need friends to be myself fully;
however, true friends are ends in and of themselves, to be treated so."[19] She
sees such friendship as a safeguard against the wrong use of power in
inter-faith engagement, which certainly rings true; but friendship for its own
sake could also be what helps people put up with the messiness, frustration
and "madness" of much dialogue.

The instrumentalizing of dialogue is one of the many threats to its integrity.
Yet dialogue does have its uses, and it would be foolish to reject them. From
my experience, there needs to be a core commitment to engagement with
each other "*l'shma*", as Jews say—"for the sake of the Name", for its own
sake, for God's sake. Different traditions, secular as well as religious, have
different analogous ways of conceiving this fundamental motive, which safeguards the purity of engagement and resists attempts to use it for inappropriate ends. In Scriptural Reasoning there is often a distinction between what
is called "formational" study, done for its own sake, or for God's sake, and
more applied, "reparative" study, in which the aim is to discern truth and
practice in such matters as debt, or gender, or violence. Formational study is
as much about the shaping of the group as of the individuals in it, and there
is a striking theme through many of the essays about the vital importance of
those interpersonal relationships. Ochs' response takes up the relation of the
l'shma to the reparative, and structures his vision of the potential of Scriptural
Reasoning around their distinction and relation.

Barnes quotes Chenu on how through the prayerful reading of texts one
can receive "a personal gift which makes it possible for a look of trust to meet
friendship and communion".[20] Dault gives examples of trust and understanding being built through text study in Memphis. Higton suggests how Christian doctrine could be enriched by theologians reading together in ways that
allow for richer devotion and sociality. The developments of Scriptural Reasoning described in my essay have had at their heart a set of overlapping
friendships and interwoven "communities of heart and mind". For all their
differences, the three practices that are the subject of these essays have each
generated and been sustained by friendships and forms of lively collegiality.
These in turn have often been supported by organizations and institutions,

---

[18] Tiemeier, p. 149.
[19] *Ibid.*, p. 151, citing Tracy Sayuki Tiemeier, "Comparative Theology and the Dialogue of
Life", *The Japan Mission Journal*, 65:2 (2011), p. 129.
[20] Barnes, p. 30.

whether religious, academic, social or civic. Besides myself, Barnes, Dault, Murray, Higton, Clooney and Ochs all comment on the importance of institutional location.

How to Engage Wisely?

Vatican II, as several essays say, opened up a great many possibilities for fresh engagement between churches and religions; understandably, it had less to say about how to go about realizing them. Comparative Theology, Receptive Ecumenism and Scriptural Reasoning can be seen as three answers to the question: How to engage wisely? The essays offer a range of answers to that "How?", mostly aimed at describing, critiquing and improving the three practices. There are the conceptual suggestions regarding shapes and habits of thinking—triadic (Adams), analogical (Moreland), alertness to multiple senses of scripture (Hughes), and more. There is the insistence on the importance of collegiality and friendship. There are practical suggestions, such as the commendation of *lectio divina* by myself and others, Dakake's description of her own initiative "Contemplating the Qur'an", Tiemeier's remarks about the choice of texts to be read together, and Murray's fundamental question to both Comparative Theology and Scriptural Reasoning as to how they might relate to Receptive Ecumenism's concern, beyond texts, with "embodied practices and structures"[21]. All converge in various ways on the need for depth. Clearly each of these young practices has huge scope for development, and this is exemplified especially in the visions of the founders, Murray, Clooney, Ochs and myself.

There is also the wisdom of combining two of them, or even all three. Murray offers an account of their mutual compatibility and complementarity, and Moreland demonstrates this. Barnes' account of Vatican II theology has room for all three. The new Institute for Comparative Scripture and Interreligious Dialogue in Beijing (see my article) has already institutionally integrated Scriptural Reasoning and Comparative Theology. Higton sees these two as complementary in Christian doctrinal theology. Tiemeier's account of Catholic-Hindu dialogue in Los Angeles resonates with the same two, and can be read as a proposal for the development of Comparative Theology in the context of dialogue with the help of group text study that has parallels with Scriptural Reasoning. Adams shows the shared logic and shapes of thinking in Receptive Ecumenism and Scriptural Reasoning. Clooney and Ochs find them complementary in different ways.

Yet such combinations are not, I think, likely to become common in practice, for a simple reason: each of the practices, and its associated collegiality, takes a good deal of time if it is to be fruitful. It may be that what is most needed is not so much that anyone should be committed to all three

---

[21] Murray, p. 81.

simultaneously as that each should be able to learn from the wisdom that the others have come to through years of experience and, as Ochs suggests, be open to specializing in one while being able to "pursue now one now another at different times in our work".[22] That is what I hope might be one result of these essays; in addition, I hope that those not involved with any of the three will also be able to learn something of value for whatever their own concerns and practices are in relation to engagements between churches and religions.

---

[22] Ochs, p. 201.

Modern Theology 29:4 October 2013
ISSN 0266-7177 (Print)
ISSN 1468-0025 (Online)

DOI: 10.1111/moth.12059

OPENING UP A DIALOGUE:
DEI VERBUM AND THE RELIGIONS

MICHAEL BARNES, SJ

In the autumn of 1967 I began my theology studies at Heythrop College, at that time splendidly isolated in an enormous mansion at the end of a long drive in north Oxfordshire. Our first course was the introduction to a new curriculum, redesigned according to principles set out by the Second Vatican Council. It was called *Revelation and the Bible* and was taught by the prodigiously learned Syriac scholar, Robert Murray. We began with the concept of faith in the Old Testament, moved into the experience of the Paschal Mystery in the early Church, considered different forms and models of revelation and ended up with knotty hermeneutical problems about inspiration and inerrancy. The mode of delivery, thirty lectures day after day, packed into some six weeks, still reeked of the traditional seminary system that was fast disappearing. The content, however, was cutting-edge. In the immediate aftermath of the Council fresh scholarship was opening up ancient tradition in a lived context of spiritual and liturgical renewal. Several decades later, that course remains one of the most stimulating theological experiences I have ever had.

No doubt it had a certain novelty value. This was, after all, the sixties and for my generation Good Pope John stood for a break with the rigidity of ultramontane Catholicism, just as JFK had drawn a clear line under the Eisenhower era. Since then the Catholic Church has learned to temper such naïve optimism by taking what historians call the long view. The first detailed descriptions of the Council which focussed on the colourful spectacle of intriguing bishops, whether of "conservative" or "progressive" persuasion, have given way to a more fiercely contested debate about how the conciliar texts are to be read and interpreted.[1] At stake now are complex and contentious questions,

Michael Barnes, SJ
Heythrop College, University of London, Kensington Square, London, W8 5HN, UK
Email: m.barnes@heythrop.ac.uk

[1] The approach of the "Bologna school" which tends to emphasise the discontinuity of the Council with what went before is to be found in the five volume *History of Vatican II*, edited by

not just about the "issues-under-the-issues",[2] especially authority, change and the development of doctrine, but also about the hermeneutics of reception. The extent to which what happened and what was decided represents a continuity or discontinuity with what had gone before continues to divide opinion.[3] All commentators are agreed, however, that the final texts were the result of a lengthy process of formation—in many, but not all, cases going back several decades. Whatever the historiographical niceties surrounding the terms "event" and "experience", text and context are intimately related. As John O'Malley has consistently shown in his studies of Trent and Vatican II, both Councils are misunderstood once the decrees and documents are separated from the particular circumstances and questions which led to their production.[4]

In this regard Vatican II is quite unique. Unlike Trent and so many of its predecessors where the prevailing literary genre was legal, laying down exact guidelines about what should and should not be said and done, the documents of Vatican II are primarily inspirational in tone. These are meditations on key themes (hope and grace, communion and collegiality, mission and dialogue, faith and the life of holiness) which are repeated in different modes and played in different keys as the Council sought to grapple with both internal and more external considerations, from the nature of the liturgy to relations with other communities of faith. The documents do not seek to define doctrine by closing off avenues of exploration; they open up new

---

Giuseppe Alberigo and Joseph Komonchak (Maryknoll, NY: Orbis Books and Leuven: Peeters, 1995–2006). From a similar perspective see also: Alberigo, *A Brief History of Vatican II* (Maryknoll, NY: Orbis Books, 2006); Ormond Rush, *Still Interpreting Vatican II: Some Hermeneutical Principles* (Mahwah, NJ: Paulist Press, 2004); John O'Malley, *What Happened at Vatican II* (Cambridge, MA: Belknap Press of Harvard University Press, 2008); and essays with a more historiographical intent by O'Malley, Komonchak, Stephen Schloesser and Neil J. Ormerod collected in David C. Schultenover (ed), *Vatican II: Did Anything Happen?* (New York: Continuum, 2007). For a sharp critique, focussing on continuities, see Agostino Marchetto, *The Second Vatican Ecumenical Council: A Counterpoint for the History of the Council*, trans. Kenneth D. Whitehead (Scranton, PA: University of Scranton Press, 2010). For a more textually-based hermeneutic see Matthew L. Lamb and Matthew Levering (eds), *Vatican II: Renewal Within Tradition* (New York: Oxford University Press, 2008).

[2] O'Malley, *What Happened at Vatican II*, pp. 298 ff.

[3] Much of the debate centres round the appropriateness or otherwise of talk about "rupture" or "reform" as interpretative keys. Following the 1985 Extraordinary Synod the then Cardinal Ratzinger insisted that "the schematism of a before and after in the history of the Church . . . must be decidedly opposed"; Joseph Ratzinger and Vittorio Messori, *The Ratzinger Report: An Exclusive Interview on the State of the Church* (San Francisco, CA: Ignatius Press, 1985), p 35. See also Ratzinger, *Principles of Catholic Theology: Building Stones for a Fundamental Theology* (San Francisco, CA: Ignatius Press, 1987), especially pp. 367–393. As Pope Benedict in his first Christmas address to the Roman Curia he reiterated his opinion that the correct hermeneutic for the Council is that of "reform"—a "combination of continuity and discontinuity at different levels" (22 December 2005); see *Acta Apostolicae Sedis*, XCVII (2006), pp. 40–53.

[4] O'Malley, *What Happened at Vatican II*, pp. 43–52. Linking Vatican II with Trent, see O'Malley *Trent and All That: Renaming Catholicism in the Early Modern Era* (Cambridge, MA: Harvard University Press, 2000) and *Trent: What Happened at the Council* (Cambridge, MA: Belknap Press of Harvard University Press, 2013).

spaces where the church can interact with a wider world which is itself understood as shot-through with the life-giving Spirit of God. As O'Malley puts it, commenting on the "style" of the Council, less important than *what* was said is the *how* of its saying.[5] When at the beginning of the Council John XXIII called for a "New Pentecost", and when years later Paul VI spoke about a "new cult" of the Spirit, they were talking about a legacy which would be rooted not in any finished set of ideas but in a certain capacity to draw from the richness of past traditions an energy which would enliven the present.[6]

Dei Verbum—*Retrieving the Sources of the Church's Inner Life*

Nowhere is this more evident than in *Dei Verbum*, the Constitution on Divine Revelation, and the topic of those Heythrop lectures. In an essay published twenty-five years after the Council ended, Robert Murray says that *DV* is "the most theologically concentrated" of the four major Constitutions "but in its wider relevance it both undergirds and touches most of the Council documents".[7] That judgement is repeated by many commentators.[8] The retrieval of a sense of scripture takes the church back to the sources of theological reflection in the Paschal Mystery itself and, in so doing, encourages a sensitivity to the ways of God's work of self-revelation throughout history. As *DV* puts it: "This tradition which comes from the apostles progresses in the church under the assistance of the Holy Spirit. There is growth in understanding of what is handed on, both the words and the realities they signify" (8).

In what follows, I am primarily interested in the effect this growth in understanding has had on the church's relations with other faith communities. The first task of this article, however, is to sketch the story of the formation of the text of *DV* and account for its centrality to the work of the Council as a whole. Very roughly, that story can be understood in terms of a shift from the propositional terms of manual-based theology to the personalism of God's own self-communication to human beings. The words of scripture are not the primary source of God's action in the world which are *then* to be interpreted by the church but *already* the living record of the incarnate Word of God forming a people which in principle embodies the whole of humankind called to a new fullness in God. In this sense my

---

[5] O'Malley, *What Happened at Vatican II*, especially pp. 147–148, 305–309.

[6] John XXIII was speaking to the clergy of the Veneto (21 April 1959); see Giuseppe Alberigo, "The Announcement of the Council", in Alberigo and Komonchak (eds), *History of Vatican II*, vol. I: pp. 1–54, especially pp. 41 ff. Paul VI was speaking at a General Audience (6 July 1973); quoted by Yves Congar in *I Believe in the Holy Spirit*, trans. David Smith (New York: Crossroad, 1997), p. 172.

[7] Robert Murray, "Revelation (*Dei Verbum*)", in Adrian Hastings (ed), *Modern Catholicism: Vatican II and After* (London: SPCK, 1991), p. 74.

[8] For detailed commentary see especially Ratzinger, Alois Grillmeier and Béda Rigaux, "Dogmatic Constitution on Divine Revelation", in Herbert Vorgrimler (ed), *Commentary on the Documents of Vatican II* (London: Burns and Oates, 1969), vol. III: pp. 155–272.

account of the legacy of *DV* and the effect it has had on practices of interreligious dialogue has a strongly ecclesial dimension.

This is a church which, according to the Council's second great dogmatic Constitution, *Lumen Gentium,* is intrinsically related to other major faith communities.[9] In the second part of this article I want to show how this vision of the single life-giving mystery of God's love in which Christians and other people of faith participate underpins that text and forms the theological background for *Nostra Aetate,* the Declaration on the Relation of the Church to Non-Christian Religions. The debate about the status of other religions has all too easily got caught up in what the Council did *not* say regarding the salvific value, or otherwise, of the religions themselves. The point I argue here is that, like all the Council documents, *NA* needs to be interpreted through the lens of *DV.* To be more specific, the task is to link *DV's* hermeneutic of revelation with the positive endorsement of the "truths and values" amongst the religions which is one of the more remarkable aspects of *NA.* As is well known, *NA* emerged after a protracted struggle within the church as a response to the Shoah and the dark legacy of Catholic anti-Semitism. My point, however, is that it would never have taken the form it did without the scholarly work in scriptural and patristic studies which took place, especially in France, in the decades before the Council. *NA's* pastoral principles are not ethical abstractions; they flow from a typically Catholic sacramental sensibility inspired by the restoration of what Daley calls the patristic "logic of signs".[10]

The third part of this article focuses on the legacy of *DV.* That biblical and patristic *ressourcement* has had an enormous impact on the liturgical and spiritual life of the church is clear, even if the depth of that reception has been patchy. I shall not, however, seek to enter into the testy debate about the interpretation of the Council. My focus here will be on a limited number of magisterial documents, including teaching documents of the Pontifical Biblical Commission and the work of the 2008 Synod of Bishops on the Word of God in the mission of the church. None of these considers the particular practices of interreligious reading and reasoning with which the articles in this collection are concerned. Nor is anything said explicitly about how the "conversations and collaboration" commended by *NA* can be regarded as somehow participating in the action of the self-revealing God. On the other hand, they do endorse and elaborate what *DV* has to say about the role of the Holy Spirit in the transmission of revelation. The Spirit ensures faithful discipleship of Christ within the church just as the same Spirit inspires the

---

[9] See *LG,* 16 which speaks about other religions being "related" or orientated (*ordinantur*) to the church.

[10] Brian Daley, "Knowing God in History and in the Church: *Dei Verbum* and *'Nouvelle Théologie'* ", in Gabriel Flynn and Paul D. Murray with Patricia Kelly (eds), *Ressourcement: A Movement for Renewal in Twentieth-Century Catholic Theology* (Oxford: Oxford University Press, 2012), p. 351.

imagination to find links, continuities and fruitful analogies with what is dimly perceived outside. It is the theological significance of that experience of new life learned through the Spirit of Christ which most needs elucidation.

The Council and the Sources of Revelation

Two words sum up the "style" of the Council: *aggiornamento*, bringing the church into the world of today, and *ressourcement*, the retrieval of theological sources which occupied so much scholarly attention in the Catholic Church between the nineteen-thirties and the nineteen-fifties. If the former is a reminder of the original vision of John XXIII, the latter is crucial in understanding the "deep structure" of the Council.[11] It is significant that the first session of the Council focussed almost exclusively on two documents: the Pastoral Constitution on the Liturgy, *Sacrosanctum Concilium*, which was accepted, and the first version of the schema on revelation, which was not. Much of the remote groundwork for the renewal of the liturgy had been accomplished by a monastic-led restorationist movement with its origins in the mid-nineteenth century. However, whereas there was general clarity and agreement about the need for liturgical reform, reactions to the renewal of biblical studies were much more ambivalent. Even as late as 1962, when two professors at the Jesuit-run Biblicum were suspended from teaching by the then Holy Office, a whiff of heresy was in the air. What O'Malley calls the "long nineteenth century" lurched between brief glimpses of tentative renewal and much longer periods of intense suspicion of anything which spoke of theological novelty.[12] Leo XIII's 1893 encyclical, *Providentissimus Deus*, seemed at first to offer a cautious welcome to the study of scripture as the authentic source of sound theological learning; with the Modernist crisis it was given a much more conservative interpretation. Pius X's encyclical, *Pascendi Dominici Gregis*, and the decree *Lamentabili*, detailing the errors of the Modernists, froze serious biblical studies for a generation. Fifty years after *Providentissimus*, Pius XII's *Divino Afflante Spiritu* offered a much broader endorsement of the historical-critical method and commended attention to literary genres in the determination of the meaning of the text.[13] But by then scholarly energies had been focussed elsewhere.

---

[11] See Alberigo, "Conclusion: Preparing for What Kind of Council?", in *History of Vatican II*, vol. I: pp. 501–508.

[12] From the French Revolution up to the nineteen-fifties, says O'Malley: "behind the placid façade that Catholicism presented to the world, a clash of epic proportions was waiting to happen" (*What Happened at Vatican II*, p. 89).

[13] *Divino Afflante Spiritu* was occasioned by ultra conservative attacks on Biblical scholars in pre-war Italy. The major responsibility for its authorship is usually ascribed to Augustin Bea, then Rector of the Pontifical Biblical Institute. In 1959 he was called by John XXIII to head the new Secretariat for Promoting Christian Unity from which position he had oversight of *NA*, *Unitatis Redintegratio* and *Dignitatis Humanae*, the Declaration on Religious Freedom, as well as exercising considerable influence over *DV*.

The term *ressourcement*, ascribed to the poet Charles Péguy, is usually understood as a retrieval of the patristic sources which were responsible for the shaping of Christian life and thought before the "science" of scholasticism drew them apart. What held together Dominicans like Chenu and Congar and Jesuits like de Lubac and Daniélou was no theological nostalgia trip, but the need to recover a way of being church which—precisely because it is in touch with the life-giving sources of faith—generates the energy to engage with the world of everyday experience. Perhaps the most influential fruit of this *ressourcement* is Henri de Lubac's *Catholicisme*, published in 1937 and still one of the most lucid theological meditations on what it means to be Catholic in a world of many ideas and cultures.[14] In 1943 de Lubac and Daniélou established *Sources Chrétiennes*—French translations of complete original works by saints and Fathers of the church. It is coincidence, of course, that this was the same year which saw the promulgation of *Divino Afflante Spiritu*—but somehow appropriate. While scripture as a body of canonical texts has a privileged place within the life and teaching of the church, it cannot be neatly isolated from the broader process of reception and interpretation which spills over, as it were, into the more strictly commentarial material of the early Fathers.

The point was not lost on critics of what disparagingly came to be called "nouvelle théologie".[15] At stake was the role of historical consciousness in theology; a deductive method which aimed to extract timeless and unchanging propositions from the flux of the Christian narrative came up against a largely inductive form of reasoning formed by a contemplative attention to scripture and liturgy. Ironically what the *ressourcement* theologians were concerned with was not some novel departure but a re-engagement with the unifying power of tradition. More ironically still, the same theologians who were censored in 1950 by the papal encyclical, *Humani Generis*, found themselves, a mere decade later, taking the lead role as the Catholic world prepared for the Second Vatican Council.[16]

Few of the more than two thousand bishops who processed into St Peter's on 11 October 1962 expected the Council to last long. Proceedings began with

---

[14] *Catholicisme: les aspects sociaux du dogme* (Paris: Éditions du Cerf, 1937); originally published as part of a series, *Unam Sanctam*, inaugurated by Yves Congar which was concerned to promote the cause of Christian unity. Translated into English as *Catholicism: Christ and the Common Destiny of Man* (San Francisco, CA: Ignatius Press, 1988).

[15] "Nouvelle théologie" was used originally as a short-hand for a new style of theology in an article in *L'Osservatore Romano* by Pietro Parente in 1942. In addresses to Jesuits and Dominicans in the summer of 1946 Pius XII spoke about the dangers of a theology which claimed to be "in constant development". Shortly afterwards it was taken up in much more trenchant terms by Réginald Garrigou-Lagrange. See Joseph A. Komonchak, "*Humani Generis* and *Nouvelle Théologie*", in Flynn and Murray with Kelly (eds), *Ressourcement*, pp. 138–156.

[16] Pope Pius XII, "*Humani Generis*" (12 August 1950), *Acta Apostolicae Sedis* XXXXII (1950), pp. 561–578. The encyclical criticised theological methods which strayed into evolutionary thinking, historicism and "false eirenism" (a reference to the ecumenical movement).

solemn High Mass and an address by Pope John. Reading that address nearly sixty years later, one is struck by its realism. There is no doubting that the Pope sees a crying need to advance the cause of truth in a world full of injustice, error and even violence. But it does not follow that a defensive and confrontational attitude is the best way forward. The message set deep in Christian doctrine does not change, but a different tone in communicating it is needed. The church, he says, "considers that she meets the needs of the present day by demonstrating the validity of her teaching rather than by condemnations".[17] A small enough change, no doubt. But it quickly became a sort of reference point and an encouragement to those who hoped for more from the Council than a ratification of the ecclesial *status quo*. In a sometimes highly contentious first session, beset by procedural wrangles about the powers of the Council, it was remarkable in retrospect that anything at all was decided. Cracks in a rather flimsy Curia-dominated consensus appeared early. After the initial success of the Constitution on the liturgy, itself hung about by some considerable unease at the level of adaptation being proposed, it was not altogether surprising that, when a less satisfactory schema on the much more contentious topic of revelation was proposed, it met with such severe criticism that the Pope intervened to have it withdrawn.[18]

The original *De Fontibus Revelationis* was constructed to defend the relationship of scripture, tradition and the Magisterium in the life of the church. It failed mainly because it lacked the pastoral dimension which was fast becoming the hallmark of the Council.[19] It was also deemed insufficiently biblical, preferring an intellectualist version of revelation as supernatural "divine speech" to the gracious act of the Word spoken in history for the salvation of humankind. The acrimonious debate which led to the schema being withdrawn was indeed a dramatic moment which changed the direction of the Council. But well before then alternative texts were being circulated. Leading theologians working as *periti* to particular bishops were coming up with different, biblically-based, theological meditations on the nature and scope of God's salvific action. Jared Wicks comments how the Council "constituted a unique case of co-operation between the theologians . . . and the Church's episcopal and papal magisterium".[20] If dialogue was to

---

[17] "Pope John's Opening Speech to the Council" in Walter Abbott (ed), *The Documents of Vatican II* (London: Chapman, 1966), p. 716. See Pope John XXIII, *"Gaudet Mater Ecclesia"* (11 October 1962), *Acta Apostolicae Sedis,* LIV (1962), pp. 786–795.

[18] See Giuseppe Ruggieri, "The First Doctrinal Clash" in Alberigo and Komonchak (eds), *History of Vatican II,* vol. II: chapter V, pp. 233–266.

[19] The intention that the Council be "pastoral" is ascribed to Pope John and goes back to the announcement in January 1959. See, e.g., Alberigo, "The Announcement of the Council", p. 37, especially note 85 for statistics of the usage in the Pope's writings. Pope John's expectations expressed in *"Gaudet"* were often used as a sort of court of last appeal in many of the discussions of the *De Fontibus* schema.

[20] Jared Wicks, "Vatican II on Revelation: From Behind the Scenes", *Theological Studies,* 71 (2010), p. 650.

become one of the great defining themes of the Vatican II "style", it began here—with the rapid growth of networks of theological conversation. As important as any retrieval or reordering of the sources of revelation was the very experience of learning together under the guidance of the Holy Spirit.

The final text of *DV*, promulgated at the end of the fourth session on 18 November 1965, still bears the marks of a tortuous process of revision and emendation.[21] But the central focus is unambiguous, substituting biblical categories for scholastic concepts.[22] The preface sets the tone, putting the Word of God first, what the church hears and then proclaims that "the whole world may hear the message of salvation" (1). The first two chapters focus on revelation itself and its transmission in the church; God's act of loving self-communication inspires movements of dialogue, communion and fellowship amongst human beings. The last four speak of the inspiration and interpretation of scripture, Old and New Testaments, and the place of scripture in the life of the church. The whole document is no more than five thousand words in the original Latin.

In retrospect it seems an innocuous and straightforward account of the biblical truth that God invites human beings to participate in God's own life. An account of faith as a personal response to a God fully involved in history and everyday life, exhortations to read the text with attention to context and literary genre, reminders that the "sacred page" is the heart of ministry and the soul of theology—all seem rather bland and obvious. Set in the context of the conciliar debate, however, *DV* witnesses to a decisive shift away from the rigidity of a "two source" theory of revelation in terms of scripture and tradition to the single source of God's continuing guidance of the Church through the Spirit of Christ. Where the rejected text of 1962 spoke of the "deposit of faith", the interpretation of which is entrusted solely to the Magisterium of the Church, *DV* says that "Tradition and scripture together form a single sacred deposit of the word of God, entrusted to the church" (10). The Magisterium, it goes on, is not above the Word of God but is there to serve it "teaching nothing but what is handed down, according as it devotedly listens, reverently preserves and faithfully transmits the word of God, by divine command and with the help of the Holy Spirit" (10). The "two sources" remain unmistakably Catholic; this is no endorsement of any principle of "sola scriptura". It is the relationship of the two which is seen in a

---

[21] See, e.g., the commentary on *DV* by George Schner, reproduced in a posthumous collection, *Essays Catholic and Critical*, edited by Philip G. Ziegler and Mark Husbands (Aldershot: Ashgate, 2003), pp. 31–43.

[22] In the background to the debate in the first session was the interpretation of Trent. Supporters of *De Fontibus* were anxious to maintain a strict "two source" theory in order to differentiate Catholic from Protestant thinking. This goes further than Trent allows. More accurately, Trent makes it clear that the teaching of Christ and the Apostles is the single source which is transmitted in two ways—"in written books and in unwritten traditions" (O'Malley, *What Happened at Vatican II*, p. 147).

new light. Tradition, and the Magisterium which serves that tradition, are not independent sources of truth but intrinsically related to the revealing power of the "sacred page" as it is read, prayed, studied and celebrated in the life of the church. In these terms *DV* is not so much a new theological synthesis of the sources of revelation for a new age as it is a meditation on the church's experience of being formed and transformed through the Word of God which goes on speaking in the world of human experience.

In telling the story of the genesis of the text—disagreement and crisis, compromise and reconstruction—it is easy to miss the heart of the matter. The painful process of drafting and redrafting which led to the final version is remarkable less for smoothing out the awkwardness of past conflicts between Catholics and Protestants than for returning the church to a more traditionally Catholic way of doing theology—rooted not in rationalist polemic but in contemplative attention to the world formed by the scriptural narrative. To that extent Rush's use of the term "micro-rupture" within the "great tradition" of the church seems entirely appropriate to speak of how a series of critical moments formed the Council, and therefore post-conciliar Catholicism, as the site of a life-giving dialogue with the wider world of human experience.[23] As the most important dimension of the learning experience which was the Council, *DV* reminds the church that at the heart of her life is the mystery of the self-revealing God himself, an act of self-revelation which is proclaimed by the apostles and their successors.

> By this link, this sacred tradition and the sacred scripture of the two testaments are like a mirror in which the church, during its pilgrimage on earth, contemplates God, the source of all that it has received, until it is brought home to see him face to face as he is (see I Jn 3, 2). (*DV*, 7)

The church cannot get back beyond itself to some original message or basic experience which can be excised from the text. Rather scripture itself is the record of the church's own experience of being confronted by the Mystery of the Risen Lord. To put the same point another way, tradition is not a set of truths which give further information about God not contained in scripture, but the process, already present within scripture itself, by which that life-giving dialogue between God and human beings is nourished and preached to succeeding generations.

Revelation, Dialogue and the Religions

DV's understated account of human speech about God made possible by God's gracious act of speaking of Godself runs through everything which the

---

[23] Rush, *Still Interpreting Vatican II*, especially pp. 7 ff.

Council produced—from the Constitutions on the Church, on Liturgy and the Church in the Modern World, to shorter but equally significant Declarations on Religious Freedom and Non-Christian Religions.[24] However, before turning to *NA* as a document indebted to *ressourcement*, we need to stay with the term with which the section above concluded—dialogue or, more exactly, conversation.[25]

Responsibility for its introduction to the language of the Council lies with Paul VI. Soon after his election in July 1963, he indicated that he was working on an encyclical which would take as its theme the mission of the church in the contemporary world. *Ecclesiam Suam* was published in August 1964 and had an immediate impact.[26] It is framed as a "conversation by letter".[27] Paul's own dialogue, with the bishops of the Council and the wider world, points a way forward for the church. Beyond the extremes of confrontation and accommodation lies a "third approach", a way of speaking which comes out of the Christian experience of God's love revealed in Christ. The second half of the encyclical is almost entirely taken up with this theme, particularly with what the Pope calls the "dialogue of salvation" which God initiates with humankind.[28] According to O'Malley *Ecclesiam Suam* "infused the word into the council's vocabulary".[29] The final version of the document on ecumenism, published little more than three months later, was transformed by the term.

---

[24] Gerard O'Collins draws attention to the way that *ressourcement* as a practice of faith becomes a theme in many of the documents of Vatican II, e.g. *Perfectae Caritatis* and *Optatum Totius*; see "*Ressourcement* and Vatican II", in Flynn and Murray with Kelly (eds), *Ressourcement*, pp. 371–391. Some editions of the Council documents (e.g. Abbott) place *LG* first; others (e.g. Austin Flannery) begin with *Sacrosanctum Concilium*—which, in terms of chronology, is correct. However, it is worth noting the *relatio* of the Doctrinal Commission of Vatican II in 1964 which spoke about *DV* as "in a certain way the first of all the Constitutions of this Council". The quotation from Augustine with which the first paragraph ends is deemed an appropriate expression of the purpose of the Council—"that the whole world may hear the message of salvation, and thus grow from hearing to faith, from faith to hope, and from hope to love" (*DV*, 1). See *Acta Synodalia Sacrosancti Concilii Vaticani II*, 4:1, p. 341.

[25] In the majority of the conciliar documents (e.g. *LG*, *NA*, *Gaudium et Spes*) the Latin is *colloquium*. The most significant exception is *UR* where the Latin is *dialogus*, with connotations of a philosophical disputation. Nolan suggests that this was to indicate a formal process between competent experts. See Ann Michele Nolan, *A Privileged Moment: Dialogue in the Language of the Second Vatican Council 1962–1965* (Bern: Peter Lang, 2006). This more formal meaning of the term had been around in ecumenical circles for decades.

[26] Pope Paul VI, "*Ecclesiam Suam*. On the Church" (6 August 1964), available at: http://www.vatican.va/holy_father/paul_vi/encyclicals/documents/hf_p-vi_enc_06081964_ecclesiam_en.html

[27] See Evangelista Vilanova, "The Intersession (1963–1964)", in Alberigo and Komonchak (eds), *History of Vatican II*, vol. III: chapter V, especially sub-section "The Impact of the Encyclical *Ecclesiam Suam* on the Council", pp. 448–457.

[28] It seems most likely that the term dialogue comes from Martin Buber and that the Pope was introduced to his thought by Jean Guitton, a French philosopher with whom the Pope had had a longstanding friendship. See O'Malley, *What Happened at Vatican II*, p, 204; Nolan, *A Privileged Moment*, pp. 164 ff. Guitton himself writes about his relationship with Paul VI in *The Pope Speaks* (London: Weidenfeld and Nicholson, 1968).

[29] O'Malley, What Happened at Vatican II, pp. 203–204.

The Declaration on Religious Freedom speaks of dialogue as a means to truth which is especially fitting for the "dignity and social nature of the human person" (3). The theme is also one of the most notable features of the Pastoral Constitution on the Church in the Modern World, the last conciliar document to be promulgated and, after *NA*, arguably the most contested.

It is, however, an ambiguous term. Sometimes (following the dominant usage in *Ecclesiam Suam*) it has instrumental connotations, implying a more suitable way of fulfilling the missionary mandate; sometimes it is used in a more open, inter-personal sense—such as we find in its single occurrence in *NA*. Here, after brief references to Hinduism and Buddhism, the text says that "the Catholic Church rejects nothing of those things which are true and holy in these religions" (2). While witnessing to their own faith, Christians should "recognise, preserve and promote those spiritual and moral good things as well as the socio-cultural values which are to be found among them" (2). Nothing is said about what such "good things" may be. There is, however, a clear practical implication. If the church is to respond generously to the imperative to enter into dialogue with people of other faith traditions, it must first listen and learn how the Spirit may be at work leading the church into a deeper understanding of God's Word. Like the Council as a whole, *NA* is pastoral in tone, concerned with promoting principles of good practice. But that does not lessen the theological significance of what is being said, however hesitantly. When read in the light of *DV*, with its theocentric focus on the personal communication which God effects in the church, engagement with other persons of faith opens up a new possibility: a participation through "conversations and collaboration" (2)[30] in the single "dialogue of salvation".

Paul VI's memorable phrase, owing as much to a retrieval of the church's lived experience of call and response as to any underlying Buberian influence, is a useful short-hand to encapsulate the Council's vision of a world already being transformed by the promptings of God's Spirit. The emphasis, however, is more on "dialogue" than "salvation"; it is God's self-revealing initiative in making speech about God possible that is properly salvific. The word "*colloquium*" only occurs once in *DV*, but the idea is foundational. The penultimate paragraph is an exhortation to priests, religious and lay-people, to engage in liturgical celebration and more personal spiritual reading of scripture. It ends with a telling quotation from Ambrose:

> Let it never be forgotten that prayer should accompany the reading of holy scripture, so that it becomes a dialogue [*colloquium*] between God and the human reader; for "when we pray, we talk to him; when we read the divine word, we listen to him".[31] (*DV*, 25)

---

[30] Norman Tanner has "dialogues and co-operation"; the Latin is *colloquia et collaborationem*.
[31] Ambrose, *De officiis ministrorum*, I, 20, 88; PL 16, 50.

The reference picks up the central theme of the opening chapter of *DV*: through the Holy Spirit who moves the heart and opens the eyes of the mind, God reveals himself to human beings. This focus on contemplative attention to what the Spirit is doing—how the Spirit is guiding the church "into all the truth" and how the same Spirit is at work in the wider world of honest and authentic human endeavour—ties together the various strands of thinking about the other which go to make up what became *NA*.

The genesis and development of *NA* is too well-known to need repeating here.[32] A mere thirty sentences in the Latin text, it has done much to repair the damage wrought by centuries of Christian anti-Semitism. At first it seems an unlikely result of *ressourcement*. While the text is peppered with scriptural allusions, nothing is developed in any detail. There are no patristic references apart from one obscure letter from Gregory VII to the King of Mauritania which speaks of the Muslim worship of the one "creator of heaven and earth" (3). Yet this act of coming to terms with the Shoah represents the experience of a learning church—not just atoning for the sins of the past but retrieving a sense of its spiritual debt to the people of Israel.

Pastorally the most important dimension of *NA* lies towards the end where the Council comes closest to issuing an old-style anathema; in guarding against any representation of the Jews as accursed or rejected, Christians should "take care that . . . they teach nothing which is not in keeping with the truth of the gospel and the spirit of Christ" (4). Theologically—that is to say, with theological consequences for the inner life of the church—it lies with the insistence that "because of their ancestors the Jews still remain very dear to God, whose gift and call are without regret" (4). However, the two points are inseparable, the one implying the other, and vice-versa. In pursuing the process of learning from its experience of the "Jewish question", *NA* introduces Paul's meditation on the fate of his sometime co-religionists in Romans 9–11 to make the point, not just that God in his providence will bring to a fullness what was begun with the promises made to Israel, but that the same God is constant and will in due time graft back the broken branches of the true olive tree which is Israel. Although not stated explicitly, Judaism is recognised as a living tradition. Jews and Christians are linked by a trajectory of faith which is rooted in a common heritage of divine revelation and human response, worked out in time through the rituals of Passover and memories of Exodus and Exile, disaster and return, loss and hope. The implication is

---

[32] The most detailed account of the development of the text is by John Oesterreicher in Vorgrimler (ed), *Commentary on the Documents of Vatican II*, vol. III, pp. 1–136. See also relevant sections in Alberigo and Komonchak's *History of Vatican II*, especially G. Miccoli, "Two Sensitive Issues: Religious Freedom and the Jews", vol. IV: chapter 2 and Mauro Velati, "Completing the Conciliar Agenda," vol. V: chapter 3. For an informative non-Catholic commentary with a careful analysis of the various texts, see Miikka Ruokanen, *The Catholic Doctrine of Non-Christian Religions According to the Second Vatican Council* (Leiden: Brill, 1982).

clear: if the Sinai Covenant has not been revoked, what Christians call the Old Testament cannot simply be regarded as an inadequate forerunner of the New.

None of this passed without heated debate and some persistent lobbying. Long before *NA* was promulgated on 28 October 1965, the original paragraphs on the relationship of the church to the Jews had been joined by a whole section on Islam, by brief but pertinent references to Hinduism and Buddhism, by the imperatives of dialogue noted above, and—not the least important aspect—an introduction incorporating ideas and themes from the disciplines of history and phenomenology of religions. Even here, biblical material is used to speak of the unity and destiny of the human race. The actual word "revelation" only appears once, in reference to the Old Testament which the church receives "through that people with whom God out of his ineffable mercy deigned to enter into an ancient covenant" (4). Nevertheless, for all its omissions and ambivalence, the framework of the whole owes more to biblical *ressourcement* than to any concern for the dogmatic problem of salvation outside the church. Speaking of the permanent validity of the revelation to the Jewish people, *DV* says that these books retain a "lasting value" (14).

> They ought therefore to be accepted by Christians, because they express a vivid sense of God, because they enshrine sublime teaching about God, salutary wisdom for human life and wonderful treasures of prayer, and finally because in the Old Testament books our salvation in Christ is hinted at under signs and symbols. (*DV*, 15)

It is also possible to detect in *NA*, amid the language of illumination, perception and awareness, traces of the shift to the single source theory of *DV*. The truths found in other religions which "frequently reflect a ray of that truth which enlightens everyone" (2) are juxtaposed with Christ the Way, Truth and Life whom the church is called to proclaim. The initial statement about all people forming one community is echoed at the end of the declaration with the reminder that all people are created in God's image (5). Interestingly any explicit mention of natural theology, such as is included in *DV* (at the end of section 6, with its reference to Romans 1:20), is absent in *NA*. The introductory paragraphs have a different purpose, not to set Nature in some sort of tension with Grace, still less to pit the natural against the supernatural, but to underscore the unity of God's creation which in Christ is being brought to a new fullness. The continuity which is stressed comes from the single action of the Word of God, spoken definitively in Jesus Christ, and the Holy Spirit, bringing to fruition the "seeds of the Word" in creation.

This theological vision, the dominating motif of *DV*, underscores two more documents which refer to other religions, *Lumen Gentium*, on the church, and *Ad Gentes*, on missionary activity. *LG* begins with the Mystery of the Church and then speaks expansively of how the People of God "is joined to those who, though baptized and so honoured with the Christian name, do not profess the faith in its entirety" (15). In the following section attention shifts to those who have "not yet accepted the gospel"; a series of relationships between the church and various "others" is sketched out, from "that people to whom the testaments and promises were given", and those like the Muslims who "worship the one merciful God who will judge humanity on the last day", to those who "search for the unknown God in shadows and images", and finally even to those who "search for God with a sincere heart" (16). In preaching and works of witness, it is important for Christians to bear in mind that "whatever goodness and truth is to be found in them is considered by the Church as a preparation for the gospel".[33]

This last point is repeated, with a vastly expanded set of scriptural and patristic references, at the beginning of *AG*. The first chapter on Doctrinal Principles picks up the opening theme of *LG*: the mission of the Son and the Spirit sent by the loving Father into the world. *AG*, expounding the "all-embracing plan of God for the salvation of the human race", speaks about the "efforts" of human beings to know God as "paving the way for the gospel message" (3) and urges Christians to seek out and make plain "seeds of the Word"—"as Christ himself searched into the hearts of people, and by a genuinely human dialogue [*colloquio*] led them to the divine light" (11). In similar ways these two documents build *DV*'s scripturally-based personalism into a rhetoric of mission as a service to the whole of humanity.

This is the context within which the theme of the salvation of the non-Christian needs to be set. The section from *LG* quoted above ends with the unequivocal statement that "these too can obtain eternal salvation" (16). Nothing, of course, is said about whether they *will* be saved; their ultimate destiny remains in the providence of God. The focus is on the church as the People of God called to preach the Gospel for the sake of the salvation of all and the overcoming of evil. That context may go some way towards explaining the absence of any such reference from *NA*. Trent had come up with its own version of the old adage, *extra ecclesiam nulla salus*, and literalist interpretations were still being peddled on the eve of the Council.[34] Vatican II produced an all-inclusive counter-vision to address the reality of a global church in the middle of a pluralist world—a more optimistic vision, as Sullivan notes, which emphasises the instrumental role of the church in what is properly the hidden work of the Holy Spirit.[35] A number of major shifts need to be noted, cultural and social as well as philosophical and

---

[33] *LG*, 16; with reference to Eusebius of Caesarea, *Praeparatio Evangelica*, 1.1.

[34] On the history of the *extra ecclesiam nulla salus* adage, from Cyprian to the Leonard Feeney controversy of 1949, see Francis A. Sullivan, *Salvation Outside the Church: Tracing the History of the Catholic Response* (London: Chapman, 1992), pp. 3–13.

[35] *Ibid.*, especially pp. 141–161.

ecumenical, not to mention what no one expected in the preparatory period: a process of learning on the part of the church which saw *NA* grow as an all too ill-defined aspiration of Pope John to the status of a declaration in its own right.[36]

To argue that in terms of status *NA* ranks below that of a dogmatic constitution such as *LG* rather misses the point. Both contain important insights and perspectives which are not to be subsumed, the one within the other, nor smoothed out into some overarching repetition of the *status quo*. My point is that the documents of the Council need to be read not as discrete proof-texts but as meditative variations on a theme—more exactly a number of themes—which develop a particular style or rhetoric. These meditations have a particular context, the emergence of what Karl Rahner called a "world Church"[37] seeking to engage with a whole variety of relationships, from the ecumenical to the interreligious, with a flesh and blood reality which is not to be encapsulated in systematic formulae and hard-edged anathemas.

However the "rupture/reform" debate works itself out, Vatican II is the story of a church coming to terms not just with the history and culture of modernity but with the radical contingency and historicality of all human living. Relations with other religions are clearly part of that reality, but it is all too easy to treat them as a "problem" which can be solved by reference to particular texts, or as an agenda which can be safely entrusted to one particular form of "dialogue", that between specialists and experts. Such a move offends against the "Catholic instinct" which, at its best, refuses to dichotomise the work of grace but seeks always the broadest bounds of God's providential action in the world. *DV* and the process of *ressourcement* have generated a movement of learning which seeks to bring the church's earliest attempts to make sense of the Paschal Mystery into a correlation with the continuing guidance of the Spirit who leads the church "into all the truth" and generates the energy to imagine new ways of engagement with the world. *NA* is just such a new engagement.

Sacred Scripture, the Holy Spirit and the Inner Life of the Church

In *NA* any theological account of the "dialogue of salvation" is muted. What I have tried to show, however, is that its original theme—the matrix of the faith and practice of the church which lies with "the patriarchs, Moses and the prophets"—is quite clearly rooted in scripture. In his commentary on *NA*, published within a year of its promulgation, Bea argues that the church finds

---

[36] On the shift in emphasis between the Councils see Jeannine Hill Fletcher, "Responding to Religious Difference: Conciliar Perspectives", in Raymond F. Bulman and Frederick J. Parella (eds), *From Trent to Vatican II: Historical and Theological Investigations* (New York: Oxford University Press, 2006), pp. 267–281.

[37] Karl Rahner, "Towards a Fundamental Theological Interpretation of the Second Vatican Council", *Theological Studies*, 40 (1978), pp. 716–727.

its proper origins in the election of Israel, as a people who are tied spiritually to another people, those born from Abraham's stock.[38] Abraham and Christ are related by a "period of long and arduous preparation which God willed".[39] Then, in reference to the books of the Old Testament, he refers to the section from *DV* 15, noted above, which speaks of the treasures of prayer in which the mystery of salvation lies hidden. What the apostles and Gospel writers first pondered as the mystery of God's self-revelation brought to a head in the person of the Risen Lord is not to be separated in any straight-forward way from the faith of Israel. That truth had been obscured by centuries of a manual-based theology. The process of scholarly *ressourcement* may have had comparatively little direct impact on *NA*. But in the wake of World War II and its aftermath it certainly did have an effect.

Thus *DV* witnesses not just to the retrieval of the church's biblical and patristic roots, but to a specific moment of learning and discovery which was experienced in the crucial early debate during the first session.[40] When Bishop Joseph de Smedt gave his all-important speech consigning the original *De Fontibus* schema to oblivion, he made a plea for a dialogical style of engagement. It is worth quoting part of Yves Congar's summary:

> For centuries, Catholics and others have thought it enough to give a clear explanation of their divergent teachings, but they both did it in *their* categories, which the other did not understand. The result: *nothing*. For some time now, a different method has been introduced: ecumenical *dialogue*. This involves paying attention to the *way* in which doctrine is expressed, so that it can be understood by the other. This is not a bargaining for unity; it is not an attempt to convert; but it is, on both sides, the giving of a clear witness which takes the other into account. It is this approach that our texts should take. It is not easy![41]

This insistence on the use of categories comprehensible to the other set up a momentum that quickly became irreversible. Dialogue with the great religious traditions was for some time included within the schema on ecumenism and remained always the responsibility of Bea's Secretariat for Christian Unity. But the development from ecumenical dialogue to interreligious conversation never lost touch with its roots in the scriptural foundations of Catholic theology. Eventually *NA* developed a broader purpose: as

---

[38] Augustin Cardinal Bea, *The Church and the Jewish People* (London: Chapman, 1966).

[39] *Ibid.*, p. 58.

[40] Schner comments that "[t]he Council Fathers integrated the practical experience of conducting such a gathering as a Council with the task of articulating foundations in a text. Thus, the history and the content of the text are mutually illuminative" (*Essays Catholic and Critical*, p. 3).

[41] Quoted in Giuseppe Ruggieri, "The First Doctrinal Clash", in Alberigo and Komonchak (eds), *History of Vatican II*, vol. II: chapter V, p. 259.

Bea puts it, to promote the "unity of the human family" by retrieving a sense of the universality of God's revelation begun in the Old Testament.[42]

In *DV* the emphasis is always on the place of scripture in the life of the church, in liturgy, preaching and prayerful study. Nevertheless, the *ad extra* dimension is never absent—nor is the specifically interreligious. Dialogue means taking the other, and other worlds of religious discourse, into account. Thus in a muted directive in its very last section, *DV* says that

> editions of holy scripture should be prepared with suitable notes which are adapted to the conditions of non-Christians also, and both pastors and Christians of whatever walk of life should take all means to distribute these imaginatively [*sapienter*]. (*DV*, 25)

From this tentative invitation to more developed contemporary practices of interreligious reading and study, such as Comparative Theology and Scriptural Reasoning, is an enormous leap. Nevertheless, the very fact that such a point could be made in a text dedicated primarily to renewing the inner life of the church is important. Most commentaries on *DV* agree that, as the foundational theology of the Council, it has had an enormous impact on the life of the church *ad intra* and on ecumenical relations. This is not to say that it maps out a complete theology of revelation any more than *NA* does something analogous for interreligious relations. Rather what both do is re-describe through a particular experience of learning-in-community what George Schner calls, with reference to *DV*, the "basic rules of Christian discourse and action".[43]

It would be a tedious process to chronicle the vast amount of teaching material, from papal encyclicals to dicasterial statements, which have sought to promote such a coherent discourse in response to the experience of interreligious dialogue in recent years. No easier would be a summary of official commentary on the place of the Bible in the life of the church. If all I do in the final section of this article is refer to a handful of documents, it is to underline the thesis I have sought to develop: theology as the recovery of a "religious world" which—paradoxically—opens the church to the possibility of new life in the Spirit.

That world is shared in complex ways with the living tradition of Judaism. *NA*'s recovery of the original formative relationship between Jews and Christians has been reinforced since the Council by several teaching documents. What for the sake of brevity are often referred to as the "Guidelines" and the "Notes" provide many pastoral directives, and acknowledge Judaism as a developing and diverse tradition with its own sources of

---

[42] Bea, *The Church and the Jewish People*, especially pp. 28 ff.
[43] Schner, *Essays Catholic and Critical*, p. 41.

religious creativity.[44] A similar point is made by the Pontifical Biblical Commission in a text published to commemorate the fiftieth anniversary of *Divino Afflante Spiritu* in 1993.[45] Catholic exegetes are encouraged to use a variety of methods of interpretation, from time-honoured approaches taught by the early Fathers to those which, while retaining their own distinct integrity, are espoused by the rabbis and Talmudic commentators. The Commission focuses on the theological issue raised by *NA*, the "internal unity" of the Old and New Testaments. Jews and Christians have different yet analogous readings of the same texts; Jewish forms of exegesis are present within the New Testament and in understanding the development of their own tradition of faith Christians have much to learn from such methods of exegesis. An important hermeneutic principle emerges from a brief discussion of inculturation: "In its transposition of the Palestinian message of Jesus into Judeo-Hellenistic culture [the New Testament] displays its intention to transcend the limits of a single cultural world".[46] This is a task of dialogue, translation, and "mutual enrichment" which is never-ending and "must be taken up again and again, in relationship to the way in which cultures continue to evolve".[47]

The integrity of this process is what has occupied much of the magisterial material—particularly from Pope Benedict. The 2008 Synod of Bishops took as its theme "the Word of God in the life and Mission of the Church". The preparatory discussion document, drawing on contributions from bishops' conferences around the world, develops and emphasises the theology of revelation hammered out in *DV* while also drawing attention to practical questions about how far the Council's call to make the "sacred page" central to the inner life of the church, both in the liturgy and in more personal prayer, has been heard.[48] Little is said about the Bible in its relation to the sacred texts of other religious traditions beyond a statutory warning about the dangers of syncretism and superficiality "because of various conceptions about the inspiration of such sacred texts".[49] More positively, however, in the preceding

---

[44] "Guidelines and suggestions for implementing the conciliar declaration *Nostra Aetate*", December 1974; "Notes on the Correct Way to Present the Jews and Judaism in Preaching and Catechesis in the Roman Catholic Church", June 1985; for an excellent summary and commentary see Eugene J. Fisher, "The Evolution of a Tradition: from *Nostra Aetate* to the 'Notes' ", in International Catholic-Jewish Liaison Committee, *Fifteen Years of Catholic-Jewish Dialogue 1970–1985* (Vatican City: Libreria Editrice Vaticana, 1988).

[45] The Pontifical Biblical Commission, The Interpretation of the Bible in the Church (1993); see Joseph A. Fitzmyer (ed), *The Biblical Commission's Document: "The Interpretation of the Bible in the Church"—Text and Commentary* (Rome: Editrice Pontificio Istituto Biblico, 1995).

[46] *Ibid.*, p. 177.

[47] *Ibid.*, p. 178.

[48] "The Word of God in the Life and Mission of the Church", *Instrumentum Laboris* (11 May 2008). Available at: http://www.vatican.va/roman_curia/synod/documents/rc_synod_doc_20080511_instrlabor-xii-assembly_en.html

[49] *Ibid.*, 56.

section, on the Word of God as the source of dialogue between Christians and Jews, it is said that

> the Jewish understanding of the Bible can be of assistance in the Christian understanding and study of the Bible. In some cases, ways to study Scripture together are being developed—and can be further developed—providing occasion to learn from each other while closely respecting each other's differences.[50]

This is hardly a ringing endorsement of practices of interreligious reading. As with the Pontifical Biblical Commission documents, however, what is being commended is the study of scripture alongside Jewish readers. *At the very least* this implies that the church can find herself enriched by sharing in the holiness and wisdom of other persons of faith.

How can such interreligious conversations be said to continue or participate in the work of revelation? *DV* stays with the Catholic orthodoxy that "no new public revelation is to be expected before the glorious manifestation of our Lord Jesus Christ" (4). In the very next sentence, however, the "obedience of faith" is described as a full and free assent to the God who reveals (5). Revelation as the perfect instantiation of God's truth in Jesus Christ is closed; revelation as the ever-continuing process by which this truth becomes known in the world through the action of Word and Spirit together is not. *NA* laid down a principle, a corollary of what is taught in *DV*, that the Church does not reject the "spiritual and moral good things" which may be found in other religions (*NA*, 2). And in line with what is expounded in *DV* and has gradually become part of post-Vatican II practice, it develops a typically Catholic sacramental sensibility which is alive not just to the revealing power of the "sacred page" itself but to the richness of religious and interreligious contexts which lead the church into a deeper understanding of God's gracious ways with humankind. In other words, wherever the church finds itself caught up in God's dialogue of love, interrogating and being interrogated by the Word, whether in the liturgy itself or in the engagements with the wider world which prayer inspires, the Holy Spirit is present, leading the church into all the truth. In his post-Synodal Apostolic Exhortation, *Verbum Domini*, Pope Benedict spoke of the mystery of the Word which is constantly present in the church by referring to *DV* and the Biblical metaphor of a nuptial dialogue:

> God, who spoke in the past, continues to converse with the spouse of his beloved Son. And the Holy Spirit, through whom the living voice of the Gospel rings out in the Church—and through it in the world—leads

---

[50] *Ibid.*, 55.

believers to the full truth and makes the word of Christ dwell in them in all its richness'.[51]

Among the many practices of the Word which can build up the church Pope Benedict commended especially the practice of *lectio divina*. DV had asked, he says, that the faithful should "go gladly to the sacred text itself, whether in the sacred liturgy . . . or in devout reading, or in such suitable exercises and various other helps which . . . are happily spreading everywhere in our day".[52] Warning of the danger of an "individualistic approach"[53], he says that the Word, while addressed to each one personally, is intended to build community; thus the privileged place for such prayerful reading is the Eucharist and it is through the liturgical setting that the criteria which should guide the practice can best be grasped. The Pope then gives his own brief commentary on the traditional four stages of the practice—*lectio, meditatio, oratio and contemplatio*. In this last stage, we find ourselves converted by the gift of God which creates within us "a wise and discerning vision of reality, as God sees it".[54]

To an extent what is being commended is a very practical *ressourcement*, a way of ensuring that significant spiritual texts of all kinds can be prayerfully embedded in the life of the church. But to say that *lectio* is an ecclesial practice is not to see it as yet another way of building a state of personal interiority. Benedict is at pains to stress that this is a communal activity. Thus he finishes the section with the reminder that "the process of *lectio divina* is not concluded until it arrives at action which moves the believer to make his or her life a gift for others in charity".[55] In recalling that "fraternal delegates"—the Ecumenical Patriarch of Constantinople and, "for the first time ever", a Jewish rabbi—had addressed the Synod, he notes that the building up of the "we" of the church comes through "mutual listening and acceptance".[56] Towards the end he speaks both of the mission of the church to proclaim the Gospel but also of the "value of interreligious dialogue", drawing attention to the close connection between the biblically-grounded vision of God's love for all peoples revealed in the Judaeo-Christian tradition and "the ethics of love for everyone [which] is found in many great religious traditions".[57] He voices the church's respect for "ancient religions and spiritual traditions of the various continents", specifically Hinduism, Buddhism and Confucianism,

---

[51] Pope Benedict XVI, "*Verbum Domini*. Post-Synodal Apostolic Exhortation" (30 September 2010), 58, quoting *DV*, 8. Available at: http://www.vatican.va/holy_father/benedict_xvi/apost_exhortations/documents/hf_ben-xvi_exh_20100930_verbum-domini_en.html

[52] *Ibid.*, 86, referring to *DV*, 25.

[53] *Ibid.*

[54] *Ibid.*, 87.

[55] *Ibid.*

[56] *Ibid.*, 4.

[57] *Ibid.*, 117.

and urges Christians and Muslims "to come to a better knowledge of one another".[58]

Nothing is said in any of these documents about how the demands of the traditional form of mission as proclamation and the more recent commitment to dialogue are to be held together. The implications of what I called earlier the Council's "rhetoric of mission" are worked out elsewhere in the official post-conciliar process of reception.[59] The legacy of *DV* does not lie with some ready-made missiology for a pluralist age but, at a prior stage, with the recovery of a more properly Catholic sense of the *single* source of revelation: God's "dialogue of salvation" with humankind which forms the church and builds up a contemplative sensitivity to the "seeds of the Word". The canonical texts which form Christian faith, and by extension the classic commentaries which they generate, have a sacramental value. Before they teach a special revelation or "message", they make the proper hearing of the Word possible by forming a discerning community sensitive to the promptings of the Spirit. If that is so, then interreligious dialogue is not a matter of looking for some analogous "message" in other places but of working with other communities in order to *learn together* something of the gracious and surprising ways of the Divine Other.

Theology of Trust and Communion

In a dense article, published originally in 1935 and in English translation in 1968, Marie-Dominique Chenu, one of the great architects of the Council, takes issue with a model of theology based on theodicy, "a metaphysical theism which distorts the ancient concept of *doctrina sacra*". Theology, he says, is not "an intellectual conquest at the end of a reasoning process" but "a personal gift which makes it possible for a look of trust to meet friendship and communion".[60] That brief quotation suggests two final summary reflections which may take us forward into the main body of this symposium.

---

[58] *Ibid.*, 119.

[59] The tension is one of many issues to do with the Church's mission addressed in Pope John Paul II's 1990 encyclical *Redemptoris Missio* (see especially paragraph 57); available at http://www.vatican.va/holy_father/john_paul_ii/encyclicals/documents/hf_jp-ii_enc_07121990_redemptoris-missio_en.html. See also "The Attitude of the Church towards the Followers of Other Religions ", issued by the then Secretariat for Non-Christian Religions, *Bulletin* 1:2 (1984), pp. 126–141, and a joint document from the Pontifical Council for Inter-religious Dialogue and the Congregation for Evangelisation, "Dialogue and Proclamation: Reflections and Orientations on Inter-Religious Dialogue and the Proclamation of the Gospel of Jesus Christ", *Bulletin* 26:2 (1991), pp. 210–250. For commentary on the relationship between the latter document and *Redemptoris Missio* see William R. Burrows (ed), *Redemption and Dialogue* (Maryknoll, NY: Orbis Books, 1993), especially Jacques Dupuis, "*A Theological Commentary*: Dialogue and Proclamation", pp. 119–158.

[60] Marie-Dominique Chenu, "What is Theology?", in *id., Faith and Theology*, trans. Denis Hickey (Dublin: Gill and Son 1968), p. 15. English translation of "Position de la théologie", *Revue des Sciences philosophiques et théologiques*, 25 (1935), pp. 232–257, quotation at p. 232.

DV ensured the triumph of the historical-critical method in the Catholic Church and enhanced ecumenical relations by retrieving a more nuanced sense of the interpretive authority of the church. More importantly, along with other documents such as *NA* which share its scriptural vision, *DV* replaced a deductive system which imposes its own categories on the other with a contemplative "logic of signs" which seeks to enter into dialogue with the other. To that extent what actually happened at the Council is less significant than the manner of its happening—O'Malley's rhetorical "style". *DV* reminds us that the primary locus for theology is the church itself which, through its customs and devotions and sacraments, contemplates the mystery of its being called to participate in God's own life. In that it was following the main thrust of *ressourcement* theologians like Chenu. To the perennial question about how human beings can be said to "know" God, Chenu points to the reading of scriptural texts where the address of a divinely-revealed truth intersects with the world of human culture in all its messy magnificence. Theology begins in a moment of gift when God speaks to the very depths of the human person and draws us out of ourselves and into a life of communion and friendship with God. Of its very nature this is an unending process, a tradition of lived interpretation of the Mystery of Christ which links Apostles, Fathers, the "believing and praying Church", and all those whom the Spirit leads into the truth.

Secondly, as Chenu reminds us, the prayerful reading of familiar texts makes possible a "look of trust". Philosophical reasoning, a sense of history, scholarship and learning, preaching and catechesis, and—Paul VI would, no doubt, want to add—the generosity of a never-ending *colloquium* with the wider world: all have a part to play in the theological enterprise. But what holds them together as *doctrina sacra* is not a set of summary propositions, however well-crafted, but the divine pedagogy which enables the community of faith to reconnect with the most vital and formative of memories *and* to be taken forward into further imaginative explorations of the depths of God's providential purposes. The lesson of this exploration, to oversimplify somewhat, is that in learning to read and reason prayerfully the church extends God's own conversation into other centres of human endeavour and interaction. In so doing the church becomes, once again, a community of learners, taught by the Holy Spirit. The implication both for the practice of faith and for theological reflection in an interreligious context is clear: the church finds and maintains its identity in relationships of mutual respect and learning. The privilege of grace enjoyed by Christians is not the possession of truths about God which sets them apart, but an entry into that mystery of God's self-communication which is generated as much by what is specific to their inner life as it is by sharing in that work of communication *ad extra*. Learning and teaching are all of a piece.

Modern Theology 29:4 October 2013
ISSN 0266-7177 (Print)
ISSN 1468-0025 (Online)

DOI: 10.1111/moth.12060

DEEP REASONINGS: *SOURCES CHRETIENNES, RESSOURCEMENT,* AND THE LOGIC OF SCRIPTURE IN THE YEARS BEFORE—AND AFTER—VATICAN II

KEVIN L. HUGHES

In the early years of Scriptural Reasoning, perhaps for reasons of historical accident, perhaps for intrinsic reasons, the Christian contributors to the practice of Scriptural Reasoning were mostly Protestant. A product of Yale himself, co-founder Peter Ochs discovered that the so-called "Yale School" of Christian theology represented by Hans Frei and George Lindbeck conceived of the work of theology in ways analogous to the rabbinic modes of thought that had served as the root-model for Jewish Textual Reasoning and then inter-traditional Scriptural Reasoning. At Cambridge, this postliberal mode of Christian thought was well-represented in the work of David Ford and Daniel Hardy. And so, for at least these genealogical reasons, Scriptural Reasoning's Christians were predominantly Protestant. It did seem, however, that there were certain obstacles beyond the accidental to wider Catholic participation in Scriptural Reasoning. In private conversation several years ago, Ochs wondered with me if it was the case that the Catholics first exposed to the practice tended to be either philosophically liberal, and so not quite so interested in the postliberal tenor, or, if not liberal, they tended to be too "conceptual and propositionalist" to embrace the pragmatist ethos at the heart of Scriptural Reasoning.

The last decade has seen tremendous development in the Catholic presence in Scriptural Reasoning. In part, I suggest, this late harvest is the fertile

Kevin L. Hughes
Department of Humanities, Villanova University, Villanova, PA, 19085, USA
Email: kevin.hughes@villanova.edu

yield of seed sown even before the Second Vatican Council, in the "movement" we generally call "*ressourcement*", the fruitful yet sometimes controversial movement associated most closely with Henri de Lubac, Jean Daniélou, and others. My argument is this: while the Second Vatican Council's clarion call to engage the wider world in *Gaudium et Spes* and *Nostra Aetate* opened the doors for Catholics to engage other religious communions in dialogue, the call itself did not present Catholics with any particular models or rules[1] for engagement. However, when this invitation is taken together with the deep scriptural logic recovered for the Catholic Church through the tireless work of de Lubac and Daniélou, Catholics can recover the internal resources, the "deep reasonings", that allow them to come to the Abrahamic tent of meeting with fitting gifts. That is, it is not only that the fruits of *ressourcement* have given Catholics a way of joining the conversation; even more, they may bring particular gifts that help to advance the work of Scriptural Reasoning in a productive way.

The Conceptual Tools for Ressourcement: *Blondel, "Catholic Modernism" and the Logic of Tradition*

Historians of the Second Vatican Council often look to *Dei Verbum*, the Constitution on Divine Revelation, as a watershed document that opened the door for Catholic Biblical scholarship—although there had been important precedents in Pius XII's *Divino Afflante Spiritu* (1943)—and, in one telling, this, together with *Nostra Aetate*, would seem to clear the way, as it were, for Catholic Scriptural Reasoning. However, the story is more complicated. The growth of historical-critical Biblical scholarship in the nineteenth and twentieth centuries had stirred up a tempest in Catholic circles. As scholars such as Alfred Loisy began to absorb elements of historical-critical scholarship into their work, influential Catholic theological voices raised the alarm that such work was essentially reductionist, eliminating the supernatural in favor of a thin historicism. However, the "traditional" voices who opposed Loisy and other "Catholic Modernists" were themselves, in their own way, altogether modern. The neo-Thomist account of revelation of those who built the case against Loisy was itself the fruit of modern Catholicism's response to the Enlightenment rationalism of Descartes and Kant with a rationalism of their own devising.[2] The nineteenth-century recovery of Thomas Aquinas under the *aegis* of Leo XIII's *Aeterni Patris* (1879) aimed explicitly at answering modern philosophy with a Catholic philosophy that delivered an

---

[1] "Rules" here should be understood in the sense of rules of grammar rather than "by-laws" or prohibitions.
[2] On this dynamic in early twentieth-century theology, see the excellent discussion in Fergus Kerr, *Twentieth-Century Catholic Theologians: From Neoscholasticism to Nuptial Mysticism* (Malden, MA: Blackwell, 2007), especially the first chapter on Vatican I and Reginald Garrigou-Lagrange.

equally-sound "clear and distinct" foundation for knowledge that remained open to divine revelation. Applied to Biblical scholarship, this contest amounted to a modern, post-Hegelian binary logic of historical facts over against a neo-Thomist binary logic of timeless propositions. Or, as Maurice Blondel called it, the opposition "History" and "Dogma".

Blondel's analysis of this dilemma, where two binary logical systems stand opposed leads him to propose (or re-propose) a third, "Tradition", which mediates between the two opposed parties, an "intermediary between history and dogma . . . which would bring about synthesis and maintain solidarity without compromising their relative independence".[3] Tradition, for Blondel, is not the transmission by writing or word of mouth of "historical facts, received truths, accepted teachings, hallowed practices, and ancient customs".[4] If this were so, tradition would simply be a conceptual deposit, conceptual content fixed in the past and transmitted to the present. The rupture between modernist historians and dogmatic theologians, in this view, would be reduced essentially to an argument over the authority of specifically determined conceptual content of the past. What the historians and dogmaticians share is a sense that tradition is fundamentally propositional or conceptual; the only matter upon which they differ is whether the concepts change or not.

In contrast, Blondel applies his developed philosophy of action to describe a notion of tradition rooted in act and practice. With the dogmaticians, Blondel will agree that tradition is, in fact, preserved as the inheritance of the apostles and fathers, but he will argue that it is preserved first and foremost in the moral and spiritual lives of the apostles, in their "moral and religious" actions "which are not unconscious and irrational, but subconscious and unreasoned, which are provisionally and partially irreducible to explicit thought".[5] The immensity and profundity of the truths of the gospel are by their very nature too great and too deep for finite human understanding (even that of extraordinary men like the apostles) to reduce into language and concept. But they are carried and handed on nonetheless in action: "A man can carry out completely what he cannot entirely understand, and in doing it he keeps alive within him the consciousness of a reality which is still half hidden from him."[6] The elements of tradition are thus not propositional or conceptual in nature, but they contain the seeds that can come to bear propositional or conceptual fruit.

---

[3] Maurice Blondel, *History and Dogma*, in *The Letter on Apologetics & History and Dogma*, trans. Alexander Dru and Illtyd Trethowan (Grand Rapids, MI: William B. Eerdmans Publishing Company, 1994), p. 264.

[4] *Ibid.*, p. 265.

[5] *Ibid.*, p. 272. Note the similarity of this argument to that advanced recently by Terence W. Tilley, *Inventing Catholic Tradition* (New York, NY: Orbis Press, 2000), who defines a tradition as a complex set of enduring practices.

[6] Blondel, *History and Dogma*, p. 273.

It is in this moral and religious action that the truths of tradition are preserved and explicated. But it is important to emphasize that the tradition is not preserved in the actions of any one individual or group within the church. Rather, tradition is discerned in the collective action of the church community, what Blondel calls the "total experience of the Church" and the "mediation of collective life". Blondel's notion of tradition is thus historical—it can account for change and development, but it cannot be reduced to an account of historical "facts". At the same time, it preserves dogmatic revelation, but argues that it is a revelation of a *lived reality* that leads to conceptual formulae, not of the conceptual formulae themselves. In the phrase that Blondel seems most nervous about, and yet most insistent upon, "one goes from faith to dogma rather than from dogma to faith".[7]

Blondel thus proposes what we might call, borrowing from Peter Ochs, a logic of repair, aiming to overcome the fractured discourse of modernity's oppositions between history and dogma:

> One has no right to set the facts on one side and the theological data on the other without going back to the sources of life and of action, finding the indivisible synthesis; the facts and definitions are simply faithful translation of it into different languages. The link between facts and beliefs can never be rationally justified by scholarship or dialectics, as though each human reason separately performed its dogmatic task. To succeed in that justification one must consider not only the efforts of each man, but the consensus of all who live the same life and share in the same love.[8]

Blondel thus articulates a capacious vision of the history of practices and communal forms of life that find expression in historical facts or events and articulation in dogmatic formulations, a vision that could fairly be called

---

[7] *Ibid.*, p. 279. It seems only fair to include Blondel's note on this phrase: "This assertion may still, despite everything, disturb some minds; but it is, after all, no more disconcerting than the following: in digging a tunnel, even in the most crumbling sand, excavation always precedes consolidation. The fixity of arguments and definitions, in the moving depths of our life and in the obscurities of our passage to God, is simply part of the unavoidable masonry required in order to keep the road open and to permit further excavations which, in their turn, will need fresh supports."

[8] *Ibid.*, pp. 286–287. Statements like these from Blondel suggest interesting convergences with American pragmatism. In fact Blondel, for a time, adopted the term "pragmatisme" to describe his project, and, in turn, William James, for a time, believed that Blondel's work did converge with his own interests. In the end, his hunch remained, even as he confessed that he could really make no sense of Blondel's argument in *L'Action*. Blondel, too, retreated a bit when he discovered that American pragmatism was beholden to a naturalism that he could not accept. But this may be more true of James than of Peirce. A full comparative philosophical study of Blondel and Peirce is a great *desideratum*. See a first step in this direction in Michael A. Conway, "Maurice Blondel and Early Anglo-American Pragmatism: The Consideration of Religion in a Pragmatic Setting", *Ephemerides Theologicae Louvanienses*, 79:1 (2003), pp. 72–96.

postliberal and pragmatic.[9] But Blondel's account does more than mediate between opposing sides in the "Catholic Modernism" debate—it aims to describe and recover a kind of logic innate to the traditional practice of "faith seeking understanding".

Sources Chrétiennes *and* Théologie: *Re-Sourcing Theology*

What Blondel, as a philosopher, lacked was the capacity to demonstrate this logic present and at work within the tradition itself. This work fell to younger scholars, deeply influenced by Blondel, but trained in the historical and theological disciplines.[10] In the midst of war and occupation, the Jesuits of the Fourvière community in Lyon, led by Jean Daniélou, SJ and Henri de Lubac, SJ, began to produce and publish two book series dedicated "to the renewal of the church". The first, *Sources Chrétiennes*, produced editions of patristic texts, many of which were homilies and scriptural commentaries from the Greek patristic tradition. The second, *Théologie*, offered theoretical discussions of traditional Christian scriptural and doctrinal principles. De Lubac's and Daniélou's zeal to bring *Sources Chrétiennes* and *Théologie* to press in the face of Nazi occupation came from their shared conviction that these deep patristic and scriptural resources were all the more vital to a church faced with persecution.[11] De Lubac wrote during the war (1943) on the need for "spiritual warfare":

> Today, the fight against Christianity is waged not only with regard to one of its foundations or to one of its consequences: it is aimed directly at the heart. The Christian concept of life, Christian spirituality, the inner attitude which, above any particular act or any external gesture, defines the Christian: this is what is at issue.[12]

Spiritual warfare against these attacks required *ressourcement*: "to the degree that we have let ourselves lose it, we have to rediscover the *spirit* of

---

[9] For the ways in which a postliberal and pragmatic vision is compatible with a theological metaphysics, see C.C. Pecknold, *Transforming Postliberal Theology: George Lindbeck, Pragmatism, and Scripture* (London: T&T Clark, 2005).

[10] De Lubac's correspondence with Blondel bears witness to the latter's influence, as does his own testimony in his memoir, *At the Service of the Church: Henri de Lubac Reflects on the Circumstances that Occasioned his Writings*, trans. Anne Elizabeth Englund (San Francisco, CA: Ignatius Press, 1989). See also Michael A. Conway, "Maurice Blondel and *Ressourcement*", in Gabriel Flynn and Paul D. Murray with Patricia Kelly (eds), *Ressourcement: A Movement for Renewal in Twentieth-Century Catholic Theology* (Oxford: Oxford University Press, 2012), pp. 65–82. Of course, there are other influential figures, e.g., John Henry Newman and Etienne Gilson. For a longer discussion of the theoretical relationship between de Lubac and Blondel, see Kevin L. Hughes, "The 'Fourfold Sense': De Lubac, Blondel, and Contemporary Theology", *The Heythrop Journal*, 42:4 (2001), pp. 451–462.

[11] De Lubac, *At the Service of the Church*, pp. 95 and 161.

[12] De Lubac, "Spiritual Warfare", in *Theology in History*, trans. Anne Englund Nash (San Francisco, CA: Ignatius Press, 1996), p. 489.

Christianity. To do so, we have to steep ourselves in its sources".[13] More specifically, De Lubac argued for a vigorous defense of the unity of the Scriptures against those who claimed to distinguish between a "Semite Old Testament" and an "Aryan New Testament"[14]:

> We are still so little accustomed to it that this new kind of offensive risks finding us dazzled at times. But it is important to recover our balance. No Christian must let himself go so far as to think that a movement of withdrawal with respect to the Old Testament would leave his faith intact. Under present conditions, less than ever.[15]

Thus, what Daniélou and de Lubac believed before the war already to be important to the renewal of Christian faith from within became a critical resource for the Christian stand against Nazism, and, after the war, for the Christian approach to the world in general.

Perhaps this is why, in the aftermath of war, both Daniélou and de Lubac turn their attention to a more detailed recovery of patristic and medieval scriptural hermeneutics. Daniélou's 1950 *Sacramentum Futuri: Études sur les origines de la typologie biblique*[16] and his 1951 *Bible et Liturgie*[17] aim to orient readers to the Biblical theology of the early church, not as the elite theological culture of the Church Fathers, but as expressed in the sacraments and liturgical actions of the Catholic Church. For Daniélou, the symbolism of the liturgy itself requires patristic scriptural exegesis to be fully understood and, more importantly, appropriated in the Christian life:

> We are not concerned with the personal theology of the Fathers; but what constitutes for us the supreme value of their work is that in them we meet apostolic tradition . . . Their sacramental theology is a biblical theology, and it is this biblical theology which we are to try to recover.[18]

For Daniélou, the renewal of the Church depends upon the recovery and renewal of a rich Biblical theology that has lain hidden, as it were, in plain

---

[13] *Ibid.*, p. 499.

[14] De Lubac, "A New Religious 'Front' ", in *Theology in History*, p. 486. De Lubac is engaging with Edmond Picard, *Synthese de l'antisemitisme* (1892; reprinted 1941). De Lubac's essay was published in 1942 in the volume *Israel et la foi chretienne*, published in Switzerland and circulated in occupied France.

[15] De Lubac, "A New Religious 'Front' ", p. 486.

[16] Jean Daniélou, *Sacramentum Futuri: Études sur les origènes de la typologie biblique* (Paris: Beauchesne, 1950); English translation: *From Shadows to Reality: Studies in the Biblical Typology of the Fathers*, trans. Wulstan Hibberd (London: Burns & Oates, 1960).

[17] Daniélou, *Bible et Liturgie: la théologie biblique des sacrements et des fêtes d'après les Pères de l'Eglise* (Paris: Éditions du Cerf, 1951); English translation: *The Bible and the Liturgy* (Notre Dame, IN: University of Notre Dame Press, 1956).

[18] Daniélou, *The Bible and the Liturgy*, p. 8.

sight, in the liturgy, carried forward by the tradition, but obscured by a particularly modern objectivist fixation. The "re-sourcing" Daniélou seeks, then, is not so much the recovery of something lost as the unveiling of a hidden, but present, wisdom—the scriptural wisdom of the liturgy.

At roughly the same time[19], Henri de Lubac produced *Histoire et Esprit* (1950), a thorough study of Origen of Alexandria's exegesis.[20] De Lubac's intent was not simply historical; indeed, it was not really historical at all: "For we are not at all concerned with the work of one solitary thinker or with a problem that in no way affects us. This work fits into a tradition that touches us ourselves."[21] Rather boldly, de Lubac rejects the narrow constraints of historical recovery altogether:

> Living the same faith as Origen, members of the same Church, afloat, so to speak, in the same stream of tradition, it would be pointless for us to wish to behave like outside observers . . . It would prohibit us a second time from understanding him.[22]

Giving particular flesh to the conceptual bones of Blondel's mediating "tradition", de Lubac reaches through the common bond of faith handed on in the church to retrieve the scriptural wisdom of Origen, but not to restore it:

> The river does not flow back to its source. No more than life itself does thought retrace itself. Yet perhaps after the long course it has just run through the parched lands of rationalism and positivism, it will find itself more likely to be understood and even taken in today . . . in order to bring to life in us what is expressed of the eternal in these forms now dead. The wells once dug by Origen have long been covered over with sand. But the same deep layer of water is still there, which he can help us find once again in order to quench the same thirst.[23]

History and Spirit reaches back through the tradition to sit at the feet of Origen of Alexandria, but de Lubac's next project endeavours to make that tradition itself visible.

---

[19] To tell the story of *ressourcement* in its entirety, we would have to discuss at some length here the censure of "la nouvelle théologie" apparently represented by de Lubac and Daniélou in the papal encyclical *Humani Generis* in August 1950 and the consequences that followed for the teaching careers of the two Jesuits. For our present purposes, this would lead us too far afield. See Joseph A. Komonchak, "*Humani Generis* and *Nouvelle Théologie*", in Flynn and Murray with Kelly (eds), *Ressourcement*, pp. 138–156.

[20] De Lubac, *Histoire et Esprit: l'intelligence de l'Écriture d'après Origène* (Paris: Aubier, 1950); English translation: *History and Spirit: The Understanding of Scripture according to Origen*, trans. Anne Englund Nash (San Francisco, CA: Ignatius Press, 2007).

[21] De Lubac, *History and Spirit*, p. 13.

[22] *Ibid.*

[23] *Ibid.*, p. 14.

From 1959 to 1964, de Lubac published four thick volumes of *Exégèse médiévale: Les quatre sens de l'écriture*.[24] Like Daniélou, de Lubac aims to recover a scriptural sensibility that was not the preserve of a spiritual and intellectual elite, but of the whole church. He writes:

Whereas I was earlier concerned with a privileged moment in time that was characterized by the blossoming forth of genius, my considerations now lie more particularly with the typical representatives of a tradition that has already been established.[25]

Studying this longer and broader tradition opened up a "whole mental universe", a "current of thought which, through multiple phases of its history, showed itself to be singularly unified".[26]

In brief, de Lubac argues that the tradition of scriptural interpretation captured in the "fourfold sense" was less the introjection of Hellenistic literary theory into the Bible than the description of a vibrant model of integration between the scripture and its interpreter. The first, "literal" or "historical" sense describes the narrative events and figures in scripture through which God acts and reveals. The reader of scripture must understand the narrative before the Bible can mean anything to him or her. The second, "allegorical" sense, for de Lubac, is not just the vague spiritual sense, but unifies the Christian scriptural witness in its testimony to Christ and the church. Understanding this testimony then allows the reader to shape his/her own life and actions in accord with its witness, and this constitutes the third, "moral" sense of scripture. And this process of integration and interiorization of the Word points to its final mystical and/or eschatological consummation, the fourth, "anagogical" sense of scripture. The theology of the fourfold sense is thus as much a spirituality as a hermeneutical rule; it names the way in which the Christian reader—and, liturgically, the whole church—discovers and deepens his/her/their own relationship to the Word as presented to Israel, focused in Christ, applied in practice, and hoped for in prayer. In de Lubac's view, the fourfold sense is thus anything but fanciful additions to the letter; on the contrary, it is the deeper understanding of the place of the Word in the Christian life.

To recover this scriptural sensibility is both to draw the scriptures closer to the center of the Christian life and to expand the semantic field of the scriptural word. Modern rationalist modes of reading tend to seek objectivity, and thus require both univocity of meaning and critical distance from the

---

[24] De Lubac, *Exégèse médiévale: Les quatre sens de l'écriture* (Paris: Aubier, 1959–1964); English translation (in progress): *Medieval Exegesis: The Fourfold Sense*, 3 vols, trans. Marc Sebanc and E. M. Macierowski (Grand Rapids, MI: William B. Eerdmans Publishing Company, 1998–2009).

[25] De Lubac, *Medieval Exegesis*, vol. 1, trans. Marc Sebanc (Grand Rapids: William. B. Eerdmans Publishing Company, 1998), p. xiii.

[26] *Ibid.*, p. xiv.

subjective reader in order to be "true". By contrast, patristic and medieval scriptural reading considers the words of scripture to be *addressed* to the reader, and thus known always in intimate relation to the knower, and, indeed, to the community of knowers, the communion of faith to whom, as one church, the scriptural word is addressed. Secondly, the hermeneutics of the "fourfold sense" names that community's deep conviction that the word so addressed is saturated with signification.

It is important to note that de Lubac recovers this "current of thought" not to replace modern Biblical scholarship: "Nothing is more vain and fruitless than such attempts to return to one of these ancient stages of growth that history makes it possible for us to know, to settle down in it, to ensconce ourselves in it as in a dream."[27] De Lubac acknowledges the shortcomings of this classic Christian approach, and he welcomes the recent progress he sees in contemporary Biblical exegesis. But he hopes that the recovery of this traditional witness will open up new connections between

> before and after . . . between historical reality and spiritual reality, between society and the individual, between time and eternity . . . a whole theology of history, which is connected with a theology of Scripture.[28]

This holistic return to "the fourfold sense" aims to place scripture at the heart of Christian thought and practice, in a way that can integrate the best scholarship without erasing the lived connections of traditional Biblical theology.

The scriptural *ressourcement* spearheaded by de Lubac and Daniélou preceded the Second Vatican Council by more than a decade, but it provided a hermeneutical key that created the conditions for the possibility of a wider engagement with religious traditions, precisely in and through a deeper recovery of its own scriptural tools. That is, it created the conditions for the development of Catholic resources for a movement like Scriptural Reasoning. However, these conditions lay hidden or dormant for some time after the Council, due to other competing narratives in mid-twentieth-century theology and culture.

Liberal and Postliberal Dimensions of Vatican II

The new openness for which the Second Vatican Council is justly praised, with John XXIII's iconic opening of the windows of the church, proceeded in the wake of the Council on a more or less modern, liberal model—that to open the windows was also to sweep out the detritus of the past, that particularities of Catholic faith and practice constrained and limited

---

[27] *Ibid.*, p. xxi.
[28] *Ibid.*, p. xix.

opportunities for dialogue. This model was helpful insofar as it was able to move Catholic thought and practice into a deeper engagement with other confessions and faith traditions, but this deeper engagement required a prior alienation from one's own roots and sources.

A case in point in Biblical Studies: *Dei Verbum*, the Dogmatic Constitution on Divine Revelation, is often cited as a key moment in opening Catholic Biblical scholarship to the results of historical-critical and other critical methodologies, and rightly so. The Catholic embrace of modern Biblical scholarship opened up a much wider horizon for these texts—we could discover the complexity of a collection of historical documents that were assembled from hundreds of different contexts and settings, with many and various authorial and editorial points of view. We could see much more of this text and context of this book than we had before, and, in theory, we could meet with Jewish and Protestant scholars on this neutral meeting ground of the text. The apparent neutrality of the text led scholars to describe their field of study in a new way. What had been "Old Testament Theology" for Christians or Torah and Tanakh study for Jews became in historical-critical scholarship expertise in "Hebrew Bible".

However, as Jewish scholar Jon Levenson has argued, this "Hebrew Bible" is a fictional academic construction—a kind of remainder-set of texts that belong properly to no religious community, neither as Tanakh for the Jews nor Old Testament for the Christians. "Hebrew Bible" names, then, not a meeting ground for faith communities, but a meeting ground free of faith, since the commitments that identify Jews as Jews and Christians as Christians are the very same commitments that give those common texts meaning and significance to each community.

> Like citizens of the classical liberal state, scholars practicing historical criticism of the Bible are expected to eliminate or minimize their communal loyalties, to see them as legitimately operative only within associations that are private, non-scholarly, and altogether voluntary.[29]

Without such communally-valued meanings, the gathering of texts in the Hebrew Bible is of only archival interest. As Levenson says, "the very value-neutrality of this method of study puts its practitioners at a loss to defend the *value* of the enterprise itself".[30]

It is in this way that these liberal models of scriptural scholarship, authorized and promoted by *Dei Verbum* and dominant throughout the twentieth century, ironically risked introducing a rift between the scriptures and the community of faith, leaving the proper interpretation of scripture solely in

---

[29] Jon D. Levenson, "Historical Criticism and the Fate of the Enlightenment Project", in *id.*, *The Hebrew Bible, the Old Testament, and Historical Criticism* (Louisville, KY: Westminster/John Knox Press, 1993), p. 118.

[30] *Ibid.*, p. 109.

the hands of authorized professional exegetes and bearing witness only to the social, cultural, and political contexts of the ancient periods that generated them. However, upon re-examination, *Dei Verbum*, perhaps more than any other major document in Vatican II, was shaped by the principles of *ressourcement* that de Lubac and Daniélou had promoted. As Brian Daley writes, *Dei Verbum* contains

> very little explicit allusion to the writings and exegetical practices of the church Fathers as the inspiration for its new perspective on revelation and biblical interpretation.... Still, *Dei Verbum's* approach to God's revealing Word bears the marks of a hermeneutical reorientation that would lead Catholic biblical study, and the rest of Catholic theology, on a journey, still underway, away from the literalism and rationalism of scholastic proof-texting and deductive argument, towards a new ability to live, reason, and worship intelligently in a world of life-giving signs. ... Scripture, tradition, and Magisterium are structural principles of a single, divinely constituted world of life-giving signs . . .[31]

This hermeneutical reorientation is precisely along the trajectory established by de Lubac and Daniélou, not in opposition to modern Biblical criticism, but with a broader context for it within a "traditioned" scriptural awareness. As Daley notes, the journey is still underway because modern liberal Biblical scholarship, left to itself, may simply replace an older, scholastic "literalism and rationalism" with a newer historical-critical one, a kind of new dogmatic slumber from which we are just beginning to awake.[32] Nevertheless, built into the Dogmatic Constitution on Divine Revelation was the potential for a radical postliberal re-centering of Catholic theology and practice on the "world of life-giving signs" through a re-connection to the tradition of patristic and medieval scriptural understanding.

The Catholic Return to Scripture and the "Re-sourcing" of Scriptural Reasoning

The broader return to scripture, as framed by *Dei Verbum*, creates the opportunity for Catholic self-understanding to return to its own deepest roots, not, as de Lubac was always careful to say, in flight from the developments of

---

[31] Brian Daley, "Knowing God in History and in the Church: *Dei Verbum* and 'Nouvelle Théologie' ", in Flynn and Murray with Kelly (eds), *Ressourcement*, pp. 350–351.

[32] Evidence for this shift in approaches to Biblical studies is abundant, dating in Anglo-American Biblical scholarship, at least, from the publication of E. P. Sanders, *The Historical Figure of Jesus* (London: Allen Lane, 1993) and Luke Timothy Johnson, *The Real Jesus: The Misguided Quest for the Historical Jesus and the Truth of the Traditional Gospels* (San Francisco, CA: HarperCollins, 1996). See Luke Timothy Johnson and William S. Kurz, SJ, *The Future of Catholic Biblical Scholarship: A Constructive Conversation* (Grand Rapids, MI: William B. Eerdmans Publishing Company, 2002) for an interesting discussion of these trends.

modern criticism, but in tandem with them, trusting in the mediating capacity of the tradition of interpretation to communicate the rooted depths of scriptural wisdom even as it engages new questions in the twenty-first century. It is in this respect that Catholic theology is most properly prepared to participate in and contribute to Scriptural Reasoning. *Nostra Aetate*, the Vatican II Declaration on the Relation of the Church to Non-Christian Religions, has a clear and fundamental role in opening opportunities for Catholic interreligious engagement, affirming "those things which are true and holy" in non-Christian religions (*NA*, 2). But in itself, it offers no models for *how* this interreligious engagement might proceed. As I have suggested above, common modern liberal attempts to find a kind of neutral territory between Jews and Christians in Biblical studies of the Hebrew Bible have often run aground short of bringing about substantive theological engagement; a deeper context from the depths of each religious tradition's wisdom is required. Scriptural Reasoning represents one such promising context, and *ressourcement* gives Catholics a fruitful path into this rich conversation. Indeed, *ressourcement* may offer a way in which Catholics may not only share in but also deepen Scriptural Reasoning's own habits and practices of shared study.

As many will know, Scriptural Reasoning began to take shape in the nineteen-nineties when Christian theologians (Daniel Hardy and David Ford) "listened in" on Jewish scholars engaged in what they called "Textual Reasoning", a mode of shared study aimed at repairing modern forms of reasoning in part by returning to the model of traditional Jewish *chevruta* study-fellowship.[33] This shared give-and-take over the scriptural text among Jews was expanded to include Christians and Jews. In essence, then, Scriptural Reasoning has always taken its basic form and inspiration from rabbinic discourse, even if it has not necessarily engaged the rabbinic tradition explicitly. Like the Christian discourse of the "fourfold sense" discussed above, rabbinic discourse presumes that the scriptural word is semantically saturated, and so multiple senses within the broader context of a tradition of inquiry and argument do not call the authority of the scriptural word into question. On the contrary, this tradition supports and affirms the rich resources of revelation. Textual and Scriptural Reasoning communities have relied upon this framing sense of the plural richness of the scriptural word to create the formal space for their cross-traditional scriptural study.

From 2003 to 2006, the Center of Theological Inquiry in Princeton sponsored a Scriptural Reasoning research project, in which I participated, that endeavored to take a further step, taking Jewish, Christian, and Islamic scriptures *and* the traditions of commentary upon them as focal points of study.[34]

---

[33] See David Ford's essay in this volume.
[34] See the fruits of this research project in Peter Ochs and William Stacy Johnson (eds), *Crisis, Call, and Leadership in the Abrahamic Traditions* (New York: Palgrave Macmillan, 2009).

This new direction provides the opportunity for Scriptural Reasoning to take its own "deep reasonings" deeper, into models of interpretation, like Talmudic commentary, Islamic *tafsīr*, and the Christian Biblical commentary tradition we have seen illuminated by the *ressourcement* theologians. These models of interpretation both place scriptures at the center of theological reflection and de-center the authority of the single modern interpreter's encounter with the text. As Steven Fraade says of Talmudic commentary:

> This collective nature of the *Sifre*'s commentary gives the impression not of a single commentator standing face to face with the text of scripture in the unmediated work of interpretation (as if such were ever fully possible), but of a collector and subtle shaper of received *traditions* who creates a commentary out of such traditions by configuring them not only in relation to the atomized texts of Deuteronomy but also in relation to one another.... This is the dialectic of continuity and innovation that characterizes the stance of sociohistorically grounded traditionality ... the multivocality of a received yet restless tradition.[35]

This recovery of each community's "received yet restless tradition", held in dialogue with each other, helps to break open the wider horizon of conversation without losing the scriptural center that unites our study and fellowship. Since the very form of thought recovered in these wisdom traditions is already a mode of engaging plural interpretations, holding varied readings in tension, seasoned through generations of study, our shared study among Jews, Christians, and Muslims could draw upon the form and logic of our own tradition-centered discourse to engage fruitfully with the plural interpretations that arise around the table over the three scriptures.

This form of Scriptural Reasoning is still in infancy, but it holds great promise. The wisdom traditions of scriptural interpretation in each of the Abrahamic faiths has relied upon this depth-dimension, this "received yet restless tradition"; without attention to this, each tradition is tempted to adopt those modern modes of interpretation that presume the sovereign activity of the solitary *cogito*. Shared Abrahamic study will be better equipped to sustain its work and repair these modern habits of inquiry insofar as that study engages the scriptures from within the deepest resources of each wisdom tradition. The Catholic contribution, in the recovery of insight from the Christian tradition's own traditional exegesis, can be substantial.

But the gift, in a certain respect, is reciprocal. If it is fair to say that the Christian tradition is continually tempted by supersessionism in its relation to Judaism, then it is also fair to be concerned that a simple *recovery* of

---

[35] Steven D. Fraade, *From Tradition to Commentary: Torah and its Interpretation in the Midrash Sifre to Deuteronomy* (Albany, NY: State University of New York Press, 1991), p. 17.

traditional Christian exegesis brings with it traditional texts and figures that can lend themselves to such supersessionist readings; indeed, one scholar has recently critiqued de Lubac, fairly or not, for uncritically receiving this dimension of the Christian past.[36] But recovering the Christian interpretive tradition *in the presence of Abrahamic fellowship* offers the discipline of encounter with others, so that it becomes more than a recovery, becoming instead a re-invigoration and re-imagination of the deep wisdom of our own tradition. This, after all, is what Catholic scholars like Blondel, de Lubac, and Daniélou always hoped for. It may be, to use an old image, that we now are like dwarves on the shoulders of giants, able to see on the horizon the prospect of interreligious peace because we are elevated by our particular tradition's best scriptural wisdom.

---

[36] See Robin Darling Young, "An Imagined Unity: Henri de Lubac & the Ironies of Ressourcement", *Commonweal*, 139:15 (14 September 2012), pp. 13–18. Available at: http://commonwealmagazine.org; last accessed 3 November 2012.

Modern Theology 29:4 October 2013
ISSN 0266-7177 (Print)
ISSN 1468-0025 (Online)

DOI: 10.1111/moth.12061

CATHOLIC REASONING AND READING ACROSS TRADITIONS

DAVID DAULT

[The church] therefore calls upon all its sons and daughters with prudence and charity, through dialogues and cooperation with the followers of other religions, bearing witness to the Christian faith and way of life, to recognise, preserve and promote those spiritual and moral good things as well as the socio-cultural values which are to be found among them.[1]

The purpose of the present article is to explore the role of the Catholic voice within the models of intra-faith hospitality put forth by the practices known collectively as "Scriptural Reasoning". Moreover, this article hopes to suggest ways in which the models of Scriptural Reasoning might be profitably incorporated into explicitly Catholic discourse and praxis.

The article will proceed by interrogating the place of the Catholic voice within present Scriptural Reasoning practices, raising inquiries as to how the models of Scriptural Reasoning account for, or elide, explicitly Catholic identity within its structures of hospitality.

A Schematic Structure of the Praxis of Scriptural Reasoning

"Scriptural Reasoning" names practices of reading together across faith traditions that find their origins in the experiments in reading conducted by members of the "Post-Modern Jewish Philosophy Network" in the nineteen-nineties, culminating in a large scale public gathering at Drew University

David Dault
Department of Religion and Philosophy, Christian Brothers University, 650 East Parkway South, Memphis, TN 38104, USA
Email: ddault@cbu.edu

[1] Declaration on the Relation of the Church to Non-Christian Religions (*Nostra Aetate*), 2.

in 1997 under the title, "Textualities: An International Conference on Postmodern Jewish Reasoning".[2] The practices developed by this network through their gatherings and online exchanges evolved into the practice now known as "Textual Reasoning".[3] The key term for the textual reasoners was *dialogue*, which Peter Ochs explained did not mean "simple agreement", but rather refers "to a relationship that persists despite difference: one that honors difference, argument and even verbal struggle as instruments of *tikkun olam* [the healing of the world], rather than as obstacles". The community created by the shared reading praxis of textual reasoning, moreover, "is not merely an end in itself, but also a means of working for a much wider world".[4]

The practitioners of textual reasoning soon realized that this "working for a much wider world" necessitated engagement with voices outside the Jewish tradition. As David Ford recounts, "this led into 'Scriptural Reasoning', which was first Jewish-Christian, and then in the late 1990s became Jewish-Christian-Muslim".[5] There is no one official description of Scriptural Reasoning, and those who write about it point out that Scriptural Reasoning praxis is experimental and pragmatic in nature, proceeding from action to reflection, rather than beginning with a well-structured theory.

That being said, some features of Scriptural Reasoning perdure and can be noted. First is the observation of Nicholas Adams that "Scriptural Reasoning is a practice of 'publicizing' deep reasonings, so that others may learn to understand them and discover why particular trains of reasoning, and not just particular assumptions, are attractive or problematic".[6] Second are the guiding metaphors of the "House", the "Campus", and the "Tent of Meeting". As David Ford explains, Scriptural Reasoning participants "are simultaneously members of a synagogue, church or mosque ('houses'), of a university ('campus'), and of a Scriptural Reasoning group ('tent')".[7] The "Tent of Meeting" is a metaphor for any temporary location used for mutual study and governed by hospitality.

---

[2] For more on the origins and development of Scriptural Reasoning, see David F. Ford, "Scriptural Reasoning and the Legacy of Vatican II: Their Mutual Engagement and Significance" in this collection.

[3] Peter Ochs, "Introduction", in Peter Ochs and Nancy Levene (eds), *Textual Reasonings: Jewish Philosophy and Text Study at the End of the Twentieth Century* (Grand Rapids, MI: William B. Eerdmans Publishing Company, 2003), pp. 4–5.

[4] *Ibid.*, p. 6.

[5] David F. Ford, "An Interfaith Wisdom: Scriptural Reasoning Between Jews, Christians, and Muslims", in David F. Ford and C. C. Pecknold (eds), *The Promise of Scriptural Reasoning* (Malden, MA: Blackwell, 2006), p. 4. I highly recommend Ford's excellent essay, as well as the essay that follows it, "A Handbook for Scriptural Reasoning", by Steven Kepnes, for those readers unfamiliar with the history and mechanics of Scriptural Reasoning.

[6] Nicholas Adams, *Habermas and Theology* (Cambridge: Cambridge University Press, 2006), p. 242, quoted in Ford, "An Interfaith Wisdom", p. 6.

[7] Ford, "An Interfaith Wisdom", p. 7.

Most of the work that results in Scriptural Reasoning occurs in the more permanent "houses" of our various faith communities. In these permanent structures, practitioners undertake what might be called "preparatory reasoning". Such reasonings might include catechesis, doctrinal training, and traditioned study of scripture. With identities formed by such communities, participants are made ready for brief forays into the space between the three houses of Judaism, Islam, and Christianity. It is in this "middle space" that the "Tent of Meeting" is erected, scriptures selected, and Scriptural Reasoning can occur.[8]

Finally, as Steven Kepnes has noted, Scriptural Reasoning "begins with the scriptural sense that the human world is broken, in exile, off the straight path, filled with corruption, sickness, war and genocide. Scriptural Reasoning practitioners come together out of a sense of impoverishment, suffering, and conflict to seek resources for healing".[9] This healing, as mentioned above, is referred to in the Jewish tradition by the Hebrew term *tikkun olam*, and has emerged as the explicit goal of Scriptural Reasoning praxis.

The Relation of Scriptural Reasoning to Preparatory Reasonings

Scriptural Reasoning is thus a cross-traditional conversational model that bridges these three Abrahamic faiths. Its praxis is built, moreover, on preparatory reasonings that occur in the context of each of these faith "houses" individually. Textual Reasoning, mentioned above, is one example of this, specific to Judaism. However, we can also note Qur'anic Reasoning, as preparatory reasoning for the Islamic practitioners of Scriptural Reasoning.

What this preparatory practice might look like for Christians, however, has proved somewhat more elusive to define. Would we call it "New Testament Reasoning"? Not without falling into the trap of Marcionism. Would we then call it "Biblical Reasoning"? Yes, but only with the caveat that the term "Bible" will be fundamentally different than its cognate term for our Jewish counterparts. Should we then call this preparatory exercise simply "Christian Reasoning"?

Perhaps "Christian Reasoning" is the best term to be found, but the use of this term will still present a distortion of the preparatory exercise being described. The term would present a simplification of a complexity and a problematic that goes to the heart of the very term "Christian" itself. Most particularly, we cannot assume that Christians share a text, at least in the manner of Textual and Qur'anic Reasonings. Tanakh and Qur'an represent relatively stable texts, around which various communities of Jewish and Muslim readers are differentiated. In contrast, Protestant, Catholic, and Orthodox Bibles are themselves composed of books of different lengths,

---

[8] See Kepnes, "A Handbook for Scriptural Reasoning", p. 24.
[9] *Ibid.*

and indeed entirely different books are included or rejected in the various canons of Christian Scripture. Moreover, if we entertain the possibility that the term "Christian" might even include groups such as the Church of Jesus Christ of Latter-Day Saints, then we have to account for an entirely additional work, The Book of Mormon, in this notion of scripture.

As practitioners of Scriptural Reasoning, we may find that there is a simplified narrative in our self-description, namely that we are "three Abrahamic traditions" coming together for mutual study in a temporary "Tent of Meeting", where "the text is our only host". Always tacitly suspended in this process, of course, is the reality that the stability of each "Abrahamic tradition" is problematized by internal tensions. Reformed, Reconstructionist, Orthodox, Conservative and other identities complicate what "Judaism" brings to the Tent of Meeting; Sunni, Shi'a, American Black Muslim, Sufi and other identities, complicate "Islam". In these cases, the frictions of identity are subdued—at least for the period of hospitality that constitutes a session of Scriptural Reasoning—by reference to the stabilized texts of the Qur'an and the Tanakh. In like manner, the "Christianity" we speak of in Scriptural Reasoning is always troubled and haunted by the shadow of the Reformation, and perhaps also by the Great Schism of 1054, but without the benefit of a stabilized and common text to which these various groups (which are always referenced, but never fully described by, the term "Christian") might refer for temporary respite.

The term "Christian", therefore, will not function well as a term of inclusion for this type of preparatory reasoning, at least in the manner that "Textual" and "Qur'anic" function in their preparatory cognates. Quite frankly, however, this has heretofore not been recognized as a problem in the discourse of Scriptural Reasoning. Scriptural Reasoning has had a form of "Christianity" as an interlocutor at the Tent of Meeting, of course, but this is largely because, both at the levels of practice and of reflection, the "Christianity" that has engaged—and been engaged by—Scriptural Reasoning has most often defaulted to a "Christianity" best defined as both Protestant and postliberal.[10]

Problematics of the Catholic Voice in the Context of Scriptural Reasoning

In March 2009 I visited the University of Virginia (UVA) to meet with Peter Ochs, spend a few days giving presentations about my research, and interact with Ochs's graduate students in the Scripture, Interpretation, and Practice program in the department of Religious Studies. Part of my schedule included participation in an exposition of Scriptural Reasoning, to which a select group of UVA faculty had been invited.

---

[10] Cf. *Ibid.*, p. 36 and Peter Ochs, "Philosophic Warrants for Scriptural Reasoning", in Ford and Pecknold (eds), *The Promise of Scriptural Reasoning*, p. 122.

The exposition took place over the course of about three hours on a Tuesday evening in an upstairs lounge in Halsey Hall on the UVA grounds. It began with a plenary session, where Peter Ochs described the basic aims and structures of Scriptural Reasoning and outlined the evening's schedule. From there, we broke into smaller assigned groups for a period of focused Scriptural Reasoning study around selected scriptural texts. Coming back into plenary after about an hour, each group shared a bit of what was discovered in reading together. This was followed by a final period, where the faculty participants were invited to ask questions and offer their responses to the Scriptural Reasoning process.

It was at this point, during the question and response period, that one participant, Slavica Jakelic, raised a concern. "This is not the way I read the Bible," she said plainly. "I am a Roman Catholic, and we do not simply sit and read Scripture, bare Scripture. There are commentaries. There is Tradition. There is preparation. These are necessary to the process of reading Scripture, for me."[11]

In the present architecture of Scriptural Reasoning, these "extra-scriptural" elements—commentary, Tradition, and preparation—are expected to be present, but present chiefly in the identity of the participant herself, rather than physically alongside the scripture being studied.[12] In other words, it is expected that the Muslim, the Jewish, and the Christian readers who gather in the Tent of Meeting will understand their traditions of reading Scripture, thanks to their *previous* participation in forms of preparatory reasoning. However, it is also expected that the participants will *not* bring these resources to the table in the Tent, except in an oblique manner.

Let me offer a Catholic critique of Scriptural Reasoning, in the vein of Jakelic's above: no matter how well-intentioned, the Scriptural Reasoning model will often appear to the Catholic participant as an example of what Katherine Clay Bassard calls the "individual loosening of the text" in the form of private, or at least non-magisterial, interpretations. "Thus, the private interpreter first shrinks the Bible to a select number of passages, then proceeds to comment on those as though they served as a representation of the whole text."[13] Moreover, even where Scriptural Reasoning might be able to encompass the "whole text" of scripture itself, there is, for the Catholic participant, always a "text beyond the text", for which an accounting must be made. This text—the Apostolic Deposit, the Sacred Tradition, or the Magisterial Faith—is by definition outside, and predecessor to, scripture. Catholic exegetes are expected to proceed "through fidelity to the great Tradition, of which the

---

[11] These comments are not meant to be taken as direct quotation. They do, however, accurately reflect the character of Jakelic's comments that evening.

[12] Aref Nayed's suggestion of the " 'internal library' ", mentioned in Kepnes, "A Handbook for Scriptural Reasoning", p. 31.

[13] Katherine Clay Bassard, *Transforming Scriptures: African American Writers and the Bible* (Athens, GA: University of Georgia Press, 2010), p. 28.

Bible itself is a witness", always toward the principal aim "which is the deepening of faith".[14]

It should be remembered that, in terms of publications, Catholic engagement with Scriptural Reasoning and Textual Reasoning has often been described by expert non-Catholics, rather than by Catholic practitioners themselves. A notable case in this regard is George Lindbeck's "Progress in Textual Reasoning: From Vatican II to the Conference at Drew".[15] As an invited observer of Vatican II, there is no reason to doubt Lindbeck's credentials to comment on the proceedings. Moreover, there is no reason to assert that, as a Lutheran, Lindbeck lacks in any way the capacity or the insight to comment on Catholic matters. Even so, as both a Catholic and a practitioner of Scriptural Reasoning, the essay continues to give me pause. My perspective on the Catholic engagement with Scriptural Reasoning, and the Catholic engagement with scripture in the wake of Vatican II, is fundamentally different from the perspective put forth by Lindbeck in this essay, and more broadly in his writings on postliberal theology. My purpose here, however, is not to contradict Lindbeck, but to complement his position with my own reportage of experiments in Scriptural Reasoning as a Catholic participant.

Of chief concern, Lindbeck's accounting proceeds from the assumption that "contemporary Jews and Christians face similar textual crises", namely that:

> Modernity's univocal and dichotomously true-or-false interpretive strategies leave only two options. One option is fundamentalist slavery to the supposedly unchangeable "literal" sense (which is in fact a historically conditioned modern claimant to the title). The other option is emancipation from that slavery through liberalism's efforts, first, to reject the authority of the text as vehicle of God's word to the believing community and, second, to replace the authority of text with the authority of experience or reason.[16]

But such an accounting, though possibly accurate with regard to "contemporary Jews and [*Protestant*] Christians", fails to describe accurately the self-understanding of contemporary *Catholic* exegetes. Where is the Catholic exegete to locate herself in Lindbeck's claim that "Christians" are trapped in these two options? She neither sees herself as caught in "fundamentalist slavery," nor as "emancipated" from the authority of the text. Indeed,

---

[14] The Pontifical Biblical Commission, *The Interpretation of the Bible in the Church* (Boston, MA: Pauline Books and Media, 1993), p. 134. See also United States Conference of Catholic Bishops [hereafter USCCB], *Catechism of the Catholic Church* (Liguori, MO: United States Catholic Conference, 1994), pp. 32–33, § 109–114.

[15] George Lindbeck, "Progress in Textual Reasoning: From Vatican II to the Conference at Drew", in Ochs and Levene (eds), *Textual Reasonings*, pp. 252–258.

[16] *Ibid.*, p. 253.

within Catholic models of interpretation, as outlined in the Pontifical Biblical Commission's *The Interpretation of the Bible in the Church* and elsewhere, there is never a bargain to be made between "the authority of the text" and "the authority of reason". To accept such a bargain would be, for the Catholic exegete, to misunderstand at a fundamental level what the task of exegesis *is*.[17]

A further dimension by which the Catholic voice and presence problematizes the identification "Christian" for Scriptural Reasoning is in the assertion that, at least as far as Catholicism is concerned, "the Christian faith is not a 'religion of the book'. Christianity is the religion of the 'Word' of God".[18] The Catholic relation to scripture, under this dynamic, is profoundly different from that of the Protestant relation to scripture. This goes beyond the rejection of *sola scriptura*, the Protestant doctrine that the Christian faith is undergirded by "scripture alone", to the rejection of the possibility of reading scripture *alone*. That is, the reading of scripture by itself, apart from the commentaries, Tradition, and preparation, is rejected, as is the possibility of reading (and interpreting) scripture as an individual, apart from the Apostolic community.

Thus, within the practice of Scriptural Reasoning, the Catholic voice always speaks as the "other" within and apart from the "Christianity" chosen by the founders of Scriptural Reasoning as their interlocutor. It is a "Christianity" neither Protestant nor postliberal. Yet it retains the respect and authority accorded scripture by Protestant Christians, while simultaneously embracing the flexibility of reading and exegesis championed by the postliberals. Catholic practices of exegesis, as outlined in the Catechism, *The Interpretation of the Bible in the Church, Dei Verbum,* and other documents, find a natural affinity with Scriptural Reasoning praxis, though not with the assumptions Scriptural Reasoning makes (and perhaps must make) about the identity of its "Christian" interlocutor.

In the remainder of this article, I will seek to outline one possible path to what might be called "Catholic Reasoning". This reasoning, then, can be seen as a cognate to both Textual and Qur'anic Reasonings, but also as a contraposition within the logic of the "Christian" Scriptural Reasoning interlocutor itself. To the default assumption of Scriptural Reasoning that "Christian" indicates Protestant and postliberal discourse, Catholic Reasoning's voice speaks as the hospitable and sympathetic "other".

Finally, then, as a form of preparatory reasoning that seeks to be identified as "Christian", what follows can be seen as an attempt to articulate "Catholic Reasoning" in distinction to the continued presence and existence (heretofore unnamed within the more "official" reflections on Scriptural Reasoning,

---

[17] The Pontifical Biblical Commission, *The Interpretation of the Bible in the Church*, pp. 104, 116 and *passim*.

[18] USCCB, *Catechism of the Catholic Church*, p. 31, § 108.

though casually discussed among practitioners) of a privileged preparatory practice we might now call "Protestant Reasoning."

The Source of Catholic Reasonings

The task of a Catholic Reasoning does not begin, then, with an agreement about the nature of texts or the nature of methods used to read those texts. Any meaningful discussion of Catholic Reasoning, and the Catholic voice within Scriptural Reasoning, must instead begin with mutual agreement on the profound need and desire for *deep healing*. Though we may eventually move to a place of mutual agreement about the nature of texts and the nature of methods used to read those texts, the Catholic engagement with Scriptural Reasoning must begin instead with a profound agreement about *tikkun olam*.

First of all, the reality of Catholicism, both since 1054 and since the Reformation, is that of a broken unity. In *Unitatis Redintegratio* (1964) the church laments:

> Even in the beginnings of this one and only church of God there arose certain rifts, which the apostle strongly condemned. But in subsequent centuries much more extensive dissensions made their appearance and large communities came to be separated from the full communion of the catholic church—for which, often enough, people of both sides were to blame.[19]

The ecclesiology of the church prizes both unity and diversity, but not division,[20] and thus the present state of separation presents a wound to the heart of the church itself.

Furthermore, the present state of intra-Catholic relations is also infected by fracture. Both worldwide and in America, the contemporary Catholic experience is one of deep division, where both "conservative" and "progressive" forces within the social body of the Church vie for legitimacy. Attempts to render the ideological "other" within Catholicism as illegitimate involve rhetorics of exclusion and exclusivity that run counter to the rhetorics of hospitality and communion that are of the essence of the marks of the church.

In the fourth and fifth centuries, the Donatist controversy erupted in North Africa over whether or not the church could be hospitable to the baptisms of those who entered the communion of the Body of Christ under the care of those declared to be heretics and schismatics. Despite the protestations of hard-liners, the church eventually answered "yes." In contemporary terms, the church now defines its unity by taking the Trinity as its essence and its

---

[19] *UR*, 3.
[20] USCCB, *Catechism of the Catholic Church*, pp. 214–215, § 813–814.

model, affirming simultaneously that the church is one, while affirming also the church as encompassing diversity and relationality.[21]

Despite this historical affirmation of fundamental hospitality within the one, holy, catholic, and apostolic church, an undeniable yearning for Donatist exclusivism persists in many corners. Whether we consider the positions of contemporary hard-liners within the church, such as Bishop Olmstead of the Diocese of Phoenix (who revoked the Catholic status of St Joseph's Hospital in 2009 because it was "not committed to following the teaching of the Catholic church"), or hard-line schismatics such as the Society of St Pius X (ultra-traditionalist followers of Archbishop Marcel Lefebvre who reject the legitimacy of Vatican II), we can find ready to hand many examples of those who wish the Catholic Church to be purified of dissent, exclusivist in nature, and monolingual in doctrine and practice. This yearning for a neo-Donatism within the church is productive of a deep binarism at the heart of contemporary Catholicism. This is coupled with the binarism of schism found in the divisions between Catholic and Protestant already mentioned.

I draw this language of "binarism" and its critique from the work of Peter Ochs, particularly his essay, "Philosophical Warrants for Scriptural Reasoning". In the essay, Ochs suggests that "the logical strategy [to be employed here] is, briefly put, to distinguish between the binary logics that help us recognize marks of both suffering and oppression and the triadic logics that help us recognize and recommend acts of repair and redemption".[22] Following the insights gained through many years of Scriptural Reasoning practice, we can begin to experiment with tactics to name and heal these binarisms, while being careful not simply to repeat and re-inscribe the binarisms by "othering" hard-liners and those who might reject the Catholic tradition of hospitality (what I am terming here "neo-Donatists") as well as those communities recognized by the church to be in schism.

It is this fundamental reality—that the one, holy, catholic and apostolic church exists in wounded unity within itself and with those who share the baptism of the church but not communion with the church—that must be primary to any undertaking of Catholic Reasoning. In sum, "the desire to recover the unity of all Christians is a gift of Christ and a call of the Holy Spirit".[23] The participation of the Catholic voice in Scriptural Reasoning, and the development of any preparatory practices of Catholic Reasoning, must both be grounded first and foremost as a response to this call. The Catholic voice joins the Tent of Meeting within Scriptural Reasoning by recognizing, in the *tikkun olam* that is the goal of Scriptural Reasoning, that same goal, which it names as the *gift of Christ*.

---

[21] See, for example, USCCB, *Catechism of the Catholic Church*, pp. 214–215, § 813–814.
[22] Ochs, "Philosophical Warrants for Scriptural Reasoning", p. 122.
[23] USCCB, *Catechism of the Catholic Church*, p. 217, § 820.

Catholic Reasoning as Response to the Call of the Holy Spirit

Having recognized the primary need for *deep healing*, and having accepted that unity of this healing is both a gift and something which the Church must "always pray [for] and work [for], reinforce, and perfect"[24], the next step is to undertake a response to this call. The Catechism outlines the requirements for any such response. They include: 1) permanent renewal of the Church and greater fidelity to its vocation; 2) conversion of the hearts of the faithful, and the hope of conversion of the hearts of the unfaithful; 3) prayer in common, and efforts toward "spiritual ecumenism"; 4) fraternal knowledge of each other; 5) ecumenical formation; 6) dialogue and meetings among the divided Christian communities; and 7) "human service"—collaborative efforts to serve humankind.[25]

Any practitioner of Scriptural Reasoning will recognize in this list of requirements some similarities with the methods and ethical commitments they have experienced in the Tent of Meeting. Ecumenical formation and fraternal knowledge are certainly hallmarks of Scriptural Reasoning, as is the goal of dialogue and "human service". Whether speaking of Scriptural Reasoning or Catholic Reasoning, the starting point of wounded unity and the need for deep healing will draw the practitioner to a similar set of practices, with similar goals. Both the Catholic Reasoner and the Scriptural Reasoner are prompted to seek communal readings and fraternal study, where deepening relationships across difference are both possible and necessary.

Models of Catholic Reasoning

In the remainder of this article, I will outline a series of approaches to Catholic Reasoning. These practices are suggestive, not exhaustive. They arise out of my own observations of Catholic Reasoning in action, and my reflections upon several experiments in practices that might be called "Catholic preparatory reasoning" in which I have participated here in the Diocese of Memphis over the last three years.

Magisterial Reasoning

Though "all the members of the Church" are affirmed in their "role in the interpretation of Scripture", the Pontifical Biblical Commission's 1993 document *The Interpretation of the Bible in the Church* makes clear that "in the exercise of their pastoral ministry, bishops, as successors of the apostles, are the first witnesses and guarantors of the living tradition within which

---

[24] *Ibid.*
[25] *Ibid.*, p. 217, § 821.

Scripture is interpreted in every age".[26] Unlike models of Christian preparatory reasoning that arise from Protestant traditions, Catholic Reasoning must
recognize that its praxis is secondary to the primary interpretive praxis of the
episcopacy of the Church. Thus Catholic Reasoners will not suppose they
have initiated the actions toward the deep healing they seek, but rather will
orient their hopes and efforts within frameworks that are always already
being undertaken by the bishops of the Church. These models of healing and
inter-faith dialogue, undertaken at the institutional level of the Catholic
Church, might be understood in the nomenclature of Scriptural Reasoning as
a form of "Magisterial Reasoning", that is, the dialogical attempts of the
Catholic Magisterium to think and reason with its religious others in the
world—Protestant, Muslim, Jew, and beyond.

The term *Magisterium* derives from the Latin *magister*, one with the authority of a teacher. According to Richard Gaillardetz, in post-Vatican II Catholicism the term is used "almost exclusively in reference to, first the unique
teaching authority of the bishops, and finally to the bishops themselves.
Today the term is commonly used as a synonym for the college of bishops
under the headship of the bishop of Rome".[27] As Gaillardetz notes, the
Second Vatican Council reawakened the operative voice of the laity, as faithful partners to the bishops, in its affirmation of the *sensus fidei* and the
consensus fidelium.[28] In the wake of Vatican II these terms, indicating both the
"instinct for faith" given to believers at baptism, and the receptive unity of
the faithful with received truths protected and interpreted by the Magisterium, become the guideposts for a secondary, but necessary, operation of the
laity in the life of the Church.

Gaillardetz explicates a dialogical model of dogmatic reception, what he
refers to as a *communio* model of reception, offering "a reciprocal give and
take between the bishops and the community".[29] The *communio* model,
moreover,

> strives to honor two ecclesial realities: (1) the unique role of the bishops
> as those distinctly empowered within the Church to offer authoritative
> determinations of the apostolic faith, and (2) the role of the whole people
> of God who share in the process of hearing and giving expression to the
> Word of God as its subtle reverberations are discerned in the received
> tradition and the ongoing life of the Church.[30]

Any attempt to integrate the Catholic voice into Scriptural Reasoning, and
any attempt to integrate Scriptural Reasoning praxis into Catholic practices

---

[26] The Pontifical Biblical Commission, *The Interpretation of the Bible in the Church*, p. 102.
[27] Richard R. Gaillardetz, *By What Authority?: A Primer on Scripture, the Magisterium, and the Sense of the Faithful* (Collegeville, PA: The Liturgical Press, 2003), p. 60.
[28] *Ibid.*, pp. 108 and 116 respectively.
[29] *Ibid.*, p. 115.
[30] *Ibid.*, p. 117.

of community reading, must make an attempt at accounting for these two ecclesial realities in their deep mutual necessity. A Catholic participant in Scriptural Reasoning, in this manner, might be said to have a dual commitment: to the text, and to the Magisterium of the church. However, if the grounding commitment of deep healing/*tikkun olam* is the starting point, then there is no reason this dual commitment should be antagonistic. The Catholic practitioner of Scriptural Reasoning will not be "serving two masters" but rather will seek to serve Christ by undertaking this reparative dialogical praxis within the Tent of Meeting, precisely *because*, by doing so, the practitioner can best demonstrate *consensus fidelium* with the Magisterium, which is itself undertaking the same reparative action in the world through dialogical praxis at the institutional level.

This, at least, is the best way in which I can understand the description given by Lindbeck of the actions of the bishops at Vatican II:

> One explanation, only slightly overstated, is that an unforeseen conjunction of circumstances turned Vatican II into a Christian version of a strange kind of yeshiva in which the bishops were drilled for months and years in textual reasoning by means of extemporized forms of something like chevruta study. Neither they nor the planners of the council intended anything of the sort, but the bishops, once they gathered in Rome, discovered to their own surprise that they as a body didn't like the agenda proposed by the Curia, the Vatican bureaucracy, and rejected its leadership. New leaders, new committees, a new agenda and new drafts of new proposals had to be chosen and approved by a huge assembly of diverse colours, nationalities and languages, communicating in their plenary sessions in ill-remembered Latin, and consisting mostly of administrative types who, for the most part, had only dim memories of the textual and theological studies of their youth which, in any case, had usually been of the traditionalist variety for which innovation in churchly matters was to be assiduously avoided.[31]

Let me say that, as a Catholic, I find Lindbeck's characterizations to be problematic at best. Though I have no reason to doubt the accuracy of his reportage of the events of the Council, of which he was a welcome and invited observer, I am less comfortable with his sweeping—and largely speculative—generalizations regarding the motivations and capacities of the gathered bishops, both at an individual and collective level.

Lindbeck's characterization of Vatican II as *chevruta*, however, is perfectly sensible (and can be best explained, in my view) as an intentional and meditated expression of Magisterial Reasoning. In other words, where

---

[31] Lindbeck, "Progress in Textual Reasoning: From Vatican II to the Conference at Drew", p. 255.

Lindbeck sees bishops arriving at this unprecedented conciliar model by accident, I see it as a matter of natural consequence. If we can assume that the bishops began the council not with a *method*, but with a *desire* for deep healing and *openness* to the Holy Spirit's call for unity, then the willingness to jettison the original design of the Council and to proceed in faith is no longer the haphazard action of those who have forgotten their Latin, but a decisive step, in faith, toward the gift promised by Christ in the face of a wounded unity.

Growing out of the Council, then, have been a series of institutional gestures toward inter-faith dialogue in the hope of healing this wounded unity. These structures of Magisterial Reasoning include the establishment in 1974 of dual commissions: the Commission for Religious Relations with Muslims, and the Commission for Religious Relations with the Jews. We might also mention the Pontifical Council for Interreligious Dialogue, the Nostra Aetate Foundation, and the Secretariat for Christian Unity. Each of these organizations, at the institutional level, seeks dialogue and healing with goals in no way dissimilar to the goal of *tikkun olam* within Scriptural Reasoning.[32]

Dialogical Models of Catholic Reasoning: Catholic Roundtables and Deep C Fishing

We turn now from institutional praxis to preparatory praxis, and experiments in Catholic Reasoning undertaken in the Memphis Diocese and at Christian Brothers University (CBU), a LaSallian college where I teach.

The Catholic Roundtables project has involved a series of experiments in text study between academics, clergy, and laity. The unifying thread in all of these experiments in reading has been that they center on Catholic encyclicals and other magisterial documents promulgated by the episcopacy of the church.

The Roundtables bring together a group of around twelve participants. We have not had the same group meet each time, but various meetings have included deacons, several members of the CBU Religion and Philosophy faculty, two undergraduates, and several laypersons.

At the suggestion of one of the lay participants, each study was centered on a short official church document. For example, at our first meeting we used "Making Moral Decisions about End-of-Life Dilemmas: A Guide Based on Catholic Teaching", prepared under the direction of Bishop Terry Steib of the Memphis Diocese.[33] The document was made available to participants several

---

[32] Space does not allow the full development of this point. For those interested in a brief but thorough overview of these organizations named, see Khaled Akasheh, "Nostra Aetate: 40 Years Later", *L'Osservatore Romano: Weekly Edition in English*, 28 June 2006, p. 8.

[33] This document can be accessed through the Diocese of Memphis website at: http://www.cdom.org/administrative/pubs-resources%20docs/Making%20Moral%20Decisions%20about%20End-Of-Life%20Dilemmas.pdf

days before the session. At the meeting, however, participants were invited to reflect on whatever portions of the document "spoke" to them or raised questions.

Under this model, small-group Catholic Roundtables are gathered around a short official text—perhaps a portion of an encyclical, but more likely a pastoral letter or episcopal document. In a fashion quite similar to Scriptural Reasoning, the group reads the text in conversation with each other. Despite the inclusion of clergy, the text is read without "expert voices" exerting mastery over the reading. Scripture reference is made and included by participants when helpful, but with the encouragement that these references not be utilized to shut down conversation but rather to open it to further dimensions of consideration.

This text-based dialogical praxis is intentionally very similar to Scriptural Reasoning, though this is not necessarily communicated to the participants. Rather, at each meeting I make some suggestions for how to proceed, and we begin the study. My suggestions are adapted from some of the guides which have been circulating at Scriptural Reasoning meetings with increasing frequency over the past several years,[34] but to this point it has not seemed necessary to mention the connection to Scriptural Reasoning praxis to the participants. It is hoped that eventually, however, that connection can be made, and some of these practitioners can be incorporated into Scriptural Reasoning groups, either at the local or regional level.

A second model of gathering has also occurred. On an institutional level within CBU, this second model has also been referred to as a "Catholic Roundtable" though its structure is different in key respects to the small-group model described above. As before, the text around which participants gather is magisterial in nature. One notable example occurred soon after the promulgation of Pope Benedict XVI's first encyclical, *Caritas in Veritate*.[35]

I organized an evening of explication and discussion around the encyclical. Two members of the CBU faculty agreed to participate. One was a professor from the Business School and a Dominican priest. The other was a professor of Ethics from the Religion Department. I selected two paragraphs from the encyclical that, though each brief, contained a good deal that could be discussed and debated. The selections were shared with the panelists beforehand, and on the evening of the event they both began by sharing prepared remarks about the paragraphs. After being given a chance to respond to each

---

[34] In addition to Steven Kepnes's "A Handbook for Scriptural Reasoning", pp. 23–39, I have in mind here the excellent ad-hoc overview handouts, suggesting ground-rules or best practices for Scriptural Reasoning, prepared by Emily Filler, of the UVA Scripture, Interpretation, and Practice graduate program, and distributed prior to the Reasonings undertaken since 2009 at UVA and other locations during Scriptural Reasoning summer trainings.

[35] Available online in English from the Holy See at: http://www.vatican.va/holy_father/ benedict_xvi/encyclicals/documents/hf_ben-xvi_enc _20090629_caritas-in-veritate_en.html

other, the floor was opened for a discussion with the audience. The venue was small enough that the audience was of an intimate size, and about two hours of discussion followed.

In this particular version of the Catholic Roundtables, the two invited speakers were allowed to function as "expert interpreters" of the document, prior to the discussion. However, they were picked precisely because they would clearly model the disparate readings—conservative and progressive—that were then circulating about the document. As such, they created a model of dialogical space, which the audience was then able to enter and populate.

Both models of Catholic Roundtables, whether the small-group model or the explication-discussion model, have their roots in the basic models of Scriptural Reasoning practice. For me, they function as experiments in application of these models within Scriptural Reasoning to explicitly Catholic contexts, where alternate ideas of Scripture obtain and explicit structures of authority must be observed, even in open dialogue around texts.

In addition to these experiments at CBU, other programs are occurring in the Memphis area. My colleague, Fr. Bruce Cinquegrani, the Episcopal Vicar for Divine Worship, Spiritual Life, and Catechesis in the Diocese, has created a program he calls "Deep C Fishing". The program is an extensive form of adult "continuing education" about the Catholic faith. Over a three-year cycle, participants will read and be taught *Dei Verbum, Gaudium et Spes, Lumen Gentium,* and *Sacrosanctum Concilium.* In short, they will have three years of exposure and analysis of the major documents of the Second Vatican Council.

All of these experiments in Catholic preparatory reasoning are text-based, but the documents that form the texts of study are not necessarily scripture. Where scripture is studied, this study occurs with tools like the New Jerome Commentary and the documents on Biblical interpretation. In all cases, then, these experiments in Catholic Reasoning take seriously the desire expressed through the Council that exegesis and catechesis occur within the clear framework of the Magisterium of the Church.

Conclusion

It has been the intent of this article to begin a conversation about the role of the Catholic voice within Scriptural Reasoning praxis, and to offer some models for a type of identity formation with Scriptural Reasoning that we might delineate as "Catholic Reasoning". This form of preparatory reasoning has cognates in Textual and Qur'anic reasoning, but cannot simply be collapsed into "Christian" reasoning. In an attempt to think through this difficulty, I have suggested that the proper starting point for any praxis of Catholic Reasoning must be in the reparative hope of deep healing/*tikkun olam* shared by Catholicism and Scriptural Reasoning, rather than in a specific text or textual methodology. Finally, I have offered some initial reflections on several experiments that attempt to enact Catholic Reasoning.

As with all reports produced within the ongoing practice of Scriptural Reasoning, these reflections are preliminary and experimental, and are not intended to present definitive closures as to what does, or does not, constitute "authentic" Scriptural Reasoning or "authentic" Catholic Reasoning. It is hoped, however, that these remarks will help to generate further reflection— both for Catholic and non-Catholic Scriptural Reasoning practitioners— about the relationship of Catholicism to the "Christian" interlocutor within the Scriptural Reasoning model, and the role of the Catholic Voice within Scriptural Reasoning itself.

Modern Theology 29:4 October 2013
ISSN 0266-7177 (Print)
ISSN 1468-0025 (Online)

DOI: 10.1111/moth.12062

AN ANALOGICAL READING OF CHRISTIAN PROPHECY: THE CASE OF MUHAMMAD[1]

ANNA BONTA MORELAND

The question of Muhammad is without doubt the most avoided question in Muslim-Christian relations. One finds no mention of this Prophet of Islam, for example, in the otherwise laudatory comments made about Muslims and their faith in the groundbreaking documents of the Second Vatican Council. They give no sense at all that this faith has a founder and a history. And since that time the hesitancy about responding could hardly be said to have diminished.[2]

The past several decades have seen a noteworthy expansion, deepening and clarification of the Roman Catholic conciliar teachings on other religions.[3] But this development certainly has been complex, with different strands within

Anna Bonta Moreland
Department of Humanities, Villanova University, Villanova, PA, 19085, USA
Email: anna.moreland@villanova.edu

[1] I would like to thank Dominic Doyle, Grant Kaplan, David Dault and Renee Massaua for reading and commenting upon earlier drafts of this article.

[2] Daniel Madigan, SJ, "Jesus and Muhammad: The Sufficiency of Prophecy", in Michael Ipgrave (ed), *Bearing the Word: Prophecy in Biblical and Qur'anic Perspective* (London: Church House Publishing, 2005), p. 90.

[3] Of particular note here is the development of the Secretariat for Non-Christians (1964), renamed the Pontifical Council for Inter-religious Dialogue in 1988. Within the several important documents published by this Council, one must highlight *Dialogue and Mission* (1984), and *Dialogue and Proclamation* (1991). Together, these two documents place dialogue within the mission of the church alongside proclamation, both necessary, indispensable elements of the church's work. For a helpful history of the Holy See's developments since the promulgation of *Nostra Aetate* (1965), see Edward Idris Cardinal Cassidy, *Ecumenism and Interreligious Dialogue: Unitatis Redintegratio, Nostra Aetate* (New York: Paulist Press, 2005), pp. 125–264. For an overview of the development of the declaration, see the 5 volume *History of Vatican II*, Giuseppe Alberigo and Joseph A. Komonchak (eds), (Maryknoll, NY: Orbis Books and Leuven: Peeters, 1995–2006), especially vol. IV: pp. 135–164, 546–559 and vol. V: pp. 211–220.

the Catholic Church constructing varying interpretations of the impact and meaning of these teachings.[4] While studies by Christian theologians have begun to draw parallels between Jesus and the Qur'an, or Muhammad and Mary,[5] I respond to Daniel Madigan's challenge by taking seriously the issue of Muhammad's prophecy. This is an essay by a Christian for Christians, but it addresses contemporary questions arising from interreligious dialogue. Muslims revere Jesus as a prophet. How far can Catholics return the favor? Can the Catholic understanding of prophecy be stretched to consider Muhammad as a prophet?[6] Do reasons internal to the Catholic tradition warrant such a move?

This article will show how the spirit and letter of Vatican II can lead us to consider Muhammad analogically as a prophet for Christians.[7] First, it outlines how the conciliar documents inaugurate the Church's emerging openness to other religions. It then draws from the practices of analogical reasoning in the Catholic tradition, exemplified in the work of Thomas Aquinas and his followers, to build its constructive argument.

---

[4] For a brief, well-documented and clear presentation of the complexity of the reception of Vatican II into the life of the Church, see Massimo Faggioli, *Vatican II: The Battle for Meaning* (New York: Paulist Press, 2012).

[5] See Daniel A. Madigan, "Mary and Muhammad: Bearers of the Word", *Australasian Catholic Record*, 80:4 (2003): pp. 417–427; Keith Ward, "Muhammad from a Christian Perspective", in Norman Solomon, Richard Harries, Tim Winter (eds), *Abraham's Children: Jews, Christians and Muslims in Conversation* (London: T&T Clark, 2005), pp. 124–131; Tim Winter, "Jesus and Muhammad: New Convergences", *The Muslim World*, 99:1 (2009), pp. 21–38.

[6] I am aware of one study that asks the question of whether Muhammad can be considered a prophet in Christianity, but its method is different than the one pursued here. Keith Trivasse "recognizes but bypasses our differences of substance and focuses on our similarities of action". See his "May the Prophet Muhammad Be a Prophet to Christianity?", *Theology*, 107:840 (2004), pp. 418–426. Kenneth Cragg puts forth an ambitious attempt to develop a theology of prophethood that Jews, Christians, and Muslims could share in *The Weight in the Word: Prophethood: Biblical and Quranic* (Brighton: Sussex Academic Press, 1999). He explores four dimensions that can be found in both Biblical and Qur'anic prophecy: personality, language, situation and circumstance. While recognizing the obvious chasm between Biblical and Qur'anic understandings of prophecy, Cragg finds reasons for hope and convergence. He outlines the "interplay of the two prophethoods by tracing the shape of the continuity between them" (p. 9). His is a creative and constructive venture, but as one particularly pointed critic put it, "if [Muslims] accommodated Cragg's terms they would cease to be Muslims" (review by Murad Wilfried Hofmann, *Journal of Qur'anic Studies*, 2:2 [2000], p. 94). One wonders at the end of Cragg's book if any one representative of the three Abrahamic traditions could be satisfied. My aim in this article is to take seriously the last chapter of Cragg's book, which names prophecy as "ongoing finality" where "[f]inality must mean that settings are not limits nor locales prisons. Prophets are not hostage to circumstance: they enlist it for posterity" (p. 139). The need to address the question of Muhammad as a prophet in Christianity arose during the third "Building Bridges" seminar of Christians and Muslims convened by the Archbishop of Canterbury at Georgetown University in 2004. In the book that emerged from this meeting, Michael Ipgrave notes that "there is urgent need for Christians to seek a generous and fair appraisal of Muhammad while retaining their commitment to the finality of Jesus"; "Bearing the Word: Prophecy in Christian and Islamic Scriptures", in *id*. (ed), *Bearing the Word*, p. 139.

[7] My own interest in this question arises both from the practice of Scriptural Reasoning with Jews and Muslims and from teaching an undergraduate course on the birth and early development of the three Abrahamic traditions.

Part I: Internal Warrants for the Project

Nostra Aetate, expressing the spirit of Vatican II, recognizes that religions outside Christianity address the "anxiety of the human heart" by offering " 'ways', that is teachings and rules of life as well as sacred rites".[8] These rules of life and sacred rites "frequently reflect a ray of that truth which enlightens everyone".[9] The famous phrase from *Nostra Aetate* asserts: "The Catholic Church rejects nothing of those things which are true and holy in these religions."[10] The document does not outline how Catholics are to recognize non-Christian truth claims or encounters with holiness in other faith traditions. But in leaving open the possibility of this recognition or encounter, this document opened up several avenues of theological inquiry.

On a practical level, *Nostra Aetate* asks Catholics to enter into dialogue and collaboration with other religious believers in order to "preserve and promote those spiritual and moral good things as well as the socio-cultural values found among them [i.e. among followers of other religions]".[11] With respect to Muslims in particular, the document affirms:

> They worship the one God, living and subsistent, merciful and almighty, creator of heaven and earth, who has spoken to humanity and to whose decrees, even the hidden ones, they seek to submit themselves whole-heartedly, just as Abraham, to whom the Islamic faith readily relates itself, submitted to God. They venerate Jesus as a prophet, even though they do not acknowledge him as God, and they honour his virgin mother Mary and even sometimes devoutly call upon her. Furthermore they await the day of judgment when God will requite all people brought back to life. Hence they have regard for the moral life and worship God especially in prayer, almsgiving and fasting.[12]

If, as *Nostra Aetate* explicitly affirms, Muslims honor the same God Christians do, and if, as the document readily acknowledges, Muslims and Christians share an overlapping web of beliefs, then we should not be surprised to find the Qur'an to be a vehicle of God's grace in Muslim communities.[13] More importantly, however, if Muslims are being sanctified through an encounter with the Qur'an, Christians should consider the possibility that acknowledging this encounter could bring Christians to a

---

[8] *NA*, 2. For a brief background on the birth and development of *Nostra Aetate*, see Thomas Stransky, CSP, "The Genesis of Nostra Aetate", *America*, 193:12 (2005), pp. 8–12.

[9] *NA*, 2.

[10] *Ibid.*, 2.

[11] *Ibid.*, 2.

[12] *Ibid.*, 3.

[13] While *Nostra Aetate* curiously does not mention the Qur'an or Muhammad, the Muslim beliefs that the document applauds did not appear in seventh-century Arabia without a messenger; they have not been preserved in Muslim religious life without being compiled in a sacred book.

deeper consideration of their own faith. Qur'anic revelations, while not adding to the deposit of the faith, might enliven the faithful at a particular historical moment, helping them more fully to understand and live out the Gospel.

Lumen Gentium is even more emphatic about the fact that Muslims and Christians honor the same God:

> But the plan of salvation also embraces those who acknowledge the Creator, and among these the . . . [Muslims] are first; they profess to hold the faith of Abraham and *along with us* they worship the one merciful God who will judge humanity on the last day.[14]

Daniel Madigan pointedly notes that we cannot say that we worship one and the same God together and then "say that we cannot or may not talk together about that God, or about the sense of adoration that God evokes in us".[15] I would push Madigan's point further to argue that if Muslims honor the same God as Christians do, the sacred text that documents the summit of the encounter between Muslims and God should have something to say to us Christians about the God we both worship.[16] For Christians, the Qur'an is not an alternative revelation alongside the revelation in Jesus Christ. The canon need not be re-opened. But Madigan helpfully suggests that we replace language of inside and outside the church with language of direction and orientation.[17] There are outsiders who are more properly oriented toward the reign of God than some insiders. At the center of Christian faith stands the revelation found in Jesus Christ. But different aspects of Christian faith and life are directed toward that center in various ways. Analogical echoes with Christian faith in facets of other religions could be one of the vectors that orient Christians toward that center.

If we argue that God chose Muhammad to be the vehicle to communicate a divine message, Christians should find language that properly acknowledges this claim. The current proposal argues that prophecy is the fitting term for such acknowledgement. But to make this novel argument, we must first widen the term "prophet" by way of analogy.

---

[14] *LG*, 16 (italics mine).

[15] Daniel Madigan, "Mutual Theological Hospitality: Doing Theology in the Presence of the 'Other' ", in Waleed El-Ansary and David K. Linnan (eds), *Muslim and Christian Understanding: Theory and Application of "A Common Word"* (New York: Palgrave Macmillan, 2010), p. 58.

[16] For an incisive critique of *Dominus Iesus* on this point see Francis X. Clooney, SJ, "Implications for the Practice of Inter-religious Learning", in Stephen J. Pope and Charles Hefling (eds), *Sic et Non: Encountering* Dominus Iesus (New York: Orbis Books, 2002), pp. 157–168, especially p. 159.

[17] Daniel Madigan, "Saving *Dominus Iesus*", in James L. Heft, SM, Reuven Firestone and Omid Safi (eds), *Learned Ignorance: Intellectual Humility among Jews, Christians, and Muslims* (Oxford: Oxford University Press, 2011), p. 270.

Part II: Thomas Aquinas on Christian Prophecy

This section will observe briefly the way Thomas deploys the term "prophecy" and the next section will apply these observations to the purposes of this article.[18] Thomas understands prophetic knowledge along the trajectory of salvation history. Prophetic knowledge helps the unfolding of divine revelation in anticipation of the end of time. This knowledge, then, is partial, transitory, hidden and imperfect. Rooted in Christ's Incarnation, it points toward the eschatological fulfilment of His Incarnation. Thomas' treatment of prophecy is marked by a continuity of concerns, where he: a) brings order and coherence to Biblical testimony that appear disparate on first reading; b) places the light of prophecy along a continuum of lights, from the natural light of the agent's intellect to the light of glory; c) gives the term an elasticity to reflect the complexity of the phenomenon.

For Thomas, Muhammad could never be a prophet in the strictest sense of the term. Prophetic revelation extends to future events, of course, but also to those beliefs relating to God that are to be espoused by all Christians and are matters of faith, and even to higher mysteries, concerning only the perfect.[19] Prophecy is "a kind of knowledge impressed under the form of teaching on the prophet's intellect by Divine revelation".[20] It is, therefore, primarily a phenomenon involving knowledge, although it involves speech in a secondary way, as the prophet declares what she was taught by God for the instruction of others. So prophecy is pedagogical in its reception and its expression. But the prophet cannot receive this revelation by recourse only to the natural light of her intellect. As a result, the Holy Spirit raises the intention of the mind to perceive divine things, preparing the prophet to receive the revelation of God.[21] This supernatural light is not in the prophet by way of an abiding form, as it is in the blessed in heaven. Rather, it occurs through a passing impression. As a result, prophets do not always prophesy; neither do they see God in God's essence.

It is important to note that prophecy is considered something imperfect in the genus of divine revelation. Placed within its proper eschatological framework, all prophecies will be made void at the end of time (1 Cor. 13:8). For now, we prophesy in part or imperfectly:

---

[18] Thomas' treatment of prophecy arises in three principal texts: the *Quaestiones disputatae de Veritate* (q.12), the *Summa contra Gentiles*, and the *Summa Theologiae* [hereafter *ST*] (II-II, 171–174), along with his Biblical commentaries on Isaiah, 1 Corinthians and Hebrews.

[19] *ST* II-II, 171, prologus: *Nam prophetica revelatio se extendit non solum ad futuros hominum eventus, sed etiam ad res divinas, et quantum ad ea quae proponuntur omnibus credenda, quae pertinent ad fidem, et quantum ad altiora mysteria, quae sunt perfectorum, quae pertinent ad sapientiam.*

[20] *ST* II-II, 171, 6: *prophetia est quaedam cognitio intellectui prophetae impressa ex revelatio divina per modum cuiusdam doctrinae.*

[21] *ST* II-II, 171, 1, ad. 4: *Sic igitur ad prophetiam requiritur inspiratio quantum ad mentis elevationem, secundum illud Iob XXXII, inspiratio omni potentis dat intelligentiam, revelatio autem, quantum ad ipsam perceptionem divinorum, in quo perficitur prophetia;*

When that which is perfect is come, that which is in part shall be done away. Consequently, it does not follow that nothing is lacking to prophetic revelation, but that it lacks none of those things to which prophecy is directed.[22]

In other words, prophecy *by its very nature* is imperfect and incomplete. In his commentary on St Paul's letter to the Corinthians, Thomas specifies that prophetic knowledge is figurative and enigmatic and will be replaced by the clarity of vision in heaven.[23]

If it is figurative and enigmatic, what kind of knowledge does prophecy provide? Beyond being imperfect and transitory, sometimes even the prophets do not properly distinguish between what is uttered by their own spirit or by the inspiration of the Holy Spirit. God instructs the prophet both by express revelation and by a mysterious instinct. The prophet has the greatest certitude about those things known by express revelation, for she has it for certain that they are revealed by God. But the prophet also knows some things by instinct. Here, it is difficult to distinguish fully whether her thoughts are conceived of divine instinct or by her own spirit. While nothing false can come under prophecy, discerning the prophetic from the human elements in any given utterance is no easy matter. Prophecy in its true and exact sense comes from divine inspiration, while that which comes from a natural cause is not called prophecy except in a relative sense.[24] Like other gratuitous graces, prophecy is inescapably ecclesial in that it is given for the good of the church.

Who is chosen for prophecy? Thomas insists that after the coming of Christ, there is still a role for prophecy in the church: "at all times there have not been lacking persons having the spirit of prophecy, not indeed for the declaration of any new doctrine of faith, but for the direction of human acts".[25] While anyone could be chosen to prophesy, an evil life provides an obstacle to prophecy; strong passions and inordinate pursuit of external things prevent the mind from being elevated in order to contemplate spiritual things.[26] But prophecy can be without charity, as it pertains to the intellect, whose act precedes the will. Prophecy, properly and simply, is conveyed by divine revelation alone; yet the revelation that is made by demons may be called

---

[22] *ST* II-II, 171, 4, ad. 2: *prophetia est sicut quiddam imperfectum in genere divinae revelationis, unde dicitur I ad Cor. XIII, quod prophetiae evacuabuntur, et quod ex parte prophetamus, id est imperfecte. Perfectio autem divinae revelationis erit in patria, unde subditur, cum venerit quod perfectum est, evacuabitur quod ex parte est. Unde non oportet quod propheticae revelatio nihil de sit, sed quod nihil de siteorum ad quae prophetia ordinatur.*

[23] Thomas Aquinas, *Commentary on the First Epistle to the Corinthians*, Fabian Larcher, OP (trans), paragraph 788, available at: http://dhspriory.org/thomas/SS1Cor.htm#133

[24] *ST* II-II, 172, 3: *prophetia vere et simpliciter dicta est ex inspiratione divina, quae autem est ex causa naturali, non dicitur prophetia nisi secundum quid.*

[25] *ST* II-II, 174, 6, ad. 3: *Et singulis temporibus non defuerunt aliqui prophetiae spiritum habentes, non quidem ad novam doctrinam fidei depromendam, sed ad humanorum actuum directionem.*

[26] *ST* II-II, 172, 4.

prophecy in a restricted sense.[27] False prophets can be led by the Spirit of truth, for "God makes use even of the wicked for the profit of the good".[28] In bearing witness to the truth, God's foes unwittingly make the truth more credible.[29] The prophet does not always know what she prophesies. Caiaphas and the soldiers who divided Christ's garments, for example, prophesied without knowing what they were saying.[30] When the person knows that she is being moved by the Holy Spirit to think, say or do something, she is properly a prophet. But when she is moved without her knowing it, this is not perfect prophecy but rather a "prophetic instinct". However, since the prophet's mind is a deficient instrument (*instrumentum deficiens*), even true prophets do not know all that the Holy Spirit means by the things they see, speak or do.

Scripture itself invites us to conclude that prophets need not be believers in Jesus. "Prophecy" is applied to them in a relative and limited sense, but scripture already documents this complex phenomenon. Thomas takes the data of scripture and shows how at the heart of prophecy stands John the Baptist, pointing directly to Christ. But closer to the borders of the prophetic instinct stand all sorts of unlikely figures, among whom we would like to consider Muhammad.

Part III: Christian Prophecy, Analogically Extended

Peter commands the early Christian community to "[a]lways be ready to give an explanation to anyone who asks [us] for a reason for [our] hope" (1 Pet. 3:15; New American Bible). He urges his listeners to give an account—in Greek an *apologion*—for the hope that is within them. Narrating our "apologias" is a primary way to encounter those of other faith traditions.[31] But this encounter cannot stop here. For our conversation to develop, we need to move from "apologia" to "analogia". In "apologia" we speak words "from" or "out of" our narrative, but in "analogia" we are taking words "up" from our narrative and seeing how those words cohere in other religious traditions.

Recalling Thomas, univocity and equivocity were the poles within which he crafted an analogical "third way" in medieval Europe. These poles re-emerge in our contemporary context as the dual challenges of Christian

---

[27] *ST* II-II, 172, 5: *Et ideo prophetia proprie et simpliciter dicta fit solum per revelationem divinam. Sed et ipsa revelatio facta per Daemones, potest secundum quid dici prophetia.*

[28] *ST* II-II, 172, 6, *ad.* 1: *Quia Deus utitur etiam malis ad utilitatem bonorum.*

[29] *ST* II-II, 172, 6, *ad.* 1: *Unde et per prophetas Daemonum aliqua vera praenuntiat, tum ut credibilior fiat veritas, quae etiam ex adversariis testimonium habet; tum etiam quia, dum homines talibus credunt, per eorum dicta magis ad veritatem inducuntur.*

[30] *ST* II-II, 174, 4, *sed contra* and *respondeo*.

[31] *Apologion* itself is already tied to one's reasons for hope; see Benedict XVI's gloss on this text in the encyclical *Spe Salvi* (30 November 2007), 2, available at: http://www.vatican.va/holy _father/benedict_xvi/encyclicals/documents/hf_ben-xvi_enc_20071130_spe-salvi_en.html.

imperialism on the one hand and the incommensurability of faith traditions on the other. Introducing analogy into the theology of religious pluralism offers us a way to resist the two extremes. It resists the temptation of univocity: forcing the beliefs and practices of other religious traditions into our own Christian terms—or rejecting them if they do not fit—in an act of imperialism. It also resists the temptation to resort to equivocity: maintaining that religious traditions are ultimately irreducible, such that one term holds no purchase across traditions. I will use David Burrell, CSC as a guide in this constructive proposal instead of becoming mired in the scholarship on the use of analogy in Christian theology.[32] Burrell embodies in practice the intellectual trajectory of his work. His first book, *Analogy and Philosophical Language* (1973), plants seeds that bear fruit years later in his groundbreaking work in Comparative Theology.[33]

Drawing inspiration from Thomas' understanding of analogy in the area of religious pluralism admittedly involves moving his work into new territory.[34] Aquinas uses analogy primarily in the arena of Divine Names. He uses analogy to balance two main commitments: 1) God is inconceivable mystery, and 2) we speak truthfully when we make claims about God. Analogy steers a middle course between univocal and equivocal language,[35] each of which is seriously deficient. In univocal language, we reduce God to one creature among others in the universe—and become idolaters in quick turn; in equivocal language, our God-talk becomes mere babble.

Thomas distinguishes between metaphor and analogy to show that while all language is wrapped in human clothing, some ways that we talk about

---

[32] For excellent work on Aquinas and analogy see: Hampus Lyttkens, *The Analogy between God and the World: An Investigation of its Background and Interpretation of its Use by Thomas of Aquino* (Uppsala: Almqvist and Wiksells, 1952); George P. Klubertanz, SJ, *St. Thomas Aquinas on Analogy: A Textual Analysis and Systematic Synthesis* (Chicago, IL: Loyola University Press, 1960); Ralph M. McInerny, *The Logic of Analogy: An Interpretation of St. Thomas* (The Hague: Nijhoff, 1961); and his more recent *Aquinas and Analogy* (Washington, DC: The Catholic University of America Press, 1996); Bernard Montagnes, OP, *La doctrine de l'analogie de l'être d'après Saint Thomas d'Aquin* (Louvain: Publications universitaires de Louvain, 1963).

[33] See in particular: *Aquinas: God and Action* (Notre Dame, IN: University of Notre Dame Press, 1979); *Knowing the Unknowable God: Ibn-Sina, Maimonides, Aquinas* (Notre Dame, IN: University of Notre Dame Press, 1986); and *Freedom and Creation in Three Traditions* (Notre Dame, IN: University of Notre Dame Press, 1993).

[34] We must recognize that this is not a move that Thomas himself makes. Given his limited knowledge of Muslim belief and practice, he includes Muslims under the category of "unbelievers" in the beginning of the *Summa contra Gentiles* (Book 1, Chapter 2). Thomas Hibbs has persuasively argued that Aquinas did not write the *Summa contra Gentiles* as a missionary manual to convert Muslims; *Dialectic and Narrative in Aquinas: An Interpretation of the Summa Contra Gentiles* (South Bend, IN: University of Notre Dame Press, 1995), pp. 9–14.

[35] *ST*, I, 13, 5: *Respondeo dicendum quod impossibile est aliquid praedicari de Deo et creaturis univoce. Quia omnis effectus non adaequans virtutem causaea gentis, recipit similitudinem a gentis non secundum eandem rationem, sed deficienter, ita ut quod divisim et multipliciter est in effectibus, in causa est simpliciter et eodemmodo; sicut sol secundum unam virtutem, multi formes et varias formas in istis inferioribus producit. . . . Sed necetiam pure aequivoce, ut aliquid ixerunt. Quia secundum hoc, ex creaturis nihil posset cognosci de Deo, nec demonstrari; sed semper incideret fallacia aequivocationis.*

God reach farther than others.[36] When we say, analogously, that "God is good", we understand that goodness applies to God in an utterly perfect way, a way unknown to us. But we believe that goodness in God is related— analogously—to goodness in humans. So our words, while not able to capture the whole meaning of how God is good, capture *something* of what this would mean. Goodness as we understand it is a pale shadow of how good God is, but if it has only the relationship of shadow to statue, then it nonetheless reflects something true about God, however vaguely or imperfectly. We can never fully express how the shadow shows us something of the statue, but we can have confidence that our speech is not meaningless.

While heeding Pseudo-Dionysius and Maimonides' warnings against idolatry, Thomas chooses not to follow their tendencies toward agnosticism. Instead, Thomas maintains that the faithful can speak about God in a true, incomplete and not fully choate way. This speech is always offered against a backdrop of radical difference between creatures and their Creator. Christians must be cautious in their language about God, but they can speak about God from observing God's pulse in the world. They must recognize continuously that these claims belie a greater ignorance of the essence of God. While religious claims must be open to further refinement, revision and even rejection, they are justified attempts at true statements about their subject, God. Whether in ordinary discourse, in religious worship, or in theological examination, Thomas assures Christians that their pursuit is not fruitless, that their proclamations really do signify something true in God. They will never have the last word, but the words they use are meaningful and true.

With Burrell, we see that Aquinas did not so much offer a theory on analogy as a practice of analogical reasoning. Certain terms can be used properly of both God and creatures, although we can never speak adequately of God by using these terms. These terms, however, cannot be univocal. They must be able to reach across "the distinction" between creatures and their Creator without dissolving it.[37]

A theology of religious pluralism must move this theological practice into a secondary sense of analogy, one that recognizes resemblances among religious traditions amidst the backdrop of radical difference. There is an implicit faith here that some of our words can have purchase across faith traditions, an implicit faith that we are all on a similar quest—not a quest that is reducible to some common denominator, but one that is framed in human terms, with human questions that inevitably reach beyond themselves. The

---

[36] *ST*, I, 13, 6: *Unde, secundum hoc, dicendum est quod, quantum ad rem significatam per nomen, per prius dicuntur de Deo quam de creaturis, quia a Deo huiusmodi perfectiones in creaturas manant. Sed quantum ad impositionem nominis, per prius a nobis imponuntur creaturis, quas prius cognoscimus. Unde et modum significandi habent qui competit creaturis, ut supra dictum est.*

[37] David B. Burrell, "Analogy, Creation, and Theological Language", *Proceedings of the American Catholic Philosophical Association*, 74 (2000), p. 35.

grounding relationship between Creator and creatures that undergirds Thomas' analogical practice re-emerges when trying to understand terms in another religious tradition in two ways. In the first, we recognize that all theological language in Abrahamic traditions—whether Jewish, Christian or Muslim—is grounded in the Creator/creature distinction, however differently each tradition might name that distinction.[38] In the second, each of the three traditions shares certain figures and terms—of which prophecy is one—but understands them in different ways. If each tradition is really naming the incomprehensible mystery that is God, then there must be a way to make sense of one another's names, even if the sense we make is limited, partial, and tentative. Metaphysical grounding for theology is shared among the three traditions, and the historical details and religious terms overlap. Christian theological discourse not only has the ability to reach beyond its native territory by speaking analogously about God; it can also reach beyond its ken into other traditions through analogical reasoning. In recognizing the backdrop of difference, it refrains from colonizing terms from the "religious other". In acknowledging similarities, it does not view differences among religious traditions as fundamentally irreducible.

Impressive attempts to negotiate religious difference on a third, objective, rational ground have been tried.[39] But with Gavin D'Costa we recognize the weaknesses of these attempts.[40] We opt instead with Burrell to accept different paths to similar conclusions, where:

we can employ the skills learned in our tradition to follow reasoning in another. Traditions, in other words, may indeed be *relative* to one another in ways that can prove mutually fruitful rather than isolating. Those traditions which prove to be so will be those which avail themselves of human reason in their development, and the patterns of stress and strain in their evolution will display their capacity for exploiting the resources of reason.[41]

---

[38] In this article I am pursuing the more modest proposal of speaking analogously in the Abrahamic traditions. There is no reason in principle not to apply this practice to other faith traditions. A creative example of this move can be found in Francis X. Clooney, SJ, *Hindu God, Christian God: How Reason Helps Break Down the Boundaries Between Religions* (New York: Oxford University Press, 2001); and his *Divine Mother, Blessed Mother: Hindu Goddesses and the Virgin Mary* (New York: Oxford University Press, 2005).

[39] See the collection of essays in John H. Hick and Paul F. Knitter (eds), *The Myth of Christian Uniqueness: Towards a Pluralistic Theology of Religion* (New York: Orbis Books, 1987); and Paul F. Knitter (ed), *The Myth of Religious Superiority: Multifaith Explorations of Religious Pluralism* (New York: Orbis Books, 2005).

[40] See Gavin D'Costa (ed), *Christian Uniqueness Reconsidered: The Myth of Pluralistic Theology of Religions* (Maryknoll, NY: Orbis Books, 1990); and *id.*, "Whose Objectivity? Which Neutrality? The Doomed Quest for A Neutral Vantage Point from Which to Judge Religions", *Religious Studies*, 29:1 (1993), pp. 79–95.

[41] David B. Burrell, CSC, "Faith, Culture, and Reason: Analogous Language and Truth", *Proceedings of the American Catholic Philosophical Association*, 77 (2003), p. 4.

The negotiating practice here is analogy, for traditions may become mutually fruitful only if they share enough terms to enable reasonable communication. Reason corresponds no longer to a set of beliefs that must be accepted by all before conversation begins. Rather, "*rationality* will then show itself in practices which can be followed and understood by persons operating in similar fashion from different grounding convictions".[42] It is the task of the theology of religious pluralism to recognize the patterns of similarities and difference through analogical reasoning. Burrell concludes:

> we can hardly appreciate the valence of analogous discourse, and its indispensability in communicating our basic human aspirations, unless we allow ourselves to be challenged by those who hold similar hopes but may express them in ways that differ widely from our own.

Analogy is crucial here because religious terms are used in multiple yet ordered ways: "the difference between ambiguous and analogous expressions lies in using them systematically—that is, so as to *show* how the many uses can be related to one".[43] Without resulting in a theory of analogy, the practice is ultimately revealed through examples.

Burrell employs the example of a married couple for whom the declaration "I love you" means something related but radically different during the second and twenty-fifth year of their marriage. What changes is the point of reference. They loved each other during their second year, but from the perspective of their twenty-fifth year, their earlier declaration seems like mere pleasantry compared to what they have come to discover over the past twenty-three years:

> Their earlier avowal seems so remote from their current paradigm—what they have discovered loving one another to be and to entail—that it seems barely to qualify for inclusion in the notion. Yet a more extended narrative—a life story—should be able to trace those shifts in a sufficiently ordered way to indicate the connections, however dramatic the shifts may have been.[44]

No concrete univocal core of meaning exists between the expression of love at the beginning of marriage and then into its maturity. What changes is the paradigm through which the couple understands the term: "And the story of those shifts—tantamount to a life story—offers sufficient coherence to assure us we are using the same notion. If no such story can be forged, of course, we

---

[42] *Ibid.*, p. 5.
[43] *Ibid.*, p. 10.
[44] David B. Burrell, "Argument in Theology: Analogy and Narrative", *Journal of the American Academy of Religion*, 49:1 (1982), pp. 45–46.

have sheer ambiguity—just as a variety of viewpoints may never become pluralistic but remain simply diverse."[45] Much as we try to construct a definition of marital love, we will always be caught resorting to ambiguous terms. And so it is in the theology of religious pluralism.

To conclude, while we cannot offer a theory of analogical reasoning, we can point to its patterns of usage. Burrell maintains:

> In the measure that we can be aware of using an expression beyond its normal reach, because we have come to experience that term's ability to render our own aspirations at various points of attainment or failure, then we can be said to be using it *properly*. It is of such awareness that analogous usage is born, and in developing that awareness it is warranted.[46]

In deciding whether another story is coherent or not, we must share something in common to make this decision. Radical cultural differences can certainly pose a barrier here. But when they do not, we use narrative in theological argument initially to recognize the kind of relationship we have to each other and, further, to help each other to notice the coherence in our faith stories. The pattern of discussion here is analogical—and I have witnessed it in action in the practice of Scriptural Reasoning.[47] When Muslims revere Jesus as a prophet, they are not revering him as Christians do, and they are not equating this prophetic role with Muhammad's singular one. I suggest that Christians can revere Muhammad as a prophet in a limited and relative sense, not one that Muslims would embrace, but one that Christians nevertheless should consider.[48]

---

[45] *Ibid.*, p. 46.

[46] *Ibid.*, p. 47.

[47] In Scriptural Reasoning sessions participants do not have to act as representatives of their home traditions; they come together, rather, as *this* Jew, *that* Christian, or *this* Muslim. In my experience, this frees me from feeling the burden of mis/representing the Catholic position, as if there were only one. At the same time, I do not have to suspend my Catholic beliefs to practice Scriptural Reasoning. The particularities of each language, history and ritual are not undermined or diluted; differences and disagreements are expressed and respected. For an introduction into Scriptural Reasoning, see David F. Ford and C. C. Pecknold (eds), *The Promise of Scriptural Reasoning* (Oxford: Blackwell, 2006). For creative work by scholars influenced by its practice see the *Journal of Scriptural Reasoning*, available online at: http://etext.lib.virginia.edu/journals/ssr/

[48] Christian Troll argues that Christians could never revere Muhammad as a prophet, understanding this in the Islamic sense, because Christians would have to obey him unconditionally. Instead, Troll invites Christians to "discern whatever is true, good and beautiful in the message of Islam and to respect the spiritual path followed by Muslims"; Christians can even "acknowledge that Muhammad was a religious and political genius and should also be prepared to admit that through God's grace, countless believers have been inspired by the Qur'an and the life of the Prophet Muhammad to live their lives in a genuine relationship with God"; "Catholicism and Islam", in Gavin D'Costa (ed), *The Catholic Church and the World Religions: A Theological and Phenomenological Account* (New York: T&T Clark, 2011), p. 97. As an alternative to this approach, I am asking Christians here to mine the conciliar documents and the Christian understanding of prophecy to revere Muhammad as a prophet in a limited and relative manner.

Conclusion

In reflecting upon *Dei Verbum*, the Pontifical Council for Inter-religious Dialogue affirms that Christians still grow into the realities of scripture in a continual and dynamic process. Interreligious dialogue becomes integral to this work, as "God, in an age-long dialogue, has offered and continues to offer salvation to humankind. In faithfulness to this divine initiative, the Church too must enter into a dialogue of salvation with all men and women".[49] Fruitful analogical reasoning is already being done from both Christian and Muslim quarters. From the Muslim perspective, Joseph Lumbard explores how an analogical approach to the Word of God in Jesus and the Qur'an helps to deepen both traditions' understanding of themselves and each other:

> perhaps we can find elements of our traditions that will help us to view the Divine Word in a manner that transcends the bounds of one particular tradition, understanding that it is infinite and therefore cannot be limited to a single revelation, or that Divine Mercy will not be confined to one religious tradition. For one thing that Christians and Muslims can agree upon is that the Divine Word is, by definition, beyond the ken of the human word. Knowledge of the Word, 'ilm al-kalām, in the ultimate sense is thus something to which we can only attain by transcending our words and being absorbed in God's Word.[50]

From the Christian perspective Pim Valkenberg reads al-Ghazālī and Said Nursi and notices analogies between both texts and between those texts and Christian theological and spiritual notions.[51]

This article is admittedly offered as a prolegomena to an extended Christian analysis of Muhammad's prophecy. And questions linger that need to be addressed: how do we analyze those passages in the Qur'an that contradict

---

[49] The Pontifical Council for Inter-religious Dialogue, *Dialogue and Proclamation* (19 May 1991), 37, available at: http://www.vatican.va/roman_curia/pontifical_councils/interelg/documents/rc_pc_interelg_doc_19051991_dialogue-and-proclamatio_en.html

[50] Joseph Lumbard, "What of the Word is in Common?", in El-Ansary and Linnan (eds), *Muslim and Christian Understanding*, p. 106. A highlighting of the analogical reasoning in this essay would have addressed Maria Dakake's concerns in her response essay in the same volume. Dakake warns that to Muslim ears the "Word" of the Qur'an never connotes creation, as in things being created through the Qur'an in the way that Christians speak of God creating through the Word. This is precisely the move that inter-faith analogous reasoning recognizes. There is a genuine overlap, resonance, between Jesus and the Qur'an as Word of God. But this happens against a backdrop of crucial differences. Outlining these points of resonance and difference is the task of creative inter-faith groups like "A Common Word" initiative. The analogical reasoning present in Dakake's essay in the same volume, which explicates the Adamic and Christic nature in all of us, is a compelling instantiation of the kind of reasoning I am suggesting here (Dakake, "Theological Parallels and Metaphysical Meeting Points", in *ibid.*, p. 135).

[51] Pim Valkenberg, *Sharing Lights On the Way to God: Muslim-Christian Dialogue and Theology in the Context of Abrahamic Partnership* (Amsterdam: Rodopi, 2006).

the narratives of the Bible?; do Catholics simply accept what coheres with their predetermined beliefs and reject the rest?; what relationship does Muhammad have to prophets in the Hebrew Scriptures? The analogical argument about Muhammad's prophecy developed here opens into these questions. These would pose a way forward in the trajectory of Comparative Theology.

Modern Theology 29:4 October 2013
ISSN 0266-7177 (Print)
ISSN 1468-0025 (Online)

DOI: 10.1111/moth.12063

FAMILIES OF RECEPTIVE THEOLOGICAL LEARNING: SCRIPTURAL REASONING, COMPARATIVE THEOLOGY, AND RECEPTIVE ECUMENISM

PAUL D. MURRAY

Introduction: Initial Grounds for Family Resemblances

In the context of the fiftieth anniversary of Vatican II, this collection of essays examines what resonance manifests between Scriptural Reasoning and contemporary Catholic theology. These examinations focus in the main on potentially fruitful relationships with the, most recently, Catholic-inspired practices of inter-faith theological learning known as Comparative Theology particularly associated with Francis Clooney and James Fredericks. As complement, this article asks after what resonance in turn exists with the again Catholic-inspired approach to intra-Christian, inter-denominational theological learning known as Receptive Ecumenism.[1]

Scriptural Reasoning, Comparative Theology and Receptive Ecumenism are all self-consciously postliberal strategies which eschew approaches premised on commonality and the priority of coming to agreement, in favour of taking seriously the particularity and plurality of traditioned commitment.

Paul D. Murray
Department of Theology and Religion, Durham University, Abbey House, Palace Green, Durham, DH1 3RS, UK
Email: paul.murray@durham.ac.uk

[1] See Paul D. Murray (ed), *Receptive Ecumenism and the Call to Catholic Learning: Exploring a Way for Contemporary Ecumenism* (Oxford: Oxford University Press, 2008), particularly Murray, "Receptive Ecumenism and Catholic Learning: Establishing the Agenda", pp. 5–25; and *id.*, "Receptive Ecumenism and Ecclesial Learning: Receiving Gifts for Our Needs", *Louvain Studies*, 33:1–2 (2008), pp. 30–45; also *id.*, "ARCIC III: Recognising the Need for an Ecumenical Gear-Change", *One in Christ*, 45:2 (2011), pp. 200–211.

Rather than seeking underlying commonalities or reconciled agreement, each seeks for learning across and from difference. Consequently, for all their differences of focus and procedure, this similar orientation suggests the possibility of some significant "family resemblances" and the potential for fruitful cross-fertilization.[2] This can be pressed further in a number of ways.

Whilst Receptive Ecumenism came to articulation independently of Scriptural Reasoning, its operative epistemological commitments and related understanding of human rationality derive from a period of doctoral research supervised by David Ford and influenced by Daniel Hardy[3] at the time when they were working towards Scriptural Reasoning in collaboration with Peter Ochs and Aref Nayed. There was doubtless collateral influence, especially around the handling of particularity and plurality.

There has been no analogous direct exchange between Comparative Theology and Receptive Ecumenism, but it is again possible to view them as jointly situated in a prior extended family conversation. This is a conversation, now running for over fifty years, as to what it means for Catholicism to receive and implement the refreshed self-understanding articulated at Vatican II, central to which is the church being "as a sacrament . . . [both] of intimate union with God and of the unity of all humanity".[4] In this perspective Catholic Christian tradition discloses the deep story of the entire cosmos. Comparative Theology, with deep roots in the 1965 "Declaration on the Relation of the Church to Non-Christian Religions", *Nostra Aetate*, represents a mature performance of this refreshed self-understanding relative to other faith traditions.[5] For its own part, following both the 1964 "Decree on Ecumenism", *Unitatis Redintegratio*, and the "Dogmatic Constitution on the Church", *Lumen Gentium*, Receptive Ecumenism offers a similarly matured engagement with the other Christian traditions.

A third reason suggesting likely resonance between Scriptural Reasoning, Comparative Theology, and Receptive Ecumenism pertains to the way Receptive Ecumenism, in its manner of addressing a significantly changed ecumenical context, has sought to learn in suitably transposed key from best practice in inter-faith engagement. There are, of course, certain fundamental differences between the inter-faith and intra-Christian contexts, particularly concerning the appropriate goals of dialogue across difference. For Christian

---

[2] For "family resemblances", see Ludwig Wittgenstein, *Philosophical Investigation*, G. E. M. Anscombe (trans), third edition, (Oxford: Basil Blackwell, 1967), §67, p. 32; also *id.*, *The Blue and Brown Books: Preliminary Studies for the "Philosophical Investigations"*, second edition (Oxford: Basil Blackwell, 1969), p. 17.

[3] See Murray, "Receptive Ecumenism and Catholic Learning", pp. 7–8; also *id.*, *Reason, Truth and Theology in Pragmatist Perspective* (Leuven: Peeters, 2004).

[4] *LG*, 1.

[5] Cf. Francis X. Clooney, SJ, *Comparative Theology: Deep Learning across Religious Borders* (Malden, MA: Wiley-Blackwell, 2010), pp. 16–17; also Clooney, "The Study of Non-Christian Religions in the Post-Vatican II Church", *Journal of Ecumenical Studies*, 28:3 (1991), pp. 482–494.

ecumenism in its classical "Faith and Order" form, the ultimate goal consists in the overcoming of historic divisions and the achievement of reconciled structural configuration and full sacramental communion. This can never be the goal of inter-faith engagement wherein the permanence of divisions between the traditions needs to be taken absolutely seriously.[6]

The inter-faith goal is not the overcoming of radical difference but learning to live it well. This extends beyond seeking increased mutual understanding and points of connection to asking what can be appropriately learned *from* the other.[7] By contrast, the classical Christian ecumenical tendency has been to seek to neutralise and overcome difference as efficiently as possible. In recent decades, however, this has increasingly appeared unrealistic as the likelihood has opened up of a prolonged interim stage of having to live with un-reconciled divisions.[8] But this recalibration of ecumenical expectation is itself opening the way to some fruitful strategic learning from the best of inter-faith engagement as the latter is exemplified by the commitment of Scriptural Reasoning and Comparative Theology to learning *from* and *across* long-term difference.

In this spirit Receptive Ecumenism advocates a shift *away* from prioritising, in the first instance, the overcoming of abiding differences and *towards* each tradition asking what they might fruitfully have to learn from the other traditions in relation *to* tangible difficulties within their own tradition. The dual conviction is that without this mode of self-critical learning no further substantive progress is possible, whereas with it all kinds of things are already possible which, if pursued, would take each of the traditions to new places wherein further things will become possible.

With all of this in view, this essay's exploration of family resemblances between Scriptural Reasoning, Comparative Theology, and Receptive Ecumenism moves through four stages. First, attention is given to the resemblances between Scriptural Reasoning and Comparative Theology in relation to the balancing of committed particularity and inextricable pluralism in the context of inter-faith theological engagement. These resemblances are considered together with the way in which the philosophical and theological archaeology of Receptive Ecumenism in turn reflects similar judgements and commitments. Second, more sustained attention is given to the relationship between Comparative Theology, Receptive Ecumenism and pertinent

---

[6] David F. Ford, *Christian Wisdom: Desiring God and Learning in Love* (Cambridge: Cambridge University Press, 2007), p. 280.

[7] See Michael Barnes, SJ, *Interreligious Learning: Dialogue, Spirituality and the Christian Imagination* (Cambridge: Cambridge University Press, 2012), p. 16; also Clooney, *Comparative Theology*, p. 10. Also significant is the work of David B. Burrell, e.g. *Knowing the Unknowable God: Ibn-Sina, Maimonides, Aquinas* (Notre Dame, IN: University of Notre Dame Press, 1986); and *Towards a Jewish-Christian-Muslim Theology* (Malden, MA: Wiley-Blackwell, 2011).

[8] See Murray, "ARCIC III: Recognising the Need for an Ecumenical Gear-Change", pp. 206–208.

Vatican II teaching. Third, in bullet-point format, a systematic summary account is given of the constructive theological principles that shape Receptive Ecumenism. Fourth, in a concluding section some attention is given to how Scriptural Reasoning and Comparative Theology might contribute to the further refining of Receptive Ecumenism and, correlatively, what Receptive Ecumenism has to offer to Scriptural Reasoning and Comparative Theology.

1. Scriptural Reasoning, Comparative Theology, and Receptive Ecumenism as Postliberal Strategies of Committed Pluralism

Scriptural Reasoning, Comparative Theology and Receptive Ecumenism are each strategies for taking seriously and living fruitfully the fact of diversely-traditioned particularity without collapsing into a closed, conflictual tribalism, or reverting to a universalising common core theory of religious traditions. In differing ways they each represent what Michael Barnes refers to as the move "from a liberal normative pluralism to a much more tradition-centred form of post-liberal theology".[9] For none of them is the solution to the "pressures of diversity," a forgetting of identities or a relinquishing of truth claims.[10] I elsewhere refer to this as a *committed pluralism*: committed to acknowledging and negotiating appropriately the pluralist reality of the world of difference in which we exist; committed also to the legitimacy and rationality of particular rooted commitments precisely in this context.[11] As Francis Clooney writes: "In our religiously diverse context, a vital theology has to resist too tight a binding by tradition, but also the idea that religious diversity renders strong claims about truth and value impossible."[12]

Core to Scriptural Reasoning, Comparative Theology, and Receptive Ecumenism alike is not only a concern to take differing traditioned identities seriously and to speak out of them, but to have them enriched through the very process of also taking another's tradition seriously. As David Ford puts it: "*the depths of one evoke the depths of the other*" through "a complex combination of what is at the core of each tradition with what is novel for each".[13] At the theological hearts of all three practices is the recognition that

---

[9] Barnes, *Interreligious Learning*, p. 9. See also Ford, *Christian Wisdom*, p. 277; Clooney, "Reading the World in Christ: From Comparison to Inclusivism", in Gavin D'Costa (ed), *Christian Uniqueness Reconsidered* (Maryknoll, NY: Orbis Books, 1992), pp. 67–68; James L. Fredericks, "A Universal Religious Experience? Comparative Theology as an Alternative to a Theology of Religions", *Horizons*, 22:1 (1995), pp. 78–82. Cf. Murray, "A Liberal Helping of Postliberalism Please", in Mark D. Chapman (ed), *The Future of Liberal Theology* (Aldershot: Ashgate, 2002), pp. 208–218.
[10] Clooney, *Comparative Theology*, p. 3; also p. 8.
[11] See Murray, "Receptive Ecumenism and Catholic Learning", p. 8.
[12] Clooney, *Comparative Theology*, p. 8; also p. 111.
[13] Ford, *Christian Wisdom*, pp. 287 and 282.

"God can speak to us in and through a tradition other than our own, even if we do not, cannot, embrace as our own the whole of that tradition".[14]

In relation to Scriptural Reasoning, the most sustained discussions of the pertinent epistemological and methodological principles are in Peter Ochs' *Peirce, Pragmatism and the Logic of Scripture*, Nicholas Adams' *Habermas and Theology*, and Chad Pecknold's *Transforming Postliberal Theology*.[15] My *Reason, Truth and Theology in Pragmatist Perspective* plays a similar role for Receptive Ecumenism. These works are variously concerned to explore the appropriate character of theological reasoning in the light of the now widespread shift to post-foundationalist understandings of human knowledge.

We are dealing here with a dual shift: firstly, *from* the image of knowledge as a superstructure progressively erected on the basis of sure and certain, discretely verifiable foundations *to* the image of knowledge as a complex, flexible, context-specific web;[16] secondly, *from* viewing truth purely in terms of cognitive understanding and conceptual articulation *to* viewing it also in performative terms of efficacy and fruitfulness.[17] Here truth is not simply about seeking to recognise and articulate the reality of things but also about discerning and living in accordance with the fruitful possibilities that the open-textured reality of things presents.

Taken together, this dual shift represents the relinquishing of rationality as an aspiration for absolute certainty built around linear modes of reinforcing progression, and the contrary embrace of rationality as a never-ending, recursively expansive process of situated, self-correcting scrutiny in service of: a) sound understanding of what is and what might be; b) reasoned evaluation of the most appropriate way forward; and c) effective practical implementation of same.[18] Here the aspiration for "objectivity" is understood not in terms of an unattainable neutrality and delusional desire for a "view from nowhere" that seeks to bracket out context and perspective but, following Donald Davidson, as a process of triangulation and mutual accountability.[19]

For present purposes this suggests an understanding of religious traditions as complex webs of thought and practice, allowing for integrity and stability across time and context but also variability, adaptability, creativity

---

[14] Clooney, *Comparative Theology*, p. 115; also pp. 3, 8, 15–16, 57.

[15] Peter Ochs, *Peirce, Pragmatism and the Logic of Scripture* (Cambridge: Cambridge University Press, 1998); Nicholas Adams, *Habermas and Theology* (Cambridge: Cambridge University Press, 2006); C. C. Pecknold, *Transforming Postliberal Theology: George Lindbeck, Pragmatism and Scripture* (London: T&T Clark, 2005).

[16] See Willard Van Orman Quine, "Two Dogmas of Empiricism" (1951), reprinted in Quine, *From a Logical Point of View: Nine Logico-Philosophical Essays*, second edition, (Cambridge, MA: Harvard University Press, 1980), pp. 20–46, particularly pp. 42–43.

[17] See Murray, *Reason, Truth, and Theology*, pp. 7, 62–63, 64–68, 75–77, 119.

[18] See *ibid.*, pp. 91–130, particularly pp. 93–123.

[19] See Thomas Nagel, *The View from Nowhere* (Oxford: Oxford University Press, 1986). Cf. Donald Davidson, "Rational Animals", in Ernest LePore and Brian McLaughlin (eds), *Actions and Events* (Oxford: Basil Blackwell, 1985), p. 480. For comment, see Murray, *Reason, Truth, and Theology*, pp. 40–49.

and, inevitably, tension. Peter Ochs appropriately identifies a therapeutic, healing concern at the heart of pragmatic modes of analysis and interpretation: to mend that which is torn; to heal and repair that which is broken, limiting and frustrating in a line of interpretation.[20] This focus on tensions within traditions of interpretation and the search for reparative readings that weave viable ways through the received webs is a core feature of Scriptural Reasoning. Similarly, a focus on textual traditions and their refined, robust yet creative interpretation is central to Comparative Theology. But a word of caution also needs voicing.

Texts and their interpretation are indeed central to traditions as their most articulate traces, shapers and carriers, but texts are not all. Most fundamentally, traditions are lived and performed; embodied in and transmitted by practices and structures as surely as in and by textual codes and associated interpretative systems.[21] If, then, the therapeutic, healing character of pragmatic modes of analysis is to be given its full rein, it must be addressed to these embodied practices and structures and the areas of difficulty, tension, incoherence, awkwardness, and dysfunction to be found there as surely as to the associated core texts and traditions of interpretation. This is a particular concern of Receptive Ecumenism which views the task of comparative ecumenical ecclesiology as a form of diagnostic, therapeutic analysis—a means of address and repair—for experienced systemic ills and which thereby deliberately seeks to be an agent of change.[22] As explored further below, Scriptural Reasoning and Comparative Theology might have something to learn here.

2. *The Vatican II Lineage of Receptive Ecumenism and Comparative Theology*

In the course of his various pursuits in Comparative Theology and in keeping with the principles just traced, Francis Clooney makes frequent reference to his own Roman Catholic context. It is readily apparent that he views the deeply Christocentric cosmology that modern Catholicism formally reclaimed at Vatican II as itself impelling towards the kind of exercises in receptive theological learning that Comparative Theology represents.[23] He points particularly to *Nostra Aetate*, section 2:

> The Catholic Church rejects nothing that is true and holy in these religions. She regards with sincere reverence those ways of conduct and of

---

[20] Ochs, *Peirce, Pragmatism and the Logic of Scripture*, especially pp. 20–50 and 253–254.

[21] See Terrence W. Tilley, *Inventing Catholic Tradition* (Maryknoll, NY: Orbis Books, 2000).

[22] For further see Murray, "Searching the Living Truth of the Church in Practice: On the Transformative Task of Systematic Ecclesiology", *Modern Theology* (forthcoming).

[23] Most significantly see Henri de Lubac, *Catholicism: Christ and the Common Destiny of Man*, Lancelot C. Sheppard and Sr Elizabeth Englund, OCD (trans), revised fourth edition (San Francisco, CA: Ignatius Press, 1988; first published in English 1950).

life, those precepts and teachings which, though differing in many aspects from the ones she holds and sets forth, nonetheless often reflect a ray of that Truth which enlightens all men.[24]

Indeed, doctrinally speaking, Clooney's entire project might be thought of as operating between this reference point and his summary closing confession:

> That for me the work of Comparative Theology finally discloses a still deeper encounter with Jesus Christ only intensifies the commitment to learn from the religious diversity God has given us. In Christ there need not be any fear of what we might learn; there is only the truth that sets us free.[25]

The same deeply Vatican II-mediated Christocentric cosmology and correlative openness to appropriate learning across difference lies at the heart of Receptive Ecumenism. Given recent debates about the appropriate hermeneutics of Vatican II, it is worth pausing to situate Receptive Ecumenism clearly in the stream of Vatican II teaching on ecumenism. Doing so will disclose the profoundly theological rather than merely strategic or epistemological roots of the familial resemblances between Comparative Theology and Receptive Ecumenism.

From the outset Pope John XXIII identified one of the core purposes of Vatican II as contributing to the unity of the churches. It was this formal entry of Roman Catholicism into the ecumenical movement that occasioned what many regard as its golden age. Despite this, recent debates mean that identifying Vatican II's precise ecumenical significance is not so straightforward. The central question presently debated is whether there is a fundamental continuity between Vatican II teaching and what went before or a radical fresh departure.

One influential rendition, the so-called progressivist, emphasises the freshness and greater appeal of the Council; a narrative that comes, perhaps, to its most sustained expression in the monumental five-volume *History of Vatican II* edited by Giuseppe Alberigo.[26] In another telling, apparently similar but really quite different, this contrast becomes pressed into radical discontinuity; most notably so by the Lefebvrists who reject the Council as a betrayal of Catholic tradition. Yet a third line of interpretation, reacting both against this fundamental denial of the Council and its more

---

[24] See Clooney, *Comparative Theology*, p. 17, quoting *NA* as available online at: http://www.vatican.va/archive/hist_councils/ii_vatican_council/documents/vat-ii_decl_19651028_nostra-aetate_en.html

[25] Clooney, *Comparative Theology*, p. 165.

[26] See Giuseppe Alberigo and Joseph A. Komonchak (eds), *History of Vatican II*, 5 vols (Maryknoll, NY: Orbis Books and Leuven: Peeters, 1995–2006).

progressivist interpretation, views Vatican II as correctly standing in strict continuity with previous Catholic tradition; so strict as to basically change nothing.[27]

In this context it is significant that Joseph Ratzinger as Prefect of the Congregation for the Doctrine of the Faith and subsequently as Pope Benedict XVI consistently maintained the need to think of reform within the continuity of the tradition.[28] The need for this dual emphasis on the freshness of conciliar teaching and its deep, if creative, continuity with earlier formulations pertains particularly to Vatican II's ecumenical teaching, for here we do appear to have a clear contrast with pre-conciliar teaching.

In the face of the rise of the modern ecumenical movement amongst the Protestant traditions (later joined by Orthodoxy), the 1917 Code of Canon Law forbad Catholics from participating in meetings with other Christians (canon 1325), let alone sharing in their rituals (canon 1258). The one true church of Christ was to be straightforwardly and exclusively identified with the Catholic Church and association with other Christians consequently rejected as suggesting a false equivalence. Unidirectional return to Rome was the only way forward, as expressed in Pope Pius XI's 1928 encyclical *Mortalium Animos*:

> for the union of Christians can only be promoted by promoting the return to the one true Church of Christ of those who are separated from it, for in the past they have unhappily left it.[29]

The same basic strict identity is to be found in Pope Pius XII's 1943 encyclical *Mystici Corporis Christi* and again subsequently in *Humani Generis*.[30] The contrast of tone and content could not be clearer when compared with Vatican II's *Lumen Gentium* and *Unitatis Redintegratio*.

Relinquishing the attitude of one-sided fault, Catholicism's complicity in the historic breaks is acknowledged (*UR*, 3). Clear recognition is given that "some, and even most, of the significant elements and endowments which . . . give life to the church . . . exist outside the visible boundaries of

---

[27] E.g. see Agostini Marchetto, *The Second Vatican Ecumenical Council: A Counterpoint for the History of the Council* (Chicago, IL: University of Chicago Press, 2010).

[28] Pope Benedict XVI, "A Proper Hermeneutic for the Second Vatican Council", in Matthew L. Lamb and Matthew Levering (eds), *Vatican II: Renewal within Tradition* (New York: Oxford University Press, 2008), pp. ix–xv, particularly pp. x and xiii.

[29] Pope Pius XI, "*Mortalium Animos*. Encyclical Letter on Religious Unity" (6 January 1928), 10, available at: http://www.vatican.va/holy_father/pius_xi/encyclicals/documents/hf_p-xi_enc_19280106_mortalium-animos_en.html

[30] Pope Pius XII, "*Mystici Corporis Christi*. On the Mystical Body of Christ" (29 June 1943), available at: http://www.vatican.va/holy_father/pius_xii/encyclicals/documents/hf_p-xii_enc_29061943_mystici-corporis-christi_en.html; also *id.*, "*Humani Generis*. Concerning Some False Opinions Threatening to Undermine the Foundations of Catholic Doctrine" (12 August 1950), available at: http://www.vatican.va/holy_father/pius_xii/encyclicals/documents/hf_p-xii_enc_12081950_humani-generis_en.html

the Catholic Church" (*UR*, 3; see also *LG*, 8). Pope John Paul II would later echo this in his remarkable encyclical *Ut Unum Sint*, saying: "To the extent that these elements are found in other Christian communities, the one Church of Christ is effectively present in them".[31]

These ecclesial elements are significant for Catholicism itself, not simply for the status of the other traditions, for the divisions prevent the Catholic Church "from realizing in practice the fullness of catholicity proper to her" (*UR*, 4). Indeed, some of these ecclesial elements may have come to fuller flower in the other traditions than they have been able to do within Catholicism: "anything wrought by the grace of the holy Spirit in the hearts of our separated fellow Christians can be a help to our own edification. . . . it can always bring a deeper realization of the mystery of Christ and the church" (*UR*, 4). John Paul II underlined this in *Ut Unum Sint*, referring to other Christian communities as places "where certain features of the Christian mystery have at times been more effectively emphasized".[32]

These lines of understanding come to expression in *Unitatis Redintegratio* and *Lumen Gentium* with an emphasis on Catholicism's own need to learn, to be renewed, purified and even reformed. *UR* section 6 speaks of ecumenism as a "renewal" (*renovatio*) and a "continual reformation" (*perennem reformationem*) and, similarly, *LG* section 8 speaks of the church as being in a state of *"semper purificanda"*, of always being purified. Whilst communion with the Bishop of Rome continues here to be viewed as an essential aspect of the unity of the church, this is no longer an ecumenism of one-sided return but of growth on both sides and mutual journeying to a new relationship: we find that "their (i.e. Catholics) especial duty is to make a careful and honest appraisal of whatever needs to be renewed in the catholic household itself" (*UR*, 4).

All this provides useful perspective within which to interpret the famous passage in *LG* section 8 about the "church of Christ" subsisting in the Catholic Church. The first seven sections of *LG*, tracing an understanding of the place of the church in the purview of creation and salvation history, speak not explicitly of the Catholic Church but of the "church of Christ". Section 8 provides the first mention of the Catholic Church. In apparent contrast to the pre-conciliar statement of strict and exclusive identity between the church of Christ and the Catholic Church, what we have is: "This church [i.e. the church of Christ] set up and organized in the world as a society, subsists in the Catholic Church . . ." (*LG*, 8). Quite apart from the linguistic awkwardness that would otherwise ensue, all the texts earlier reviewed demonstrate that "subsistit in" cannot simply mean strict and exclusive identity—"is"—given

---

[31] Pope John Paul II, *"Ut Unum Sint*. On Commitment to Ecumenism" (25 May 1995), 11; available at: http://www.vatican.va/holy_father/john_paul_ii/encyclicals/documents/hf_jp-ii_enc_25051995_ut-unum-sint_en.html

[32] *Ibid.*, 14; also 48.

the full and repeated acknowledgement of there being real elements of the church to be found outside the Catholic Church.

Equally, nor is it cogent to claim that this freshness amounts to a complete relinquishing of there being something distinctive about the Catholic Church, all churches being equal subsistences of the one church of Christ, as it were. *LG* and *UR* are quite clear that whilst there might be elements of the church in the other traditions, something essential is also missing: for they "are not blessed with that unity which Jesus Christ wished to bestow on all those who through Him were born again into one body" (*UR*, 3). Whereas, "We believe that it [i.e. this unity] subsists in the Catholic Church as something she can never lose" (*UR*, 4).

Here, then, Catholicism is refreshing its self-understanding in a way that both recognises the dignity of other traditions and the real potential for appropriate Catholic learning from them whilst also continuing to maintain—as do, analogously, many other traditions in their own regard and in their own way—what Catholicism understands to be its own distinctive gifts. The deeper point, however, is that even a relatively cautious reading—one guided throughout by the principle of "reform within the continuity of the tradition"—needs to recognise that Vatican II maintains an appropriate orientation to receptive ecumenical learning on Catholicism's behalf and clear recognition that Catholicism is itself engaged on a continuing story of reform, growth, and renewal.

As *Nostra Aetate* has been of fundamental significance for the development of Comparative Theology, so these principles have been of fundamental importance in the shaping of Receptive Ecumenism. To demonstrate this, as well as the relevance of the epistemological and methodological principles identified earlier, it will be helpful to review in summary systematic form the distinctive core theological principles of Receptive Ecumenism.

3. Receptive Ecumenism's Core Theological Principles in Systematic Purview

No attempt is made here either to repeat or substantively to supplement the various extended accounts of Receptive Ecumenism's guiding principles cited in note 1 earlier. We simply summarise in ordered point-form the most important of these principles. By so doing their relationship with the various factors here identified as influencing the development of Receptive Ecumenism comes all the more clearly into view. These principles are:

- as called forth by and held within the Trinitarian communion of God, the churches are called to grow ever more visibly together in order to express this union-in-relation in appropriate structural and sacramental unity;
- "Life and Works" ecumenism—doing things together—is vitally necessary but alone insufficient;

- authentic Christian ecumenism can never be a matter either of simply *bearing with* communion-dividing differences or of *collapsing* and *eradicating* such differences; it must rather be a matter of so learning *from* and *across* such differences that they can with integrity be brought into configured, mutually enriching communion;
- whilst always in need of being tested by the "head"—by critical theological scrutiny—all effective ecumenical learning consists most deeply in an affair of the "heart", through being attracted by, desiring and falling in love with something of the grace-filled beauty of another tradition and being impelled to move towards this focus of desire, even at cost;
- the authentic Spirit-led vitality of Christian life and tradition consists not in identical repetition of received articulations but in preparedness to return to core callings and to ask what fresh performances and articulations are appropriate to the specific challenges and opportunities of current times and contexts;
- the dynamic integrity of Christian tradition consists not merely in always doing the same things in different ways and different locations but in doing, as required, genuinely fresh things that properly cohere with the form and patterns of received tradition;
- we should resist exclusively past-oriented views of tradition and associated problem-solving understandings of the ecumenical task and engage also future-oriented understandings of the Christian tradition as *all it is and might be* relative to the saving purposes of God in Christ and the Spirit: we are responsible for the tradition's future as well as its past;
- traditions are better understood as dynamic webs rather than as inflexible structures;
- our traditions are limited as well as life-giving, wounded as well as grace-bearing: we need to show our wounds rather than to hide them and to ask our others to minister to us in our need from their specific gifts;
- the openness to growth, change, examination of conscience and grace-filled conversion at the heart of Christian life properly pertains as much to the ecclesial as to the personal: to allowing one's tradition to be challenged to expand and re-think how it understands and does things in relation to specific issues;
- this emphasis on the ecclesial dimension of conversion needs to extend beyond the doctrinal-theoretical to include also the organisational, the structural, the cultural, and the broadly practical;
- truth is ultimately something lived and not simply thought;
- whether personal or ecclesial, the call to conversion requires to be lived through attentive hospitality to the truth of the other in specific circumstances;
- Christian living and ecclesial existence is not a zero-sum game: the call to graced conversion is always the call to greater life and flourishing, never, fundamentally, to diminishment;

- receptive ecumenical learning, when pursued with dynamic integrity, is not about becoming less but about becoming more deeply, more richly, more fully, more freely what we already are: about our becoming all that we are called to be;
- rather than worrying unduly about what others may need to learn, each should take responsibility for their own learning, mindful that "We cannot change others, we can only change ourselves but doing so can also promote change in others";
- with this, receptive ecumenical learning requires a move away from the presupposition of mutuality—"we'll move if you move"—to the embrace of a certain unilateral willingness to walk the path of ecclesial conversion for the sake of the greater flourishing of one's own tradition and regardless, to some extent, of whether others are currently prepared to do likewise;
- the primary aim is not the promotion of increased mutual understanding and appreciation *between* traditions but continuing ecclesial conversion, deepening and expansive growth *within* traditions by receptive learning *from* and *across* traditions;
- the conviction is that pursuing this primary aim will in time move each tradition, with integrity, to a new place and so open up fresh possibilities for overcoming currently communion-dividing differences *between* traditions;
- throughout, it must always be remembered that progress towards our ecumenical goal is fundamentally God's work and calling into which we are being drawn rather than any merely human project of our own creation, possession and control;
- living this requires *both* active trust that we are being resourced for this and led into it in the ways we require *and* patient recognition that any real receptive learning necessarily takes time to be realised;
- as such, the ecumenical scene is best viewed not simply as a problem-strewn field but as one of open possibilities, across which the only path is one of long, slow learning into greater life and maturity: this is not a "second-best" accommodation compared with a supposedly alternative faster route but the only route possible—*the* golden highway of receptive ecumenical growth;
- the time we have is a time of grace for the present anticipating of an eventual unfolding of God's success, not a time of irredeemable failure;
- the fact that some problems and differences now appear as insuperable divisions does not mean they will always so appear;
- we must neither give up on the God-given calling to be one, nor allow it to mutate into merely getting along with each other but must seek to live courageously and imaginatively in hope;
- we need to "lean-into" the promise of God's purpose and the presence of God's Spirit and ask what it means in practice for us to enter into this more fully in the here and now;

- we are changed by love not by anger and if we are in turn to effect creative ecclesial change then it must be through the sustained passion of love rather than frustration: "by love alone" is the way of ecclesial transformation.

4. Concluding Unscientific Postscript: On what Scriptural Reasoning, Comparative Theology and Receptive Ecumenism Might Fruitfully Learn from Each Other

This essay started by identifying various initial grounds for assuming positive family resemblances between Scriptural Reasoning, Comparative Theology, and Receptive Ecumenism as ways of engaging with and learning from one's religious other. First, it was noted that they each represent a certain postliberal holding of particularity and plurality in dynamic tension. Second, a certain genetic relationship was identified between the groundswell of conversation that led to the articulation of Scriptural Reasoning and that which led to Receptive Ecumenism. Third, as regards Comparative Theology and Receptive Ecumenism, a more tangible, common-shaping influence was flagged in terms of the shared context of contemporary Catholic self-understanding promoted by Vatican II. Fourth, it was claimed that Receptive Ecumenism can appropriately be understood as applying to the intra-Christian, inter-denominational context principles about the need to learn *from* and *across* long-term difference more commonly associated with the best of inter-faith engagement as exemplified by Scriptural Reasoning and Comparative Theology alike. Subsequent sections then gave closer attention to the first, third, and fourth of these in turn.

With all of this in view, it is now appropriate to ask how Scriptural Reasoning, Comparative Theology, and Receptive Ecumenism, as three distinct yet related modes of receptive learning from the religious other, might in turn have significant things to learn from *each other* as they respectively seek to pursue the way of receptive learning. Four points are explored: 1) the centrality of textual engagement in Scriptural Reasoning and Comparative Theology alike and what the practice of Receptive Ecumenism might learn from this; 2) the near inevitable professionalism of Scriptural Reasoning and Comparative Theology and whether there might be something to learn from the democratisation of receptive learning that is one facet of Receptive Ecumenism; 3) the assumed communal context of receptive learning in both Scriptural Reasoning and Receptive Ecumenism and what Comparative Theology's more individualist ethos might learn from this; and 4) whether Receptive Ecumenism's explicit concern to address the wounds within the practice, the organisational, structural and procedural realities of traditions, might be appropriately absorbed into Scriptural Reasoning and Comparative Theology.

At the core of Scriptural Reasoning is a central focus on practices of shared reading of hallowed textual traditions and of seeking to learn across these traditions; texts are reverenced as sacred scripture for the members of at least one of the participant traditions and as potential vehicles of God's guidance and blessing for the others. Whilst these texts are explicitly situated within and read-out-of and across the traditions they shape and distinguish, the proximate focus is texts and the core activity their interpretation. Similarly, although the practice of Comparative Theology might quite conceivably take as its primary focus and point of departure such things as ritual, architecture, art, organisation, observed practice and behavioural codes, in the way in which Francis Clooney has consistently practised it, comparative analysis of defining texts has again been central.[33]

This emphasis on the centrality of learning through the medium of core texts is without question the primary contribution and challenge that Scriptural Reasoning and Comparative Theology can each make and pose to Receptive Ecumenism, which is more typically focussed, in the first instance, on matters of practical, structural and organisational difference between traditions and how they each might learn from the other. In this context—one in which some Christian traditions find themselves incapable of breaking the bread of Eucharist together—this emphasis on already being capable of breaking the nourishing word of hallowed scripture across and between such divisions is highly significant. Alongside the opportunities this affords for real learning in the here and now, it can act as counterbalance to any unintended possibility there might be of Receptive Ecumenism focusing narrowly on the purely structural and pragmatic, without due attention being given both to the primary context of spiritual and religious life such structures serve and to the forms of sustenance already available *in via*. It is for such reasons that David Ford, Peter Ochs and Aref Nayed were invited to speak at the second international Receptive Ecumenism conference in 2009 and that a form of small group Biblical reasoning was built into the daily process of the conference.

Indeed, at the level of formal bilateral dialogue, daily scripture-sharing has long been an established ingredient in the overall context and habitus out of which such dialogue operates. At this level the potential contribution of Scriptural Reasoning in particular is that it might helpfully promote a more self-conscious attention to the divergent histories of interpretation and reception of the texts in question as factors in historic divisions and sites for potential fruitful learning.

Similarly, at the local level, scripture-sharing groups have long been part of the stock-in-trade of fruitful ecumenical engagement. But here a part of the attraction of such ecumenical scripture-sharing has been that it has appeared

---

[33] See Clooney, *Comparative Theology*, p. 58.

to offer a way beyond focussing on the doctrinal, the organisational and the divisive by focussing rather on a common source by which Christians of diverse affiliations are respectively nourished. The challenge of how to incorporate analogous aspects of Scriptural Reasoning and Comparative Theology into these local scripture-sharing practices and so turn them in a more explicitly receptive direction is to ask whether aspects of diverse traditioned readings might in some way be effectively introduced (e.g. by comparing the different readings of the Pastoral Epistles and the classic Petrine texts in relation to matters of ecclesial order and structure). This in turn raises the challenge as to how the refined resource of scholarly expertise can best help promote practices of effective local ecumenical scripture-sharing that absorb something of Scriptural Reasoning and Comparative Theology and place this at the service of real receptive ecumenical learning.

This takes us into a second difference between Scriptural Reasoning and Comparative Theology relative to Receptive Ecumenism, one that provides a fruitful point of potential learning from Receptive Ecumenism. Given the shared emphasis in Scriptural Reasoning and Comparative Theology on the need for sensitive, sophisticated, and appropriately fresh interpretations of core scriptural texts, always situated against the relevant reception history and context of application, both have an inevitable bias towards the professionalization of inter-faith engagement that opens them, as Francis Clooney acknowledges, to the charge of a certain elitism.[34]

In itself such sophistication and elitism is no bad thing, at least provided we can overcome the unfortunate pejorative connotations that "elite" has gained in English as distinct from the more basic sense of leadership that "*elan*" retains in French. For its own part Receptive Ecumenism also depends upon and accords a proper place to the need for rigorous and sophisticated theological scrutiny, testing and discernment, drawing upon expertise in all the traditional sub-disciplines of theology as appropriate. Alongside this, however, Receptive Ecumenism is also quite clear that asking the basic receptive ecumenical question (as to what in a given situation can appropriately be learned from one's other) is not the exclusive preserve of an elite caste of theologians. On the contrary, a basic principle is that everyone at every level of church life is capable of asking in relation to any given issue, problem, area of understanding, or responsibility, what might fruitfully be learned from one's ecumenical others in this specific regard. Certainly such pondered potential learning always needs due testing and informing in the most refined and sophisticated of ways but the point is that the basic process is one in which all can share and of which all can properly be initiators in relation to specific live issues. Advocates of Scriptural Reasoning and Comparative Theology would do well to ask

---

[34] See *ibid.*, p. 67; also pp. 12, 154, 163; also Barnes, *Interreligious Learning*, p. 262.

whether and how an analogous democratising of these approaches might similarly be possible and appropriately facilitated.

A further corollary of Clooney's recognition of the "demanding" and sophisticated level of religious and theological bilingualism required for successful explorations in Comparative Theology is his assumption that the task will generally therefore fall to a small number of particularly well-resourced individuals rather than being a more communal endeavour.[35] This arguably places Comparative Theology one step further removed from the level of interpersonal exchange that is the normal sphere of ecclesial and religious conversation. In this, the basic tenor of Clooney's Comparative Theology contrasts significantly with the explicit priority diversely accorded to collaborative processes of exploration, analysis, and judgement in Scriptural Reasoning and Receptive Ecumenism alike. This might, then, represent a further area of fruitful peer-learning for Comparative Theology but one, as Michael Barnes' own highly significant and deeply resonant work demonstrates (rooted in sustained practices of small group face-to-face encounter), that is entirely compatible with the basic tenets and very significant strengths of Comparative Theology.

The final area of difference and possible fruitful learning between these three kindred modes of receptive religious learning takes us back to the central textual focus of Scriptural Reasoning and Comparative Theology alike. Earlier it was noted that engagement with Scriptural Reasoning has already been encouraging Receptive Ecumenism to place clearer emphasis on and to make space for Biblical reasoning, when duly situated within reception history, as a fruitful site and resource for receptive ecumenical learning. But this also needs to be turned around.

If the core-focus in Scriptural Reasoning and Comparative Theology is on specifically textual traditions of understanding and application and how they might mutually inform each other, the core focus in Receptive Ecumenism is on the lived practice of traditions, their organisational, structural and procedural realities, and the wounds and tensions to be found there that call out for repair through potential receptive learning from another's particular gifts. As such, the textual and the explicitly theological come in as the appropriate means of systematically analysing these wounds, diagnosing their causes, and assessing the possibilities for their healing and cure. The intention is that receptive ecumenical learning should not simply be a highly theorised endeavour, somewhat abstracted from the ordinary lived practice of the traditions concerned and feeding, in the main, only the understanding and practice of its specialist participants. Rather, the intention is that the impulse towards receptive ecumenical learning should arise out of the felt needs and experienced difficulties of the participant traditions and, with all due

---

[35] See Clooney, *Comparative Theology*, pp. 14 and 155.

expertise, rigor and sophistication brought to bear, should explicitly seek to perform a reparative ministry addressing these wounds.

The emphasis here on practice and repair is, of course, far from alien either to Scriptural Reasoning or to Comparative Theology. David Ford recurrently emphasises the ways in which Scriptural Reasoning is in service of "transforming the public sphere for the better" by "being a site where Jews, Christians and Muslims can work out in dialogue the considerable ethical and political implications of their scriptures".[36] Again, the notion of reparative reason aimed at addressing wounds, whether in traditions of textual understanding (Ochs) or in the "human world" viewed as "broken, in exile, off the straight path, filled with corruption, sickness, war and genocide", is central to Scriptural Reasoning.[37]

In this context what Receptive Ecumenism distinctively does is to attend to tears and tensions, wounds and dysfunctions in search of healing and repair not only in the reading and reception of the treasured texts of a tradition and in the wider society in which the communities that read these texts are situated but in the lived practice and structural, organisational and procedural realities of the traditions themselves. This represents a radicalized version of the pragmatic concern already deeply at work within Scriptural Reasoning. It is to release the full transformative potential of this concern by turning it self-referentially in service of the greater flourishing and witness whereby each tradition might, through appropriate receptive learning, discern within itself a need to learn from another's gifts.

The challenges standing in the way of such transformative learning even in the relatively closer context of intra-Christian, inter-denominational learning are already very considerable. Whether such practically, structurally, procedurally-oriented receptive learning can have any role at all in the even more challenging context of inter-faith learning is yet to be discerned. This represents Receptive Ecumenism's core challenge to Scriptural Reasoning and Comparative Theology alike. It needs to be remembered, however, that whilst family resemblances there may be, uniformity there most certainly is not.

---

[36] Ford, *Christian Wisdom*, p. 301.

[37] Steven Kepnes, "A Handbook for Scriptural Reasoning", in David F. Ford & C. C. Pecknold (eds), *The Promise of Scriptural Reasoning* (Oxford: Blackwell, 2006), p. 24; also *ibid.*, p. 28: "*Scriptural Reasoning practitioners come together out of a sense of impoverishment, suffering, and conflict to seek resources for healing*" (original italics).

Modern Theology 29:4 October 2013
ISSN 0266-7177 (Print)
ISSN 1468-0025 (Online)

SCRIPTURAL REASONII
THE LEGACY OF VATIC.
THEIR MUTUAL ENGAC ____ . _
AND SIGNIFICANCE

DAVID F. FORD

The Second Vatican Council was a seminal event that in retrospect, as debates intensify around its legacy, comes to appear ever more complex. This article discusses three aspects of that ramifying legacy that have become increasingly interrelated: *ressourcement* through the Bible, response to the modern world, and engagement with other faiths. These are brought into conversation with the development, understanding and practice of Scriptural Reasoning.

The history relevant to the relationship between the legacy of Vatican II and Scriptural Reasoning is only partly chronicled in print. Vatican II has been well studied,[1] and that literature, together with Michael Barnes' article in this volume and the assessment of George Lindbeck discussed below, all show how important it is to understand the eventful context in which the Council's documents were produced. Scriptural Reasoning, however, has no comparable written resources.[2] There have been many events that have contributed

David F. Ford
Faculty of Divinity, University of Cambridge, West Road, Cambridge, CB3 9BS, UK
Email: dff1000@cam.ac.uk

[1] The most comprehensive account of Vatican II is the five-volume work *History of Vatican II* edited by Giuseppe Alberigo and Joseph A. Komonchak (Maryknoll, NY: Orbis Books and Leuven: Peeters, 1995–2006). For two recent reassessments of Vatican II see Matthew L. Lamb and Matthew Levering (eds), *Vatican II: Renewal Within Tradition* (New York: Oxford University Press, 2008), which takes its cue from Pope Benedict XVI's December 2005 address to the Roman Curia "Ad Romanam Curiam ob omnia natalicia" (published in *Acta Apostolicae Sedis*, XCVIII (2006), pp. 40–53) in which he said that a proper hermeneutic for Vatican II should be a "hermeneutic of reform" rather than a "hermeneutic of discontinuity and rupture"; and John W. O'Malley, *What Happened at Vatican II* (Cambridge, MA: Belknap Press at Harvard University Press, 2008). I am grateful to my colleague Professor Eamon Duffy for assistance in researching and understanding the history of Vatican II.

[2] I among others have given a brief account if its origins in David F. Ford, *Christian Wisdom: Desiring God and Learning in Love* (Cambridge: Cambridge University Press, 2007). Perhaps the

ing but about which there are only fragmentary records,[3] and e accounts are oral. This is because Scriptural Reasoning is not only recent and smaller in scale than Vatican II but it has also been far less lic and has had little "official" status. It is probably premature to attempt any comprehensive account of the early history of Scriptural Reasoning, but already there are academic and other debates about the practice and this thinking needs to be historically informed. Significant judgements, decisions and developments are already happening ahead of any thorough history being written.

In the first part of this article I offer brief descriptions of and commentaries upon five seminal events, four of which belong primarily to the history of Scriptural Reasoning, one to the legacy of Vatican II. Each is so far known only to a restricted circle,[4] with little overlap between the circles; these events are here linked together for the first time. These five events are in my judgement especially instructive in relation to the theme of the Council's legacy, and they are all the more helpful because they are accompanied by texts.[5] From them arise most of the issues to be addressed in the second part of the

---

best description of the actual practice of Scriptural Reasoning so far is that of Mike Higton and Rachel Muers in *The Text in Play: Experiments in Reading Scripture* (Eugene, OR: Cascade Books, 2012), in particular chapter 9 which includes a semi-fictionalized script of a study session.

[3] Besides the five events selected for comment in this article others that would need to be noted include: the mid-nineteen-nineties expansion of Scriptural Reasoning from being Jewish-Christian to including Muslims; a series of summer meetings between 1996 and 2007 at the holiday home in Connecticut of Daniel Hardy; the first residential three-faith meeting in Long Island in 1999; the founding and incorporation of the Society for Scriptural Reasoning; the development of the online Journal of Scriptural Reasoning; successive meetings of the American Academy of Religion (AAR) in which first Textual Reasoning and later both it and Scriptural Reasoning featured, and both moved from being fringe meetings to official units on the annual programme; the gatherings held before the AAR annual meetings; the annual residential conferences held in Cambridge University, and sometimes combined with an international summer school for young Jewish, Christian and Muslim leaders; the establishment of the first graduate programme in Scriptural Reasoning in the University of Virginia; the introduction of Scriptural Reasoning to other academic institutions; the second international Receptive Ecumenism conference in Durham in 2009 (mentioned by Paul Murray in his piece in this volume); the spread of Scriptural Reasoning to settings beyond the academy—schools and prisons in UK, hospitals in Israel and the Palestinian territories, local synagogue, church and mosque congregations in many countries; civil society initiatives by London Citizens and the Thousand Cities movement; contributions to the statement by Jewish scholars about Christianity, *Dabru Emet*, in 2000 and its aftermath, and to the Muslim letter to Christians, *A Common Word Between Us and You* in 2007 and its aftermath; the visit by Peter Ochs to Beijing in May 2012; the international Scriptural Reasoning gathering in Minzu University of China in May 2013.

[4] This may seem more obvious with regard to the small-scale, "unofficial" and largely unpublicized Drew, Princeton, Salzburg and Beijing events, but less true of the 2008 Rome Synod. Yet the reception of that has been largely restricted to Catholics, and even among them there has been little recognition of those inter-faith aspects to which I draw attention.

[5] The edited volumes produced by the Drew, Princeton and Salzburg events are discussed below, as are the documents emerging from the 2008 Rome Synod. The more recent Chinese event has been described by me in a website posting that is due to be published in Chinese by the Institute of Comparative Scripture and Interreligious Dialogue and is drawn upon in this article. See: http://www.interfaith.cam.ac.uk/en/resources/papers/sr-in-china.

article, concerning the mutual significance of the legacy of Vatican II and Scriptural Reasoning, and their future potential.

Both the history and the strategic thinking about inter-faith engagement in this article are permeated with hermeneutics and theology, and I give fuller accounts of my thinking on these elsewhere.[6] The distinctive elements of the present article are its interconnection and interpretation of the five events, and its discussion of the relationship between the legacy of Vatican II and Scriptural Reasoning, which includes suggestions for the future.

Part I—Reading Together: Five Seminal Events

1. Drew 1997: Vatican II and Textual Reasoning Compared

In the early nineteen-nineties a group of Jewish text scholars and philosophers formed a group called Textual Reasoning that used to gather as a fringe meeting at the American Academy of Religion (AAR) annual meeting. They held a conference entitled "Textualities: An International Conference on Postmodern Jewish Reasoning" in June 1997 at Drew University, attended by about ninety Jewish academics from many disciplines and traditions of Judaism. With George Lindbeck and Daniel Hardy, I was one of the three Christian respondents to the conference. The conference included intensive *chevruta* (small group) study of scripture and Talmud, academic papers and discussions,[7] playful expositions of Talmud, and a great deal of formal and informal argument.

In his response,[8] Lindbeck drew a suggestive analogy between Textual Reasoning and Vatican II, in which he had taken part as an official Lutheran observer.[9] He described the Council as "a Christian version of a strange kind of yeshiva in which bishops were drilled for months and years in textual reasoning by means of extemporized forms of something like chevruta study".[10] Lindbeck drew attention to the process that the bishops and their scholarly and theological advisers developed: studying and conversing interminably around texts in larger and smaller groups; learning skills of interpretation, argument, deliberation and application; combining historical-critical

---

[6] See especially Ford, *Christian Wisdom*, particularly chapters 2, 3, 4 and 8.

[7] Some of these are published in Peter Ochs and Nancy Levene (eds), *Textual Reasonings: Jewish Philosophy and Text Study at the End of the Twentieth Century* (London: SCM Press, 2002). This volume of Drew papers is very important (though usually neglected) for understanding the origins of Scriptural Reasoning, especially the chapters by those who have been active in Scriptural Reasoning: Steven Kepnes, Aryeh Cohen, Robert Gibbs, Peter Ochs, Shaul Magid, Martin Kavka, Randi Rashkover and Laurie Zoloth.

[8] George Lindbeck, "Progress in textual reasoning: From Vatican II to the conference at Drew", in Ochs and Levene (eds), *Textual Reasonings*, pp. 252–258.

[9] In his essay in this volume, "Catholic Reasoning and Reading Across Traditions", David Dault takes issue with some of what Lindbeck said, but affirms "Lindbeck's characterization of Vatican II as *chevruta*" (p. 57), which is for me the essential point. Dault's examples of "text-based dialogical praxis" reinforce this point (p. 59).

[10] Lindbeck, "Progress in textual reasoning", p. 255.

study and "spiritual reading"; and, through all this, building a community within which bishops could become convinced of conclusions they would not have imagined coming to in advance.[11]

Lindbeck saw the enthusiasm for the Council having waned by 1997, and a "modern divisiveness" having reasserted itself. He was clear about one key factor in this:

> With the disbandment of the Council, there were no environments in which its reading practices could propagate . . . Those skills were present in abundance, but their existence as identifiable, rule-governed and deliberately transmissible behaviour was unknown. Not even an apprentice system was envisioned, and the spontaneous growth of textual reasoning in our society such as occurred at Vatican II is even more unthinkable now than forty years ago. It is only efforts such as those that produced this book and convened the conference at Drew that give hope for the future. The results of these efforts are so far quantitatively unimpressive, but the qualitative progress has been immense. Recognition, contrary to modern biases, that theory must grow out of practice, not the other way around, is a key to this progress. The more groups of textual reasoners there are and the better their practices, the more data will be available for descriptions and analyses that can help retrieve and improve the tradition-and-community restoring and reforming habits of thought and discourse that our society and religious bodies badly need.[12]

The two other Christian respondents at Drew, Daniel Hardy and myself, were by then already closely involved with some of the Textual Reasoning group in beginning Scriptural Reasoning.[13] In the light of Lindbeck's parallel it is instructive to examine what both Textual Reasoning and Scriptural Reasoning have in common with Vatican II.

It is, I think, a helpful oversimplification to see all three sharing in three interrelated dynamics, which in Vatican II terminology might be named as *ressourcement*, *aggiornamento* and *conversazione*—taking the latter as intensive conversation around texts, closely connected with what Lindbeck calls "reading skills".[14] It is notable that in 1997, at an early stage in its development, Scriptural Reasoning's elder sibling and paradigm, Textual

---

[11] *Ibid.*, p. 256.

[12] *Ibid.*, pp. 257–258.

[13] See our responses: David F. Ford, "Responding to Textual Reasoning: What might Christians Learn?" and Daniel W. Hardy, "Textual Reasoning: A Concluding Reflection", in Ochs and Levene (eds), *Textual Reasonings*, pp. 259–268 and 269–276.

[14] Lindbeck's downbeat verdict was that "without those skills, *aggiornamento* (i.e. 'updating', as the Council's opening to the modern world was generally called) was no longer rooted in *ressourcement* (return to the sources), [and] the spirit of Vatican II did not survive" (Lindbeck, "Progress in Textual Reasoning", p. 257). Certainly, the neglect or distortion of one or more of these three dynamics does threaten the spirit of the Council and of its intra-faith and inter-faith

Reasoning, was not only being compared by Lindbeck with Vatican II, but the main focus of the comparison was on such practices of reading and associated conversation in connection with these two other fundamental dynamics of the Council, *ressourcement* and *aggiornamento*.

I see these three dynamics as a sort of "DNA" that is shared by Vatican II, Textual Reasoning, and Scriptural Reasoning in analogous, tradition-specific forms. Thus, Textual Reasoning can be characterized as seeking to combine return to Tanakh and Talmud with a critical and constructive engagement with modernity, open to dialogue around texts with others who, in their own ways, are seeking contemporary wisdom through *ressourcement*, *aggiornamento* and *conversazione*. As Scriptural Reasoning continued after the Drew conference, with many members of Textual Reasoning as participants, it took up all three of these dynamics, and in combination they can act as a shorthand summary of points of correlation between it and Vatican II.[15]

2. Princeton 2003–2006: Abrahamic Study and Fellowship

Between 2003 and 2006 the Princeton Center of Theological Inquiry hosted and funded a group of sixteen Jewish, Christian and Muslim scholars, philosophers and theologians who came into residence together for a week twice a year. Apart from the annual Scriptural Reasoning in the University conferences in Cambridge,[16] this is probably the nearest Scriptural Reasoning has come thus far to Vatican II's periodic residential collegiality around texts, leading to textual production.[17] In line with the concerns of this article I will draw special attention to the resonances between Vatican II and the reading practices of the group, as articulately described by themselves.

The most obvious resonances are in the group's enactment of the three elements of what I have described above as the "DNA" of Vatican II and Scriptural Reasoning, often in ways that bring out even more parallels.

The Princeton group's *ressourcement* drew not just on scriptures but also on traditions of interpretation, especially medieval commentaries and other works. There was a vigorous Catholic presence: Kevin L. Hughes, drawing on Thomas Aquinas, Ambrose, Augustine, Ruusbroec and Henri de Lubac to

---

analogues. Yet, as is clear from many of the contributions in this volume, those three dynamics are by no means absent from contemporary Catholicism that is in the tradition of Vatican II.

[15] It is worth noting that the Textual Reasoning pattern of collegial meetings, combining gathering at the AAR with the Drew conference, was continued in Scriptural Reasoning. The Scriptural Reasoning in the University (SRU) group has met annually for a couple of days before the AAR (and, since the AAR invited Scriptural Reasoning to become an official unit of its annual meeting, also at sessions during the meeting), and there has also been an annual conference in the University of Cambridge.

[16] The Princeton pattern was modelled on the residential Cambridge conferences. I have chosen to focus on the Princeton group because it met over a shorter period of time than the Cambridge conferences, it was more stable in its membership, and it produced a text on behalf of all.

[17] The book produced by the Princeton group is: Peter Ochs and William Stacy Johnson (eds), *Crisis, Call, and Leadership in the Abrahamic Traditions* (New York: Palgrave Macmillan, 2009).

interpret Matthew 26:11, "The poor are always with you"; Ann W. Astell, bringing together Bonaventure and Dorothy Day on Lazarus "in the bosom of Abraham" (Luke 16:22); and R.R. Reno, reading Paul's first letter to the Corinthians alongside William Langland's *Piers Plowman*, with a view to "a spiritual politics of poverty"[18].

Aggiornamento was a pervasive concern of the group.[19] This was evident in the five chapters of the book produced by the group which focused on aspects of "Abrahamic Traditions and Modernity", and also in the ways they faced contemporary questions of leadership, conflict, poverty and politics. Such issues resonate with the pastoral, practical thrust of Vatican II, and with the Jewish *tikkun olam* (repairing the world) which, with Christian and Muslim analogues, has been part of Scriptural Reasoning from the first.

But, as in Lindbeck's account of Vatican II, it is the *conversazione* and associated practices of study, "interpretive hospitality" and conviviality, that are most striking in accounts of the group. The editors of the group's book speak of these in terms that might stand as a classic description of the process of academic Scriptural Reasoning:

> Each week of work began with *formational study*: sustained periods of unfettered discussion of a few verses from each of the three scriptural canons. Before each meeting, each participant was responsible for preparing larger portions of scripture, reading for the plain sense as well as examining text historical studies and traditional commentaries. After hearing an introduction to each selection by an appropriate text scholar, participants then broke into small groups of three to six . . . for hours of close textual study and dialogue. This study would be interspersed with one or two plenary sessions: occasions to discuss texts that proved particularly challenging and themes that proved particularly compelling. The group considered this initial work "formational" because it shaped the kind of fellowship that would unfold the rest of the week: how participants heard the plain sense of each scriptural text; how they experienced interrelations among the texts; how they spoke and listened to one another; and how they began to reason together.[20]

The editors go on to describe how this helped form the participants into a "*community* of care and of inquiry: directing its energies, at once, to friend-

---

[18] Reno, "*Lawe, loue and lewete*: The Kenotic Vision of Traditional Christian Political Theology", in Ochs and Johnson (eds), *Crisis, Call, and Leadership*, p. 182.

[19] The leading statement of the Council on this is *Gaudium et Spes*, the Pastoral Constitution on the Church in the Modern World (7 December 1965). Its inter-faith significance lies in its address to all humanity, its vision of the church in the service of the common good of all humanity, its recognition of the scale and profundity of the changes the world has been going through in recent centuries, and its clear commitment to conversation and collaboration with all who work for peace and human flourishing.

[20] William Stacy Johnson and Peter Ochs, "Introduction: Crisis and the Call to Leadership in the Abrahamic Traditions", in *id.* (eds), *Crisis, Call and Leadership*, p. 5.

ship, to careful study of scriptures and commentaries, and to discovering the unexpected kinds of dialogue that emerge both within and across the borders of each religious tradition".[21]

Beyond formational study, the focal work of the group was "re-examining medieval scriptural commentaries in light of today's crisis of relations among the three Abrahamic traditions of faith", which was largely carried out in three sub-groups.[22] The members of these produced chapters composed in line with each author's faith tradition, modelling a form of Abrahamic peace that is not about agreement so much as it is about shared space for fellowship and discussion. Here is a sharp difference from Vatican II: the non-syncretistic character of Scriptural Reasoning, and its search for "better quality disagreement", contrasts with the sort of consensus that Vatican II had to reach.[23]

Clearly the two gatherings differ both substantively, in the contrast between a huge global church in official conclave and a small group of academic Jews, Muslims and Christians, and formally, in the distinction between one-faith and three-faith gatherings.[24] Recognizing these vast differences, I nonetheless want to conclude this section by drawing out two further analogies with Vatican II.

The first is the God-centredness of each gathering. In Vatican II this was most obviously expressed by the Council worshipping together. For the Princeton group, common worship in that sense was not possible, and "God" was identified in very different ways by members. Yet it is fascinating to observe how these religiously serious academics[25] enacted and expressed their faith in God as a group. Primarily this is seen in the approach to text study itself: it is a quasi-liturgical activity, explicitly conducted before God

---

[21] *Ibid.*

[22] *Ibid.*, pp. 6–7.

[23] My description here is abundantly filled out by the comments of others in the book: e.g. Hughes, Astell, Aryeh Cohen, and Timothy J. Gianotti.

[24] Lindbeck's parallel is, appropriately, between Vatican II and the intra-faith practice of Textual Reasoning.

[25] Aryeh Cohen speaks of their "religious seriousness, academic integrity and conviviality" (Cohen, "Hearing the Cry of the Poor", in Ochs and Johnson (eds), *Crisis, Call and Leadership*, p. 109). Scriptural Reasoning as such does not carry any requirement of a particular sort of religious commitment, and study and conversation around the three scriptures can be done by those who identify themselves with one of the three traditions and those who do not. It began among academics who were also practising Jews, Christians or Muslims, and in many settings beyond the academy this has also been the norm; but, as the rest of this article and the other articles in this volume show, there have been many variations on this pattern. Indeed, study of scriptures and other texts has in some settings proved an attractive form of dialogue across religious-secular divisions, as well as across the boundaries of faiths other than the Abrahamic. Most reflection so far, as in this volume, has been about specifically interreligious reading, in which participants self-identify with one strand of one of the three traditions. There remains a challenging task of developing, in analogous ways, both long-term practice of other forms and reflection about those forms.

(however God is identified) and open to divine illumination.[26] Peter Ochs' essay, "Moses in the Sea: Reading Scripture as Liturgical Performance" gives a Jewish angle on this, and other essays have many analogous comments. William Stacy Johnson writes:

> One thing I discovered is that the deeply theocentric character of the version of Reformed Christianity in which I was reared, especially with its insistence on knowledge of Hebrew and its ecumenical emphasis, enabled me to find deep resonances with both the Jewish and Muslim participants in our group.[27]

This amounts to a fundamental motivation in reading these scriptures primarily "for God's sake", combined with a recognition of doing so in the presence of God. This may be as far as most practising Jews, Christians and Muslims are willing to go in the direction of shared worship. Yet one should acknowledge just how far this took them in terms of a God-centred inter-faith engagement.[28]

The second analogy concerns the eschatological dimension. This is closely related to theocentricity insofar as it is about orientation towards God's future for the world. Vatican II was considerably affected by the renewal of eschatology in twentieth-century Christian theology. So also the Princeton group was alert to the lively eschatological consciousness in many forms of Judaism and Islam. Michael Signer summed this up in discussing a statement Bertold Klappert made to him:

> "Michael, we must live our eschatology." He explained that he meant we ought to always attempt to create an atmosphere where the prophetic promise of shalom and harmony is the foundation of our interaction. My own idea of that eschatological moment has always been that people from different religious communities should study their sacred scriptures and share them with one another. We explain our own particularity without apology . . . Balancing our own desire to communicate our teaching is our eager anticipation of hearing what Christians and Muslims teach. Scriptural Reasoning at the Center of Theological Inquiry opened this eschatological horizon for me.[29]

Eschatology is not only a rich focus for study and discussion within and between each of the Abrahamic traditions; it also challenges any notion that

---

[26] Cf. the account of Paul Griffiths in *Religious Reading: The Place of Reading in the Practice of Religion* (New York: Oxford University Press, 1999).

[27] Johnson, "Three Voices, One Response: Here I Am: A Reformed Christian's Perspective on Abraham's Dilemma", in Ochs and Johnson (eds), *Crisis, Call and Leadership*, p. 71.

[28] A further aspect of quasi-liturgical practice is that of *lectio divina*, also practised by the Princeton group, and discussed below.

[29] Signer, " 'These Are the Generations': Reasoning with Rabbi Samuel ben Meier", in Ochs and Johnson (eds), *Crisis, Call and Leadership*, p. 59.

we have arrived at finality in teachings or practices, and is open to surprises from God. Both Vatican II and Scriptural Reasoning might be seen as exemplifying transformations which demonstrate that our traditions have not reached their final forms.

3. The 2008 Rome Synod: Developing the Scriptural Legacy of Vatican II
In October 2008 the General Assembly of the Synod of Bishops on "The Word of God in the Life and Mission of the Church" took place in Rome.[30] Michael Barnes in his contribution to this volume has made a number of important points relating to the Synod. He has shown its roots in *Dei Verbum* and in the *ressourcement* that fed the whole of Vatican II, describing the Council's "vision of the single life-giving mystery of God's love in which Christians and other people of faith participate".[31] That vision connects directly with the Council's strong emphasis (articulated most authoritatively by Pope Paul VI) on dialogue and conversation, complementing *ressourcement* and *aggiornamento*, with commitment to dialogue with other faiths in the context of the "single dialogue of salvation" between God and humanity. The implications are clear: *put together scripture-centred* ressourcement *in one's own tradition, an inclusive, God-centred vision of salvation, and dialogue with other religions that have scriptures, and the result should be scripture-centred inter-faith conversation.*

This result is reinforced by a range of other points made by Barnes, Hughes, Dault, Higton and Murray in this volume. The points include: the shift from predominantly scholastic to more Biblical terminology; the official encouragement of many approaches to interpreting scripture, including learning from Jewish practices; the horizon of a "world church"; the desirability of avoiding the neutral, faith-free ground of secularized Biblical Studies; the complementarity of scripture study and doctrinal theology; the intensification and mutual enhancement through deeper scripture study of both intra-Christian ecumenism and inter-faith engagement; and the ideal of mutual respect and friendship grounded in learning from each other. The conclusion is that the legacy of Vatican II, as expressed in the 2008 Synod, can be seen as a theological vision in search of appropriate Bible-related practices, and that Scriptural Reasoning (when, as in the Princeton group, it involves Catholics who take

---

[30] The principal official documents produced are the *lineamenta*, the preliminary statement and questions sent out to the bishops and others; the *instrumentum laboris* of the Synod (a preparatory document based on responses to the *lineamenta*); the message of the bishops to the church after the Synod; and the post-Synodal message of Pope Benedict XVI, *Verbum Domini*. These are available (respectively) at: http://www.vatican.va/roman_curia/synod/documents/rc_synod_doc_20070427_lineamenta-xii-assembly_en.html; http://www.vatican.va/roman_curia/synod/documents/rc_synod_doc_20080511_instrlabor-xii-assembly_en.html;http://www.vatican.va/roman_curia/synod/documents/rc_synod_doc_20081024_message-synod_en.html; and http://www.vatican.va/holy_father/benedict_xvi/apost_exhortations/documents/hf_ben-xvi_exh_20100930_verbum-domini_en.html

[31] Barnes, p. 13.

part in the spirit of Vatican II) is well suited to being one such practice. I would add to these observations three further comments on the 2008 Synod.

(i) A strong endorsement?

The first is that I read the Synod documents as pointing somewhat more strongly towards the conclusion just drawn than does Barnes. Commenting on the statement in the *instrumentum laboris* about Jews and Christians ("In some cases, ways to study Scripture together are being developed—and can be further developed—providing occasion to learn from each other while closely respecting each other's differences") Barnes' verdict is: "This is hardly a ringing endorsement of practices of interreligious reading."[32] On the contrary, it seems to me to be a properly cautious yet definite and positive affirmation. I would also point to other statements emerging from the Synod, which need to be read together, such as:

> Study and meetings, especially in interreligious and intercultural exchanges, urgently need to give an appreciable place to the Word of God in relation to culture and the human spirit.[33]

> I wish to state once more how much the Church values her dialogue with the Jews. Wherever it seems appropriate, it would be good to create opportunities for encounter and exchange in public as well as in private, and thus to promote growth in reciprocal knowledge, in mutual esteem and cooperation, also in the study of the sacred Scriptures.[34]

> I express my hope that the trust-filled relationships established between Christians and Muslims over the years will continue to develop in a spirit of sincere and respectful dialogue.[35]

> Frequently we note a consonance with values expressed also in their religious books, such as, in Buddhism, respect for life, contemplation, silence, simplicity; in Hinduism, the sense of the sacred, sacrifice and fasting; and again, in Confucianism, family and social values.[36]

One thrust of those statements is towards interreligious reading of each other's core texts, which might be either in a form such as Comparative Theology or, if there is more emphasis on live *conversazione* as practised by the Council itself, Scriptural Reasoning.

---

[32] *Ibid.*, p. 28.

[33] "The Word of God in the Life and Mission of the Church", *Instrumentum Laboris* (11 May 2008), 32.

[34] Pope Benedict XVI, "*Verbum Domini*. Post-Synodal Apostolic Exhortation" (30 September 2010), 43. Cf. "Message to the People of God of the XII Ordinary General Assembly of the Synod of Bishops", 14.

[35] Pope Benedict XVI, "*Verbum Domini*", 118.

[36] *Ibid.*, 119.

(ii) Re-engagement with the Bible

The second comment concerns the Synod's long-term significance. It can be seen as the culmination to date of one of the most important events in the history of Christianity: the twentieth-century re-engagement of the Roman Catholic Church with the Bible. This began mid-century, was formative in Vatican II, and since then has been sustained with considerable consistency, energy and practical effect on liturgy, ecclesiology, mission, religious orders, spirituality, theological and religious education, and much else. Vatican II emphatically encouraged study of the Bible by laity, clergy and religious, scholars and theologians. It stressed the importance of good translations (and of cooperating with other Christians in producing them). It also insisted on the vital importance of the Bible for preaching, catechetics and Christian instruction. Overall it hoped that the church's "spiritual life will receive a new impulse from increased devotion to the word of God" *(DV, 26)*.

A series of official documents,[37] together with the prominence of the Bible in the teachings of Popes John XXIII, Paul VI, John Paul II and Benedict XVI, are among many indications of this momentum being maintained after the Council. Fresh interpretation of the Bible has been essential to rethinking major issues in fundamental, doctrinal, liturgical, pastoral, moral and political theology. Perhaps the most pervasively influential transformation in the reception of the Bible among the world's Roman Catholics has been the post-Vatican II changes in the lectionary and the liturgy of the Mass.

The 2008 Synod is the most concentrated official effort so far to ensure that the Bible, understood in Catholic terms, is utterly pervasive in the life and thought of the church. Two of its distinctive features are its concern with how the Word of God (inseparably linked to the Bible) might in practice be pervasively formative, and its embrace of other faiths and their scriptures under the heading of discussing the Word of God. To connect a renewed Biblical culture in the church with new practices of interreligious reading opens up possibilities for the twenty-first century that go beyond anything any other Christian church has so far undertaken.[38] Intra-Christian ecumenism (for which Vatican II and its scriptural turn were so important) was one of the religious surprises of the twentieth century, bringing about a turning among many denominations from confrontation and conflict to conversation and

---

[37] Notably *On the Historical Truth of the Gospels* (1964), *The Interpretation of the Bible in the Church* (1993) and *The Jewish People and Their Sacred Scriptures in the Christian Bible* (2001). See http://www.vatican.va/roman_curia/congregations/cfaith/pcb_doc_index.htm.

[38] The nearest is probably *Generous Love: the truth of the Gospel and the call to dialogue. An Anglican theology of inter faith relations*. A report from the Anglican Communion Network for Inter Faith Concerns (London: The Anglican Consultative Council, 2008) which welcomes Scriptural Reasoning.

collaboration. The 2008 Synod as an expression of the legacy of Vatican II could help to bring about something analogous among the religions.[39]

(iii) *Lectio divina*

If that is to be realized, while there is need for a great many forms of inter-faith engagement besides interreligious reading of each other's core texts,[40] yet Vatican II and the 2008 Synod do suggest that the latter is essential. This leads into a third comment on the Synod, about its repeated, strong recommendation of the practice of *lectio divina*. Time and again the documents see it as a good way to read the Bible habitually, culminating in Pope Benedict warmly advocating it and outlining its four key elements.[41] *Lectio divina* is also commended as a shared practice with other Christians, but is not explicitly mentioned in relation to the scriptures of other faiths. I suggest, with reference to a particular experience, that it is well suited to interreligious reading of a sort that differs from Scriptural Reasoning but can complement it, and that their combination might be an especially fruitful Catholic contribution to inter-faith dialogue.

The experience was an event in England in September 2011. Some Benedictine nuns from Turvey Abbey, Bedfordshire, had come to an Open Scriptural Reasoning session that was part of a Cambridge University "Festival of Ideas". After the session, they contacted the Cambridge Inter-faith Programme with a suggestion: they had greatly appreciated Scriptural Reasoning but wondered whether it could be done alongside their own habitual practice of *lectio divina*. The result was a gathering for a day at Turvey Abbey of more than twenty Jews, Christians and Muslims. We divided into two groups, each of which read the same texts from Tanakh, Bible and Qur'an, engaging first through one practice and then through the other. We then gathered in plenary to discuss together, and the unanimous verdict was that it was a fruitful form of "stereophonic" interreligious reading. The Scriptural

---

[39] With Paul Murray, I see ecumenism and inter-faith engagement as deeply interrelated; cf. David F. Ford, *The Future of Christian Theology* (Malden, MA: Wiley Blackwell, 2011), chapter 7.

[40] The ecumenical movement is a good parallel here, requiring many modes of interaction at interpersonal, local, regional, national and international levels, besides the building of appropriate institutions. For a summary of modes of inter-faith engagement including joint scriptural study, see the final section, "Seeking Together in the Way of God" in *A Common Word for the Common Good*, the response by the then Archbishop of Canterbury, Rowan Williams, to the Muslim letter, *A Common Word Between Us and You*. Available at: http://www.acommonword.com/category/site/christian-responses

[41] He sums up each element in a question: *Lectio*—"*what does the biblical text say in itself?*"; *meditatio*—"*what does the biblical text say to us?*"; *oratio*—"*what do we say to the Lord in response to his word?*"; *contemplatio*—"*what conversion of mind, heart and life is the Lord asking of us?*" (Pope Benedict XVI, "*Verbum Domini*", 87). He continues: "The word of God appears here as a criterion for discernment: it is 'living and active, sharper than any two-edged sword, piercing to the division of soul and spirit, of joints and marrow, and discerning the thoughts and intentions of the heart' (Heb 4:12). We do well also to remember that the process of *lectio divina* is not concluded until it arrives at action (*actio*), which moves the believer to make his or her life a gift for others in charity" (87).

Reasoning method of conversation and argument around texts is an adaptation of the ancient Rabbinic *chevruta*; *lectio divina* is rooted in monastic traditions of meditation and contemplation, and excludes discussion. All agreed that, done together successively, they gave a richer appreciation of both the texts and of each other.

In retrospect, I would now add two reflections about this experiment relevant to the legacy of Vatican II.

First, it makes sense for traditions to share their habitual reading practices as well as their classic texts. If part of fruitful interreligious reading is seeking to go deeper into both one's own texts and the texts of others, then not to bring into the engagement one's habitual ways of going deeper into one's own scripture impoverishes the encounter. To do so, of course, raises complex questions; there was extensive discussion in advance of the day at Turvey Abbey, and no doubt if the practice of joint Scriptural Reasoning and *lectio divina* were to continue it would evolve and mature over many years by trial and error, as each has independently. Nevertheless, in principle it is wise to explore the use of such practices. The enthusiasm for *lectio divina* expressed by Vatican II and the 2008 Synod suggests that, in line with the Synod's other statements, it could also play an inter-faith role.[42]

Second, it is noteworthy that the Princeton group discussed above, which included Catholic medieval scholars, also drew upon *lectio divina*.[43] For Catholic theology, the Middle Ages is a classic period, still immensely important, in which (in ways that are often not recognized) the Bible was of fundamental significance. The story[44] of the Bible in the Latin Church after Ambrose (339–97), Jerome (347–420) and Augustine (354–430), moving through Cassiodorus (c. 485–585), Benedict (c. 480–585), Pope Gregory the Great (c. 540–604), Bede (c. 673–735), Julian of Toledo (642–90),[45] and the creation of a Biblical culture in the Carolingian Empire in the eighth to tenth centuries,[46] into the expanding network of cathedral, diocesan, monastic and

---

[42] It is noteworthy that at the 2011 Christian-Muslim Building Bridges Seminar in Doha, chaired by the then Archbishop of Canterbury, Rowan Williams, which I attended, Dom Timothy Wright presented a paper on *lectio divina*.

[43] See Johnson and Ochs, "Introduction", in *id.* (eds), *Crisis, Call, and Leadership*, p. 6: "participants were instructed by the medieval Church traditions of *lectio divina*: giving voice to images that the scriptural texts brought to mind and, thereby, sharing personal religious reflections alongside more academic analyses of the texts' rhetorical forms and semantic force."

[44] See the chapters by John J. Contreni on "The Patristic Legacy to c. 1000", Guy Lobrichon on "The Early Schools, c. 900-1100", William J. Courtenay on "The Bible in Medieval Universities" and Mary Dove on "Scripture and Reform", in Richard Marsden and E. Ann Matter (eds), *The New Cambridge History of the Bible*, vol. 2: *From 600 to 1450* (Cambridge: Cambridge University Press, 2012), pp. 505–595.

[45] "Julian's confident pedagogy is a reminder that the culture of one book in the early Middle Ages was a culture of debate, analysis and the application of critical reasoning" (Contreni, "The Patristic Legacy", in Marsden and Matter (eds), *The New Cambridge History of the Bible*, p. 519).

[46] *Ibid.*, p. 525: "The Bible became one of the most prominent features of the Carolingian landscape, informing contemporary thought, literature, art, law, political and social policy, as well as Carolingian notions of religion, spirituality and reform."

parochial schools at the beginning of the second millennium, and then into the medieval universities, is one in which meditative and argumentative reasoning practices developed together.

The 2008 Synod, with its insistence on scholarly and theological rationality that engages with the Bible and is integrated with liturgy, *lectio divina* and other scripture-centred practices, could be seen as recreating what I judge to be the single most important condition for the golden age of Catholic theology. Arguably, none of the many types of Thomism in the past century has succeeded in being as thoroughly Biblical in contemporary terms (including relating the Bible to modern scholarship, philosophy, theology, liturgy, spirituality, politics and culture) as Bonaventure or Thomas Aquinas was in medieval terms. I see the central challenge of Benedict XVI's response to the 2008 Synod, together with some of his other pronouncements, being to realize a theology and a church that is both thoroughly scriptural and thoroughly rational, an inter-faith analogue of which might be Scriptural Reasoning. In realizing this vision it might be that a contemporary engagement with Jews and Muslims who are likewise committed to being thoroughly scriptural and rational could act as a stimulus comparable to that received by Aquinas through his mostly philosophical engagement with Jewish and Muslim thought—but with the important difference of being able today to engage face to face across the religious boundaries in contexts of mutual hospitality where no one faith exercises hegemony. The Pope Emeritus' doctrinal concern could be met by Mike Higton's account in this volume of the practice of Scriptural Reasoning being, for its Christian participants, part of their discipline of "doctrinally-governed scriptural reading".[47]

4. Salzburg 2009: Scriptural Reasoning Alongside Comparative Theology

In April 2009 about a hundred scholars attended a three-day conference of the European Society for Intercultural Theology and Interreligious Studies in the University of Salzburg, Austria, on the theme of interreligious hermeneutics in a pluralistic Europe. This conference later gave rise to a volume of papers.[48] There were several sub-themes in the conference, but two of the main ones were Scriptural Reasoning (four papers) and Comparative Theology (six papers). So the two were brought alongside each other in a conference for the first time, and each was served by one paper that deserves to become a classic on the practice it discusses: Nicholas Adams on "Scriptural Reasoning and Interfaith Hermeneutics", and Francis

---

[47] Higton, p. 135.
[48] David Cheetham, Ulrich Winkler, Oddbjørn Leirvik and Judith Gruber (eds), *Interreligious Hermeneutics in Pluralistic Europe: Between Texts and People* (Amsterdam: Rodopi, 2011).

Clooney on "Comparative Theology—As Theology".[49] "Alongside" is the appropriate term: the post-conference papers do not give a sense of deep engagement between the two practices, but suggest a need for conversation such as is conducted elsewhere in the present volume (as does the founding in China of an institute that is inspired by both Scriptural Reasoning and Comparative Theology, discussed below). Nor did the conference result in substantial further development of the practices individually. It was a short conference with a very varied agenda, and any expectation of such development would have been unrealistic in relation to long-term practices. Nonetheless the Salzburg event can be seen as significant in several respects.

First, there was its largely continental European membership. There were some participants from the UK and the US, where both Comparative Theology and Scriptural Reasoning began, but most were from a range of European countries: Austria, Germany, Scandinavia, France, Belgium, Holland, and elsewhere. The world of inter-faith engagement tends, despite dealing with global religions, to be curiously regional in its approaches and in how it largely looks to local thinkers and practitioners. The conference connected these worlds within worlds. It both advanced the "inculturation" of Scriptural Reasoning and Comparative Theology in continental Europe, and also brought these practices into contact with interreligious thinkers and practitioners who are not well known in the UK and the US.[50]

Closely tied to this diversity amongst the participants were the cross-disciplinary and cross-institutional interconnections represented by the conference. The very name, European Society for Intercultural Theology and Interreligious Studies, indicates one of its fundamental strengths: the determination not to separate theology from religious studies. The Chinese situation discussed below shows a similar determination. Whereas in German-language, Dutch, Belgian and Scandinavian universities the main traditional bias has been towards theology and not religious studies, the main Chinese university bias has been against theology. What appears to be happening in both settings is a new convergence of the two. For those convinced of the worthwhileness of Comparative Theology and Scriptural Reasoning, it is important to argue for shaping and strengthening institutional contexts in which theology and religious studies can come together. Plural societies that are both multi-religious and secular need spaces where those committed to particular religions and to none can come together in study, teaching and learning, research, multi-disciplinary engagement,

---

[49] The other papers on Comparative Theology tended to be more substantial than those on Scriptural Reasoning, partly because they were more thoroughly researched. The Scriptural Reasoning side was especially affected by the lack of Jewish and Muslim contributions, and by the absence of anyone other than Adams who had long-term experience of the practice.

[50] The bibliographies accompanying the papers are a good indicator of this.

critical and constructive thinking, conversation and dispute.[51] Both Comparative Theology and Scriptural Reasoning can be carried on in many settings, but essential to their "ecology" are those niches where there are many disciplines engaging with many religions in ways that allow also for deep conversation and theological thinking. It is worth noting that Comparative Theology germinated at Harvard, and that Scriptural Reasoning has had its main academic homes in the University of Cambridge and the University of Virginia: in all three there is theology with religious studies.

The Salzburg gathering was also notable for its multiple discourses, by which I mean not only a variety of academic disciplines but ways of understanding, analyzing and thinking that transcend particular fields. The leading discourse was hermeneutics, but in addition there were feminism and other gender-related approaches, culture and media studies, phenomenology, empirical methods, postmodern deconstruction, postcolonial critique and polemics. From the point of view of Scriptural Reasoning and Comparative Theology such discourses not only help to ensure constant alertness and self-critique but also open up debates across the various religious-secular divides.

All of these points about the Salzburg conference also relate to the legacy of Vatican II: this global church is seeking to encourage its regions to learn from each other; its members are involved in complexly multi-religious and secular societies, and are having to live and think their faith in the midst of people of many faiths and none; its *ressourcement* and *aggiornamento* require *conversazione* with many discourses. Above all, what one glimpses through some of the Salzburg conference papers is the richness, rigour and depth of what has been, at least until the late twentieth century, the most fruitful and weighty double tradition of modern Christian theology: that which was developed in German-language universities, in both Catholic and Protestant faculties, since the nineteenth century, and was joined by that generated through French-language Catholic institutions. The ways in which Vatican II engaged in *ressourcement* and *aggiornamento* are unthinkable without this continental European tradition. If it does not draw on this, any twenty-first-century Christian Biblical interpretation and theology is impoverished. In both Catholicism and Protestantism it has already made a huge contribution to ecumenical theology between the churches. Salzburg gave some hints of what its potential might be in the inter-faith field,[52] but also underlined the challenge it faces to transcend, without betraying, its confessional mode.

---

[51] For my advocacy of "new theology and religious studies" see *The Future of Christian Theology*, chapter 8, and *Shaping Theology: Engagements in a Religious and Secular World* (Oxford: Blackwell, 2007).

[52] I think especially of the chapters by Sigrid Rettenbacher, Hendrik Rungelrath, Ulrich Winkler and Judith Gruber. There are at present promising initiatives in some German universities in the teaching of Islamic theology, with the possibility that a Muslim academic theological tradition might be developed there alongside and in dialogue with Christian theology.

5. Beijing and Jinan 2012: Six-text Scriptural Reasoning

In 2008, following a visit to China, the then Archbishop of Canterbury, Dr Rowan Williams, hosted a symposium at Lambeth Palace for Chinese and UK academics in the field of theology and religious studies, at which there was a paper on Scriptural Reasoning. The respondent was Yang Huilin, Vice-President of Renmin University of China and Professor of Comparative Literature and Religious Studies there, who through this was introduced to Scriptural Reasoning. Back in Beijing, he and You Bin, Professor of Christianity and Director of Research at Minzu University of China, set up the Institute of Comparative Scripture and Interreligious Dialogue (ICS) in the Faculty of Philosophy and Religious Studies within Minzu University. Minzu is the "University of the Nationalities/Ethnicities"—the dozens of non-Han ethnic groups (numbered in tens of millions) recognized by the Chinese government—so its whole ethos is to do with diversity. Since many of the groups also are religious in distinctive ways, it is well suited to a practice that tries to deepen relationships and understanding across deep differences.

Modelled on Scriptural Reasoning and Comparative Theology, the ICS aims

to conduct comparative research in the classical or scriptural traditions of the great world religions and to engage in interreligious dialogue . . . The Institute not only focuses on a purely academic or scientific comparison of texts, but also allows for a study of one's own scripture as authoritative Scripture in the context of one's faith community as well as of other faith communities (Institute brochure).

Already it has launched a new Journal of Comparative Scripture Studies, and it holds regular Scriptural Reasoning sessions.

I visited China in 2012 and took part in Scriptural Reasoning in Minzu University and in the Jinan campus of Shandong University. I recognized familiar elements in these sessions, such as energetic conversation and argument around short texts on related themes, a mixture of scholarly, hermeneutical, ethical and theological points, all sorts of translation issues, and frequent laughter. Yet this Chinese practice is also an improvisation upon Scriptural Reasoning, marked by four main innovations.

The most obvious innovation is that the participants are adding scriptures that are important in China: Confucian, Daoist and a variety of Buddhist texts. Since Scriptural Reasoning was developed through reading together three "sibling" scriptures, the addition of three scriptures unrelated to the Abrahamic ones, and more distantly related to each other, poses new challenges. Notably, however, the participants are not using the numerical scarcity of Jews in China to drop or marginalize Judaism.[53] A second innovation

---

[53] The Professor of Jewish Studies in Shandong University, Fu Youde, is a member of the Academic Committee of the ICS and at the time of my visit had studying with him two Israeli

is in drawing on Comparative Theology as well as Scriptural Reasoning. Francis Clooney is an International Advisor on the Academic Committee of ICS. A third innovation is in using Confucianism as a relatively uncontroversial Chinese point of reference. A fourth is a new disciplinary setting for Scriptural Reasoning: Comparative Literature. Scriptural Reasoning's main institutional location in China is in the Department of Philosophy and Religious Studies in Minzu University, but another is in Comparative Literature in Renmin University, due largely to Professors Yang Huilin and Youzhang Geng. They have seen that Comparative Literature is a natural home for Scriptural Reasoning, and are also introducing it to the international academic Comparative Literature community.[54]

What have been the conditions for this to happen in Chinese universities? One of the main architects of a remarkable transformation in academic religious studies in China is German-educated Professor Zhuo Xinping, since 1998 Director of the Institute of World Religions in the Chinese Academy of Social Sciences (CASS)[55] and since 2001 Chair of the Chinese Association of Religious Studies, covering all the university departments that study religions. In a paper given during my visit he summed up the transformation:

> Before the reform era, religion in China was characterized as a private affair, which should have no connection with the society. So the study of religion was mainly from an ideological perspective. Nobody paid special attention to the academic study of religion. But now, the academic study of religions in China plays a leading role.[56]

Professor Zhuo traced the evolution of official attitudes from "religion as opium" through "religion as culture" to "religion as religion", with religious studies moving from being a "dangerous discipline" to a "promising discipline". The wider context is the new international context of "reforming China", including "the rapid revitalization of religions in contemporary China" which is being affected by globalization and world religions. Professor Zhuo saw this as "the beginning of open religions in an open society of China", but frankly named a range of dilemmas this is posing regarding Chinese Marxism and its ideological role, the growth of Chinese cultural and

---

Jewish doctoral students who played an active role in the three-hour Scriptural Reasoning session.

[54] E.g. a day-long Round Table on Scriptural Reasoning at the International Comparative Literature Association annual meeting in July 2013 in Paris, sponsored by Professor Yang Huilin.

[55] CASS is the highest academic research organization in the fields of philosophy and social sciences in China. It has thirty-one research institutes and more than fifty research centres, which carry out research activities covering about two-hundred and sixty sub-disciplines.

[56] Unpublished, delivered in a co-lecture with me on "The Future of Religious Studies"; this paper is also the source of other quotations from Zhuo.

religious nationalism, large numbers of Chinese joining world religions, political control of the religions, religious freedom and human rights.

The result of all this is that China has recognized that a world-class university system needs to engage well academically with the religions without excluding confessional religious voices. There is no sense that religious studies in universities is only for non-believers, nor, of course, is it only for adherents of religions. Rather, it is taken for granted that a department will be a plural space, embracing those of many religions and none. It is also taken for granted that there can be theology in those departments, in the sense of both studying theological thinking and exploring issues raised in current discussions. A common Chinese perception of Scriptural Reasoning is that it can mediate between theology and religious studies. This is because it allows for discussion of contemporary issues of interpretation and application whilst also requiring the scholarly disciplines related to texts and contexts.

Scriptural Reasoning has three further features that seem to suit at least some Chinese departments well. First, it is intrinsically hospitable to many traditions, enabling a plural collegiality and encouraging conversation. China is emerging from a relatively non-conversational culture as regards religions. Second, it does not insist on coming to conclusions. Scriptural Reasoning tends to operate in an interrogative and exploratory mode, and while individual participants may come to conclusions there is no demand for agreement. Third, it allows for self-description by religious people and for the use of "native" categories. Students and staff in our Scriptural Reasoning sessions in China self-identified naturally as Muslim, Christian, Buddhist, Confucian, Daoist, Jewish, or no faith tradition. The two main ways until now of relating across religious traditions in Chinese departments of religious studies have been through philosophy and the social sciences, both for many years largely Marxist, though now diversifying. A disadvantage of both is that they are external to the religions, and tend to interpret or explain them through "foreign" categories. Such categories may be illuminating but are ultimately inadequate for enabling in-depth understanding of the particularity of specific traditions. Scriptural Reasoning not only allows for the use of native categories from one's own tradition but also enables participants to learn the categories of others.

Finally, how might all this relate to the legacy of Vatican II? It seems like a whole people is going through *ressourcement* (after the traumas of the twentieth century many yearn for an identity with roots and spiritual substance) and *aggiornamento* (but often suffering from the darker sides of modernity). Learning anew to engage in *conversazione*, with academic discourse that takes religion and religious people seriously, is quite a recent development. In the midst of all this, one small new institute, supported by some of the architects of an academic religious studies hospitable to scriptures and theology, has discerned the potential in combining Scriptural Reasoning with Comparative Theology. In this way something of the "DNA" of the Council is, mostly anonymously, being introduced to China, and many possibilities are opening up.

Part II—The Mutual Significance of the Legacy of Vatican II and Scriptural Reasoning

Scriptural Reasoning's Contribution to the Legacy of Vatican II

What might Scriptural Reasoning have to contribute to the legacy of Vatican II? I have shown it bringing together in a specific practice three core dynamics of the Council: *ressourcement, aggiornamento* and *conversazione*. It does so with special attention to three key concerns of the Council: the Bible, the modern world and the encounter with other religions. In relation to these three, Scriptural Reasoning offers a form of receptive learning whose most distinctive feature is an apprenticeship in intensive, text-centred conversation, which Lindbeck identified as a vital generative practice of the Council. *Scriptural Reasoning thus resonates with and realizes more fully what is already present in the legacy of Vatican II.* This pattern of echoing and enhancing themes of the Council can also be seen in relation to: ecumenism[57]; Judaism[58]; Islam[59]; the desire to increase and deepen the significance of the Bible in the church[60]; the desirability of a twenty-first-century version of the golden age of medieval theology drawing on both *lectio divina* and philosophical and theological discussion of the *sacra pagina*[61]; and the multi-dimensional practice of dialogue.

Yet there are also complications in the relationship between the legacy of the Second Vatican Council and Scriptural Reasoning. I will mention just two.

First is the question of an institutional setting for academic Scriptural Reasoning in relation to Catholics. The strong preference of the Catholic Church is, understandably, for its theological thinking and teaching to be done in Catholic institutions. This is a sensible preference for any religious

---

[57] Cf. Paul Murray in this volume on how inter-faith scriptural study and intra-Christian Biblical reasoning can be mutually beneficial.

[58] The most notable inter-faith achievement of the Council was in relation to Judaism, and this has been well followed through, especially in the area of interpretation of scripture. Scriptural Reasoning, with its roots in Textual Reasoning, allows this engagement to become habitual in the mode of *conversazione*, and to generate further dialogue and collaboration.

[59] The tentative beginnings of *Nostra Aetate* have developed considerably, culminating in the twice-yearly gatherings of Vatican representatives with Muslim signatories of *A Common Word Between Us and You*; and, as argued above, the various official documents, such as those emerging from the 2008 Synod, can be read as offering theology and guidelines in search of appropriate practices, with Scriptural Reasoning well suited to meet the need.

[60] One of the most striking experiences associated with Scriptural Reasoning is that of deepening engagement with one's own scripture as one engages with those of others—see my conclusion below.

[61] The challenges include doing justice to: post-medieval developments in Biblical studies and *ressourcement* in line with Vatican II; philosophy and science beyond Plato and Aristotle; Abrahamic engagement beyond polemics; inter-faith engagement beyond the Abrahamic; and institutional settings and spheres of life beyond the Catholic Church and Catholic universities.

community, and it means that the vast majority of institutions around the world where theology (or its equivalent in other traditions) is taught and researched are controlled by the authorities of a particular religious tradition. Members of these institutions can, and do, take part in Scriptural Reasoning. Yet it is no accident that Scriptural Reasoning and Comparative Theology have, as mentioned above, been nurtured in settings not controlled by one tradition, where there is both theology and religious studies, and students and staff come from many religions and none. These are quite rare niches in the academic world, but where they exist they often in fact contain many Catholic students and academics. In line with my interpretation of the legacy of Vatican II, there is a case for official Catholic Church support for such settings, and for encouragement to be given to Catholics to see participation in such institutions as a recognized form of theological vocation, without in any way comparing these settings, favourably or unfavourably, with confessional ones.

The second, more serious, complication can be summed up as the challenge of *Dominus Iesus*, the Declaration of the Congregation for the Doctrine of the Faith in 2000, signed by Cardinal Ratzinger, later Pope Benedict XVI.[62] Its points include: the Christian imperative to evangelize, with interreligious dialogue seen as part of this mission (1, 2, 22); a rejection of "the tendency to read and to interpret Sacred Scripture outside the Tradition and Magisterium of the Church" (4); a "distinction between theological faith and belief in the other religions" (7); a denial that other scriptures than the Bible are inspired by the Holy Spirit (8); a denial that other ways of salvation are "parallel or complementary" to that of Jesus Christ (14)[63]; a declaration that "One can and must say that Jesus Christ has a significance and a value for the human race and its history, which are unique and singular, proper to him alone, exclusive, universal, and absolute" (15); and an affirmation of the church's "indispensable relationship with the salvation of every human being" (20).

Alongside a first strand represented by such points are two other strands, which the style of the declaration makes clear are subsidiary. The second strand is a nuancing of those points listed above: affirming with Vatican II that the "Catholic Church rejects nothing of what is true and holy in these religions", and that interreligious dialogue "requires an attitude of understanding and a relationship of mutual knowledge and reciprocal enrichment" (2); refining the proclamation of the "definitiveness and completeness" of

---

[62] Congregation for the Doctrine of the Faith, *"Dominus Iesus. On the Unicity and Salvific Universality of Jesus Christ and the Church"* (6 August 2000). Available at: http://www.vatican.va/roman_curia/congregations/cfaith/documents/rc_con_cfaith_doc_20000806_dominus-iesus_en.html

[63] Citing here Pope John Paul II's encyclical, *"Redemptoris Missio. On the Permanent Validity of the Church's Missionary Mandate"* (7 December 1990). Available at: http://www.vatican.va/holy_father/john_paul_ii/encyclicals/documents/hf_jp-ii_enc_07121990_redemptoris-missio_en.html

Christian revelation as taught by the Catholic Church by indicating that "the depth of the divine mystery in itself remains transcendent and inexhaustible" (6); in the context of discussing other sacred writings, affirming with Vatican II that they "often reflect a ray of that truth which enlightens all men" (8); affirming with Vatican II that "the unique mediation of the Redeemer does not exclude, but rather gives rise to a manifold cooperation which is but a participation in this one source" (14); insisting on the mysterious character of how grace and salvation are accessible to non-Christians, and of their relationship to the church (15, 21); and nuancing the rejection of complementarity or equivalence in relation to salvation through other religions by the qualification, "even if these are said to be converging with the church toward the eschatological kingdom of God" (21). The asymmetry between the first and second sets of points is well summed up in the penultimate paragraph:

> If it is true that the followers of other religions can receive divine grace, it is also certain that objectively speaking they are in a gravely deficient situation in comparison with those who, in the Church, have the fullness of the means of salvation. (22)

The third strand is one of openness to further dialogue, reflection and research. In an early paragraph there is an interweaving of *conversazione*, *ressourcement* and *aggiornamento*:

> In the practice of dialogue between the Christian faith and other religious traditions, as well as in seeking to understand its theoretical basis more deeply, new questions arise that need to be addressed through pursuing new paths of research, advancing proposals, and suggesting ways of acting that call for attentive discernment. In this task, the present Declaration seeks to recall to Bishops, theologians, and all the Catholic faithful, certain indispensable elements of Christian doctrine, which may help theological reflection in developing solutions consistent with the contents of the faith and responsive to the pressing needs of contemporary culture. (3)[64]

That statement combines a robust, primary assertion of essential Christian doctrine with the practice of dialogue, theoretical reflection and responsiveness to current needs.

How might all that accord with Scriptural Reasoning? The perhaps surprising answer is: remarkably well. Scriptural Reasoning takes deep, even absolute, long-term and apparently irresolvable differences as part of the

---

[64] Cf. 14 on the invitation "to explore if and in what way the historical figures and positive elements of these religions may fall within the divine plan of salvation. In this undertaking, theological research has a vast field of work under the guidance of the Church's Magisterium".

reality of inter-faith engagement.[65] It does not assume consensus or aim at it (though, of course, where it is possible it welcomes it); far more important is improvement in the quality of disagreements. *Dominus Iesus* is a clear official Catholic statement of distinctiveness that has already evoked a great deal of disagreement within and beyond the Roman Catholic Church. In a Scriptural Reasoning setting the many Biblical texts quoted by the declaration in support of its assertions could be studied and argued about. It is possible that Catholics, as those who consider they should be able to arrive at a consensus, would have some of the most passionate arguments among themselves. Nothing in the declaration implies the inappropriateness of Catholics who assent to *Dominus Iesus* taking part in Scriptural Reasoning as generally practised. They are encouraged to engage in dialogue and be open to the truths contributed by others; Scriptural Reasoning does not rule out anyone claiming universality, absoluteness, uniqueness or other forms of superiority for their own tradition; in a Scriptural Reasoning setting Catholics are free to interpret the Bible in accordance with the Magisterium of their church; and the declaration says enough about the inexhaustible depth and mystery of God's ways, about the truths others might share, and about the hope of eschatological convergence in the kingdom of God, to make a dialogical practice centred on scriptures very attractive—especially when considered alongside later documents such as those of the 2008 Synod.

In short, a tradition that can subscribe to a document such as *Dominus Iesus*, and also to the importance of dialogue with those with whom it deeply differs, needs a practice, such as Scriptural Reasoning, that specializes in facing deep disagreements.

Perhaps the most difficult issue is the relationship of dialogue to evangelism. The Declaration could be read as encouraging interreligious dialogue only for the sake of proselytizing and converting people to Roman Catholicism. For those of other traditions, including other Christian traditions, this is one of the strongest inhibitors of participation in dialogue with Catholics. However, that is not a necessary interpretation, especially the "only". In addition it is important to mention that Scriptural Reasoning has in fact included, and should in theory be able to include, those (nearly always Christians or Muslims) who are committed to missionary activity on behalf of their community. It is one of the most sensitive and explosive issues between and within the Abrahamic faiths. Yet, if the protocols of Scriptural Reasoning are observed,[66] there can be a space where even this is explored and argued about with reference to the scriptures of each tradition.

---

[65] Cf. Nicholas Adams, "Scriptural Reasoning and Interfaith Hermeneutics," in Cheetham et al. (eds), *Interreligious Hermeneutics in Pluralistic Europe*, pp. 59–78, which emphasizes the importance of the quality of disagreement.

[66] As described, for example, in Steven Kepnes, "A Handbook for Scriptural Reasoning," in David F. Ford and C. C. Pecknold (eds), *The Promise of Scriptural Reasoning* (Oxford: Blackwell, 2006), pp. 23–40; Higton and Muers, *The Text in Play*, pp. 93–114; and the websites

The Contribution of the Legacy of Vatican II to Scriptural Reasoning

The pattern of echoing and enhancement that is noted in the previous section can also be seen in the contribution of Vatican II and its legacy to Scriptural Reasoning. I would draw attention to seven particularly significant areas:

1. Already, some Scriptural Reasoning groups have met on occasion with Biblical commentaries, doctrinal statements and church documents (together with analogous Jewish and Muslim texts) on the table alongside scripture. The Catholic presence in Scriptural Reasoning (as in the Princeton group, above) and official statements (such as those of the 2008 Synod and *Dominus Iesus*) encourage this to be taken further.[67]

2. Already, Scriptural Reasoning groups embrace Christians of many traditions.[68] The Council and its legacy repeatedly emphasize ecumenical relations alongside interreligious relations, and Scriptural Reasoning can be encouraged by this to develop its intra-Christian potential, not least in improving the quality of disagreements among Christians through meeting with those of other faiths.

3. Already, Scriptural Reasoning has on occasion moved beyond Abrahamic scriptures (as in China, above). The global horizon of Vatican II documents and their successors, not least the 2008 Synod's consideration of the scriptures of non-Abrahamic religions, encourages this to be taken further.

4. Already, Scriptural Reasoning has sought to learn from the reading practices of its members (such as *chevruta* study and *lectio divina*, above). The documents and practices of Vatican II, and the emphasis on the pervasive importance of the Bible, encourage more such learning from both Christian practices and others.

5. Already, there has been intensive hermeneutical and philosophical discussion by and among participants in Scriptural Reasoning.[69] Among Christian traditions Roman Catholic teaching since Vatican II has been especially insistent on the inseparability of hermeneutics and philosophy from the understanding of the Bible, but so far this Catholic discourse has not had much impact on the debates surrounding Scriptural Reasoning.

---

www.scripturalreasoning.org and www.scripturalreasoning.com and their links. Note that there are other websites bearing similar names which are not affiliated to the Scriptural Reasoning movement described in this article.

[67] That this is by no means only a Catholic concern is seen, for example, in Muers' use of Quaker tradition in Higton and Muers, *The Text in Play*. It is also a strong concern of many Jews (especially regarding Talmud) and Muslims (especially regarding Hadith and legal traditions).

[68] From my own knowledge, besides Roman Catholics: Anglican, Churches of Christ, Lutheran, Mennonite, Methodist/Wesleyan, Pentecostal, Quaker, Reformed and Russian Orthodox. The suggestion that Scriptural Reasoning has on the Christian side been predominantly Protestant does not ring true. In its early years, it had, if anything, a preponderance of Anglicans, many of whom were more on the Catholic side of Anglicanism.

[69] Cf. Peter Ochs on Descartes and Peirce, Nicholas Adams on Habermas, Kant and Hegel, Basit Koshul on Mohammed Iqbal and Weber, Robert Gibbs on Cohen, Rosenzweig and Levinas, Daniel Weiss on Cohen, Randi Rashkover on Rosenzweig.

6. Already, Scriptural Reasoning has, on occasion, been related to rich embodiments of meaning in more than one tradition in multiple genres, such as liturgy (Steven Kepnes), law (Robert Gibbs and Anver Emon), art (Ben Quash), music (Peter Ochs and Oded Zahavi) and poetry (Micheal O'Siadhail). The legacy of Vatican II encourages this to be taken even further, with its vision of scripture pervading whole cultures.[70]

7. Already, Scriptural Reasoning has moved beyond the academy into local synagogues, churches and mosques, schools, prisons, hospitals, leadership programmes, and into initiatives connected to peacebuilding, religious literacy, environmental issues, and more. What Benedict XVI called "the immense horizons of the Church's mission and the complexity of today's situation"[71] are a Christian stimulus to extend Scriptural Reasoning even further, in particular attending to those who are suffering, poor or otherwise disadvantaged, so that understanding and action in such matters can be collaborative across faiths, drawing on the deepest sources of motivation and vision in each tradition.

Yet it is not imaginable that such enhancements to Scriptural Reasoning might be smooth developments, simply carrying on along lines already laid down. Scriptural Reasoning does not have a Vatican-like official consensus[72]; it is a varied practice that embraces many arguments, debates and ongoing disagreements. It creates a space for relating across such differences in ways that allow participants to be true to their own traditions. This continually raises awkward, often irresolvable, questions, and, whilst there is no pressure for them to be resolved consensually, integrity requires that the questions be faced. Among those involved in Scriptural Reasoning there is at present intensive discussion about such questions, and about meta-issues such as which questions should be on the agenda and what are the appropriate settings for their discussion. I will offer my agenda of questions before concluding with a brief discussion of what I consider the most important issue of all. I do not wish by any means to imply that these questions must be resolved before reading together can proceed: Scriptural Reasoning is practice-led, and practitioners have tended (rightly) to resist suggestions that they should suspend practice in order to clarify theory.

Questions facing Scriptural Reasoning

Among the main questions facing Scriptural Reasoning if it is to take the legacy of Vatican II seriously are the following, correlated with the seven points above:

---

[70] Cf. the strong statement of Pope Benedict XVI in *"Verbum Domini"*, 109–116.

[71] *Ibid.*, 97.

[72] That, of course, is not monolithic, but the differences are nothing near as deep as among those in Scriptural Reasoning.

1. (a) How should commentaries and other documents from the various traditions be treated in interreligious reading together? Their presence implies that each participant brings their whole tradition to the table, and remains fully embedded within it; but some in Scriptural Reasoning argue that the reading group is more like a separate space, a laboratory, where one can bracket out aspects of one's allegiance in order to "experiment" or "play"[73] with a small set of "bare" texts.

   (b) Closely allied to that are questions of authority and innovation. What is the text on the table? Is it Sacred Scripture? Who, if anyone, "owns" the text? What about God in relation to the text and those reading it? Does it retain its authoritative status for members of its own faith community? Or does it take on a new "temporary" identity for them (which might permit "experiments")? If new interpretations are proposed, what status do they have?

2. What are the most serious intra-Christian disagreements about Scriptural Reasoning? Is there any way of handling them other than "Biblical Reasoning", i.e. Christians gathering in order to do the sort of study and argument required to improve the quality of their disagreements and perhaps find some agreements?

3. What is involved in moving beyond the Abrahamic? The Abrahamic scriptures are siblings, and Scriptural Reasoning has been developed so far with close attention to their particularity. How might a comparable attention to the classic writings of other traditions, such as Buddhism, Hinduism, Confucianism or Daoism, do justice to their particularity? How might, or ought, Scriptural Reasoning change when these new texts are studied together? What is to be learnt from Comparative Theology about this?

4. What other Christian, Jewish and Muslim practices around scripture might contribute to Scriptural Reasoning? Given the constitutive practice of *chevruta* study and successful experiments with *lectio divina*, might there be a distinctively Muslim contribution (perhaps to do with recitation)?

5. What about "reasoning"? Is there any shared paradigm of what "reasoning" is? Are some philosophies or hermeneutical theories incompatible with Scriptural Reasoning, and, if so, why?

6. Is the Vatican II vision of the Bible pervading whole cultures hegemonic, and bound to come into conflict with competing (usually Christian or Muslim) hegemonic visions? Can Scriptural Reasoning really contain disagreements on this scale, such as are indicated by *Dominus Iesus*?

7. Is it wise of Scriptural Reasoning as a movement to become more involved in practical projects, programmes and causes, rather than leaving it up to individual readers to decide which to support? If it does go this way,

---

[73] Interestingly, the book on Scriptural Reasoning that most uses the language of experiment and play, Higton and Muers, *The Text in Play*, does not make this connection with being temporarily "disembedded" from one's tradition.

how does it avoid fragmentation around particular causes and ways to support them?

In addition to these questions, there are also many questions and challenges that are shared by Scriptural Reasoning and the contemporary Catholic Church, especially those which come under the headings of *ressourcement, aggiornamento* and *conversazione*. I conclude with one that I consider fundamental.

Conclusion: The Challenge of Multiple Deepening

This article has drawn upon key events during the past two decades in order to explore the interplay between the legacy of Vatican II and Scriptural Reasoning. One result is a triple proposition: that Scriptural Reasoning needs and is ready for a richer relationship with post-Vatican II Catholicism; that post-Vatican II Catholicism might benefit from Scriptural Reasoning; and that this mutual engagement would be good for our world in the twenty-first century. Realizing this potential crucially depends on the quality of Scriptural Reasoning and of Catholic life and thought.

In conclusion I return to the theme of deepening that has already occurred at several points.[74] One of the distinctive features of Scriptural Reasoning is that, at its best, it enables participants to go deeper into their own texts, deeper into the texts of others and deeper into the common good of our world. These deepenings can be correlated with *ressourcement, conversazione* and *aggiornamento* respectively, and so can also be found in Vatican II and its legacy. What this might mean and how it might happen more fully is perhaps the core challenge for both Scriptural Reasoning and the Catholic Church today.

There is also a fourth deepening: the deepening of relationships among those who come together in the first three deepenings. What is true of inter-religious learning can also be true of these relationships. Just as awareness and learning can be intensified through the dynamic between oneself, the other and the wider society, so love, friendship and delight in each other can also intensify.[75]

There is even a fifth deepening. Through being stretched in mutual understanding and, whether with fellow Christians or with those of other faiths, facing apparently irresolvable differences, it is possible for the mutual understanding of disagreements to be deepened to the point where there is something like a miracle: there is still disagreement, but there is also friendship.

---

[74] For further reflection on this theme see Ford, *Christian Wisdom*, especially chapters 2, 3, 4 and 7, and *The Future of Christian Theology*, especially chapters 4, 5, 7, 9 and 10.

[75] See Ford, *Christian Wisdom*, chapters 8, 10 and Conclusion.

Modern Theology 29:4 October 2013
ISSN 0266-7177 (Print)
ISSN 1468-0025 (Online)

DOI: 10.1111/moth.12065

SCRIPTURAL REASONING AND THE DISCIPLINE OF CHRISTIAN DOCTRINE

MIKE HIGTON

Introduction

In the fourth Pope John Paul II Annual Lecture on Interreligious Understanding at the Angelicum in Rome in 2011, David Ford drew attention to the deep relationship possible between two dynamics of post-Vatican-II Catholic theology: the engagement with scripture called for in *Dei Verbum*, and the engagement with other faiths called for in *Nostra Aetate*. Deep calls to deep, according to Ford, and the journey deeper into the scriptural sources of one faith receives additional impetus when undertaken alongside journeys deeper into the scriptural sources of others.[1]

In this article, I will ask whether and how Christian doctrine, and Christian doctrinal theology, can fruitfully become part of this relationship. I will begin with a brief comparison between two recent inter-faith practices, Comparative Theology and Scriptural Reasoning.[2] The former, as developed by Francis X. Clooney, SJ, draws sustenance from the kinds of scriptural reading that have come to the fore in post-Vatican II Catholic theology, but is also able to delve into an eclectic range of non-scriptural texts in a variety of genres and registers—and approaches doctrinal questions by means of extended contemplative attention to the texts in which they are broached.

Mike Higton
Department of Theology and Religion, Durham University, 16 South Bailey, Durham, DH1 3EE, UK
Email: mike.higton@durham.ac.uk

[1] David Ford, "Jews, Christians and Muslims Meet around their Scriptures: An Inter-faith Practice for the 21st Century", available online at http://www.interfaith.cam.ac.uk/en/resources/papers/jpii-lecture; last accessed 29 August, 2012.

[2] Michael Barnes, "Reading Other Religious Texts: Intratextuality and the Logic of Scripture", *Journal of Ecumenical Studies*, 46:3 (2011), pp. 389–410.

In Comparative Theology, the primary site for wrestling with doctrinal questions is in the internal dialogue of the comparative theologian's own rumination, albeit fed by the experience of live inter-faith dialogue. By contrast, Scriptural Reasoning is a practice in which the primary form of engagement is in live conversation, albeit fed by the internal deliberation of the individuals involved. In Scriptural Reasoning it has proved much harder to make doctrinal questions a focus for discussion or in other ways to expose doctrinal commitments directly to the rigours of the encounter. Two questions therefore emerge from this comparison. Does Comparative Theology's success in addressing doctrinal questions depend upon the ability of the Christian comparative theologian to set the agenda, and to arrange his reading of the texts of other traditions around it? And, is there a way in which doctrinal questions can appropriately be addressed in Scriptural Reasoning, where both the agenda and the modes of conversation by which it is pursued are subject to constant negotiation between participants from multiple traditions?

The bulk of the article focuses on the second question. I look more closely at what is meant by "doctrine" and by "doctrinal theology", and propose that doctrinal theology itself be envisaged as a practice of devout scriptural reading. Renewed engagement with scripture since Vatican II has, after all, deeply shaped Catholic doctrinal or dogmatic theology—not simply in the sense that such theology now draws more intensively on the results of biblical exegesis and criticism, but in the sense that the practice of such theology is (for some, at least) becoming inseparable from the kind of ruminative, contemplative steeping in scripture found in *lectio divina*. Doctrinal claims belong in the context of such reading: they emerge from it and discipline its continuation, and they are properly understood by tracing that emergence and participating in that continuation.

I then argue that, if Christian doctrinal theology is understood in this way, what is needed for Christian doctrinal questions to be exposed to the rigours of Scriptural Reasoning dialogue is simply the presence in that dialogue of Christian doctrinal theologians steeped in the practices of scriptural reading that constitute their discipline and that no additional focus or mode of discussion is required, beyond the intense attention already central to Scriptural Reasoning: attention to the way the words run in particular scriptural texts.

I finish by noting that the existence of Christian doctrinal theologians steeped in the practices of scriptural reading that constitute their discipline cannot be taken for granted—and suggest that the experience of Scriptural Reasoning might indicate one practical way in which that steeping might be further pursued: in cells of argumentatively devout discussion of Christian scripture, analogous to Scriptural Reasoning groups, but made up of people committed to the discipline of Christian doctrinal reading. Such cells would meet to explore together (and disagree about) how the reading of scripture is properly disciplined by doctrine—what those doctrines mean as forms of such discipline, and where such disciplined reading leads. Such a practice might form Christian scriptural readers in whose habits of reading Christian doctrinal commitments would be made more fully present to the Scriptural Reasoning conversation: those commitments would, as it were, be closer to the surface of their reading practices. It might also provide a context in which the implications of readings explored in Scriptural Reasoning could be appropriately tested, making practical sense of the claim that, for Christian readers, Scriptural Reasoning is an inter-faith discipline within a Christian discipline of devout reading.

Scripture, Inter-faith Engagement—and Doctrine?

Dei Verbum concludes with the aspiration that "by reading and study of the sacred books . . . the treasure of revelation, entrusted to the church, [may] fill human hearts ever more and more", such that "we may hope that . . . [the church's] spiritual life will receive a new impulse from increased devotion to the word of God".[3] Ford notes that this deeper engagement with scripture has been visible in many ways in the subsequent life of the Catholic Church, and draws particular attention to its liturgy, and to the renewal and world-wide spread of *lectio divina*. In Luke Dysinger's words, *lectio divina* is

> a slow, contemplative praying of the Scriptures which enables the Bible, the Word of God, to become a means of union with God. . . . [It] enables us to discover . . . an increasing ability to offer more of ourselves and our relationships to the Father, and to accept the embrace that God is con-tinuously extending to us in the person of his Son Jesus Christ.[4]

It is, in other words, a means of plunging deeper, by means of Scripture, into the particularity of the Christian faith, or of taking that particularity more deeply to heart.

On the basis of his experience of Scriptural Reasoning,[5] Ford claims that such a scriptural journey deeper into Christian particularity, into Christian *difference*, does not need to be achieved at the expense of, or in opposition to,

---

[3] *DV*, 26.

[4] From Luke Dysinger's widely circulated description of *lectio divina*: "Accepting the Embrace of God: The Ancient Art of *Lectio Divina*" (1990), available online at http://www.valyermo.com/ld-art.html; last accessed 29 August 2012.

[5] There are plenty of descriptions of Scriptural Reasoning in the literature, and I will assume that the basic form of Scriptural Reasoning discussion of scripture is understood. See David F. Ford and C. C. Pecknold (eds), *The Promise of Scriptural Reasoning* (Oxford: Blackwell, 2006), especially the essays by Ford, Kepnes, Adams and Quash. See also Mike Higton and Rachel Muers, *The Text in Play: Experiments in Reading Scripture* (Eugene, OR: Cascade, 2012). For a more popular introduction, see the materials on http://www.scripturalreasoning.org. Note that there are other websites bearing similar names which are not affiliated to Scriptural Reasoning move-ment referred to in this article.

the deeper engagement with other faiths called for in *Nostra Aetate*. In fact, the opposite turns out to be true: the two "deepers" ("going deeper into the faith of others [and] deeper into one's own faith") can animate and impel one another. When members of one faith read its scriptures devoutly, ruminatively, and prayerfully in company with members of other faiths reading their own scriptures in similar ways, a sustainable conversation becomes possible in which the scriptures and reading practices of each faith are thrown into relief, questioned, tested, and explored. Such conversation is impelled rather than impeded by attention to the animating particularity of each faith.

In practice, however, one limit has been discovered in the conversations of Scriptural Reasoning. Bringing explicit doctrinal statements to the conversation tends to kill it—though not because they cause disagreement (there is plenty of disagreement in Scriptural Reasoning, and it is not normally regarded as a problem to be overcome). In my own experience in several Scriptural Reasoning groups, there have been occasions when two or more of the Christian participants have discussed some facet of a passage in explicitly doctrinal terms, and the other participants have inevitably become spectators, removed from the flow of the conversation (just as in, say, an explicitly legal discussion between two Jewish participants, Christians might tend to become spectators). Such moments work as asides, eddies of "in-house" speech curling off from the main flow of the conversation, but it has proven difficult in practice to find fruitful ways—ways that allow a continued intensive conversational interchange across faith boundaries—of bringing explicit doctrinal discourse into the heart of Scriptural Reasoning discussions. References to formal Christian doctrine have therefore been infrequent, irregular, and fragmentary in Scriptural Reasoning discussions of particular scriptures, and in most conversations *about* Scriptural Reasoning, even on the lips of Christians from doctrinally-shaped traditions.

The situation with Comparative Theology is rather different. In his recent apologia for the practice, Francis Clooney discusses its relation to doctrine or dogma. Comparative Theology "does not disrespect doctrinal expressions of truth" but

neither does it merely repeat doctrinal statements as if nothing is learned from comparative reflection. Rarely, if ever, will comparative theology produce new truths, but it can make possible fresh insights into familiar and revered truths, and new ways of receiving those truths.[6]

Elsewhere, he says that doctrinal claims "need to be tested and purified through interreligious, comparative, and dialogical practices", while

---

[6] Francis X. Clooney, SJ, *Comparative Theology: Deep Learning Across Religious Borders* (Malden, MA: Wiley-Blackwell, 2010), p. 112.

insisting that "[a] proper theology is always the work of believers who may be expected to adhere to the truth of their faith positions as expressed theologically".[7]

Comparative Theology's distinctive feature, over against some other practices of doctrinally-focused inter-faith dialogue, is that it does not abstract doctrinal claims from the differing practices of religious reading within which they are made. Its operating assumption is that doctrinal claims belong in the context of such reading, that their meaning is properly grasped only by a meditative tracing of the ways they emerge from and are handled by relevant religious texts. Comparative Theology's basic practice, then, is extended ruminative reading of texts from two or more religious traditions, placed alongside one another, in the light of the traditions of religious commentary in which the course of such ruminative reading within each tradition is displayed.

The range of texts explored by Comparative Theology is wide and eclectic —much wider than the scriptural canons that provide the bread and butter of Scriptural Reasoning discussion. Comparative Theology explores scriptural texts, commentaries, liturgies, philosophical treatises and more, its only restriction being its tendency to focus on texts that have been the subject of repeated ruminative reading within their own traditions. A particular Comparative Theology exploration

> ordinarily starts with the intuition of an intriguing resemblance that prompts us to place two realities—texts, images, practices, doctrines, persons—near one another, so that they may be seen over and again, side by side. In this necessarily arbitrary and intuitive practice we understand each differently because the other is near.[8]

Live dialogue—"[l]iving interaction among people of different faiths"— is an important accompaniment to this process,

> [b]ut even a seriously theological dialogue among learned believers is not enough. The comparative theologian must do more than listen to others explain their faith; she must be willing to study their traditions deeply alongside her own, taking both to heart.[9]

Clooney therefore says, in the introduction to one Comparative Theology exploration, that it

> is not filled with accounts of firsthand theological conversations, although I have engaged in more than a few over the years. Rather, it

---

[7] Francis X. Clooney, SJ, *Hindu God, Christian God: How Reason Helps Break Down the Boundaries between Religions* (New York: Oxford University Press, 2001), p. 11.
[8] Clooney, *Comparative Theology*, p. 11.
[9] *Ibid.*, p. 13.

reflects the interior dialogue, more common in theological circles, that occurs when theologians read and ponder what they read.[10]

It is this interiority that makes possible Comparative Theology's relatively greater ability to treat matters of doctrine, in comparison to Scriptural Reasoning. The individual theologian, who intuits an intriguing resemblance that might be worth pursuing, can set his own agenda; he can organise the ruminative reading that is the heartbeat of Comparative Theology's method around his perception of resemblance, and explore assiduously whatever texts allow him to probe it more deeply. It is this freedom to explore wherever the resemblance leads that makes possible the remarkable achievements of Comparative Theology—and, where the resemblances intuited are doctrinal, it is this freedom that makes possible its fresh insights into doctrinal claims.

This interiority is also, however, the reason why Comparative Theology's success in approaching doctrinal claims cannot easily be matched by Scriptural Reasoning: when the agenda, the texts studied, and the modes of discourse preferred are subject to constant negotiation between the members of multiple traditions who participate in Scriptural Reasoning, it has proved impossible to organise the conversation around a perceived doctrinal resemblance, to select texts that allow that doctrine to be kept in the foreground, and to bring the conversation back regularly to a doctrinal register. It would be impossible, for instance, to arrange a Scriptural Reasoning symposium on God around the questions that organise Clooney's *Hindu God, Christian God*: "Is there a God who is maker of the world? Can God's true identity be to some extent known? Can God become embodied? Is revelation the norm by which to judge religions?"[11] Certainly Scriptural Reasoning groups could choose to study scriptural texts that, to an eye informed by Christian doctrine, seem to treat these themes—but the wisdom of experienced practitioners of Scriptural Reasoning is that the attempt to frame the discussion of those texts in these terms, and the attempt to return to these questions (in however nuanced a way) as the touchstone of the study, kills the conversation.

---

[10] Clooney, *Hindu God*, p. 10. Comparative Theology therefore coheres most easily with forms of Christian doctrinal theology in which such an interior dialogue is the primary form taken by devout reading. Cf. Dysinger's claim that "the most authentic and traditional form of Christian *lectio divina* is the solitary or 'private' practice" even if there are also "many different forms of so-called 'group lectio' " which have their own usefulness as "means of introducing and encouraging the practice of *lectio divina*", but which "should not become a substitute for an encounter and communion with the Living God that can only take place in that privileged solitude where the biblical Word of God becomes transparent to the Very Word Himself—namely private *lectio divina*" (Dysinger, "Accepting the Embrace of God").

[11] Clooney, *Hindu God*, p. 12.

If we are to understand the potential relationship between Scriptural Reasoning and Christian doctrine, we will have to travel by another route—and the first step on that route is a closer examination of what we mean by "doctrine".

The Discipline of Christian Doctrine

When I speak of "Christian doctrine", I mean, first of all, to refer to doctrines as statements of Christian belief, that are corporately acknowledged, and that function as an authoritative code—a discipline—for Christian speech and practice, or to crystallise and express the disciplined form of such speech and practice. Paradigmatically, one might think of doctrinal statements in creeds, as the statements of councils whose abiding authority is acknowledged, or as liturgical declarations providing corporate summaries of faith.

Christian doctrine is discussed in the academic discipline (to use the word "discipline" in a second sense) of doctrinal theology or systematic theology. Doctrinal theology is not itself doctrine, though it might from time to time have contributed to the formation or formulation of doctrine. Much that is said in doctrinal theology will not itself be an authoritative statement of belief, corporately acknowledged, and much of it will not succeed in authoritatively disciplining Christian speech and practice, or expressing their existing disciplined form. Rather, doctrinal theology is that scholarly practice by which doctrine is examined, tested, and expounded, and its connections to Christian speech and practice explored.

Even if we stick to these definitions, however, Christian doctrine is no one thing. The forms and locations of authoritative statement, the forms and locations of corporate acknowledgement, and the processes by which the authoritative doctrinal disciplining of practice and speech takes place, have all differed from time to time and place to place. The history of Christian doctrine is a history not only of changing doctrinal claims, but of the changing nature of doctrine—and of changing construals, amongst doctrinal theologians, of that nature.

Any attempt by a doctrinal theologian in the present to construe the nature of doctrine—to provide an account of the kind of discourse that Christian doctrine is, its proper location and function—cannot simply be descriptive. Different construals will highlight different features and tendencies in the history of Christian doctrine and in its present operation, and organise the whole field around them. So, for instance, a Lindbeckian postliberal and a proponent of analytic theology might approach the Christological definition produced at the Council of Chalcedon rather differently, prior to any detailed engagement with its content. Each would take it to be a different kind of text, functioning in a different kind of way, and properly subject to differing kinds of analysis; each would be able to appeal to real features of the history of Chalcedon, and would need to downplay others. Each construal would enable and organise a different programme of doctrinal theological work, exploring, testing and expounding the Chalcedonian definition in different ways—and it is unlikely that there would be any knock-down argument available to dictate a choice between the two approaches.

What I offer in the remainder of this section is one such construal of the nature of doctrine. The construal that I favour is easiest to see against a foil—a contrast model that is perhaps no more than a straw man. One can imagine a construal of Christian doctrine in which it would be the authoritative summarising and organising of the data found in the sources from which doctrine is properly drawn (let us say scripture, tradition, reason, and experience, appropriately weighted and ordered). Christian doctrine would be the yield of these sources, and to hold fast to these doctrines would be a significant part of what it is to know God.[12]

Against that foil, Christian doctrine can be thought of as a discipline within the discipline of Christian living. Christian life can be thought of as itself a form of discipline, where that word is being used in a third sense to name a spiritual regimen by which holiness is pursued. Christian life can be thought of as a discipline by which deeper and fuller knowledge of God is received and pursued—and Christian doctrine can be construed as a disciplining of that discipline. To know God by means of Christian doctrine is not so much a matter of understanding and affirming those doctrines as it is a matter of accepting their discipline—a matter of moving in the direction that doctrine marks out. To say this is not to abandon the idea that doctrinal statements are true, of course. They have the capacity to guide into truth only if they respond to and get hold of the way things truly are; but their truthfulness is properly grasped by accepting their discipline; they are true insofar as they guide truly.

This basic construal of doctrine can be elaborated in more than one way. A fuller account of doctrine—a theology of doctrine, as we might call it—would need to consider Christian doctrine as a disciplining of scriptural reading, a disciplining of worship, and a disciplining of ethical action, and possibly more. Here, however, I am pursuing only the first of these aspects: Christian doctrine not as a summarising and organising of the yield of scriptural reading, but as a guiding and impelling of an ongoing practice of delving into scripture.

The basic practice here is, in the broadest sense, *lectio divina*; it is what Paul Griffiths has called "religious reading".[13] To read religiously is to read "as a lover reads, with a tensile attentiveness that wishes to linger, to prolong,

---

[12] This is similar to the "cognitive–propositionalist" account of doctrine described (and rejected) by George Lindbeck in *The Nature of Doctrine: Religion and Theology in a Postliberal Age* (Philadelphia, PA: Westminster, 1984)—though my purpose is somewhat different from his.

[13] Paul J. Griffiths, *Religious Reading: The Place of Reading in the Practice of Religion* (New York: Oxford University Press, 1999); see also the discussion in Clooney, *Comparative Theology*, pp. 58–59, and in Michael Barnes, "Reading Other Religious Texts".

to savor, and has no interest at all in the quick orgasm of consumption".[14] It is reading in which

> the work read is understood as a stable and vastly rich resource, one that yields meaning, suggestions (or imperatives) for action, matter for aesthetic wonder, and much else. It is a treasure-house, an ocean, a mine: the deeper religious readers dig, the more ardently they fish, the more single-mindedly they seek gold, the greater will be their reward. The basic metaphors here are those of discovery, uncovering, retrieval, opening up: religious readers read what is there to be read, and what is there to be read always precedes, exceeds, and in the end supersedes its readers. There can, according to those metaphors, be no final act of reading in which everything is uncovered, in which the mine of gold has yielded all its treasure or the fish pool has been emptied of fish. Reading, for religious readers, ends only with death, and perhaps not then: it is a continuous, ever-repeated act.[15]

Such reading is a curriculum, a form of pedagogy—and it is a form of pedagogy that is comprehensive, unsurpassable, and central: for the religious reader, *everything* falls within the compass of this pedagogy, there is no moving on from it to some higher or deeper curriculum, and it is held to give the reader's life its most basic orientation.[16]

Such reading requires an extravagant and open-ended commitment from the reader. There is no ground on which a reader may stand to survey multiple candidates for such commitment before choosing the most fruitful; the very criteria by which fruitfulness can be identified will be shaped by this reading. Nor is it an experiment that the religious reader designs for him- or herself; he or she submits to a discipline—to what Griffiths calls

> the presence of some acknowledged constraints upon what and how religious readers should read and compose, as well as (by entailment) upon the kinds of conclusions that can properly be drawn and taught from this reading and composition.[17]

Doctrine is, under the aspect that I am considering, precisely such a set of acknowledged constraints upon the reading of scripture—a set of rules for reading that have emerged from the practice of such reading and that shape its continuation. Christological doctrine, for example, will be understood as

---

[14] Griffiths, *Religious Reading*, p. ix.
[15] *Ibid.*, p. 41.
[16] *Ibid.*, pp. 7–13, 67.
[17] *Ibid.*, p. 63.

just such a set of rules for reading—a set of constraints guiding Christian readers into a more penetrating reading of the gospels, for the sake of their conformity to Christ. Christological doctrines teach Christians, for instance, to read the gospels in such a way as to acknowledge who the acting subject is when they read of the actions and passions of the man Jesus of Nazareth. One has not understood Chalcedonian doctrine well when one has learnt to manipulate the conceptual machinery of natures and persons that it sets into motion; one has understood Chalcedonian doctrine well when one has begun learning how it teaches one to read pronouns and active verbs in the gospels, how to read statements of Christ's weakness alongside statements of his power, how to read claims about our sharing in Christ's death and resurrection—and one is Chalcedonian when those practices of reading have become habitual shapes in one's continuous, ever-repeated practices of devout reading.

These practices of reading are not primarily solutions to problems in the text, as if their adoption allows a relaxation in attention to the difficult ways that the words run; they are disciplines by which one's nose is held against the grindstone of the text, bindings by which one is disabled from holding the text at arm's length.

Living within doctrinal discipline is considerably more widespread than is technical understanding of doctrine (indeed, there might be a smaller overlap between the two than we doctrinal theologians would care to admit). Someone may have a technical understanding of doctrine, and enjoy firm intellectual assent to it, who does not live by its discipline; equally, someone may be formed into habits of reading that lie within this discipline without being schooled in technical understanding of the doctrine, or without being able to connect their habits to the words they speak in the creed each Sunday. The latter, not the former, is the one who understands the truth that doctrine teaches. A Christian who knows how to read the gospels well, when measured by the standards of doctrinal discipline, lacks nothing of the knowledge of God that could be supplied by a deeper understanding of those standards—though the fact that some in a community have a deeper understanding of those standards may well prove to be a contribution to keeping the discipline alive.

Christian doctrine disciplines holy reading for the sake of that holy living which is knowledge of God. The reading that it promotes is, however, as fundamentally corporate as the living. One learns to read more richly—to fish more ardently, seek gold more assiduously, mine more deeply—by reading in the company of others. One learns to read, for instance, by the light of those whose lives have become commentaries, and who by inhabiting and embodying the Christian discipline of reading teach what it means to read well.

One also learns to read in the company of those who read *differently*, who unsettle and question the readings one has settled with, whose ways of reading differently lead one in new directions within the inexhaustibility of scripture—they send one back again to the text, to look more deeply. But one's doctrinal discipline shapes (or should shape) one's reception of another's reading; it holds one accountable to the wider community of reading, and to the tradition of religious reading that one is called to inhabit—a pattern of testing and discernment provided to ensure that Christian readers are not led back from deep water into the shallows.

If Christian doctrine is construed in this way, the question of its relation to Scriptural Reasoning can be transformed. Instead of asking whether it is possible, without inhibiting the flow of Scriptural Reasoning practice, to bring Christian doctrine into it, one can ask whether it is possible for the practice of Scriptural Reasoning to become, for its Christian participants, part of their discipline of Christian doctrinal reading. If Christian doctrinal discourse functions to discipline ongoing scriptural reading (not simply to codify and express its results), then to bring those disciplined forms of scriptural reading into Scriptural Reasoning discussion *is* to bring doctrine into those conversations. That is not to say that one thereby brings the discourse of doctrinal theology—the explicit discussion of doctrinal claims—into the discussion, so that those claims are directly examined and questioned by the other participants. But it does mean that one can participate in Scriptural Reasoning quite directly *as* someone under doctrinal discipline. The real substance of Christian doctrinal deliberation can therefore be present in those dialogues, and can be exposed to the questioning and challenge that those dialogues bring.

Does it make sense, however, to regard the practice of Scriptural Reasoning as, for its Christian participants, part of their discipline of Christian doctrinal reading—a discipline within their primary discipline? At first blush, this must sound like an imperialist gesture on the part of Christian participants: an attempt to define the whole practice in terms that are obviously exclusive to them. In order to understand why this is not so—or at least why it does not *need* to be so—we have to understand more clearly what role is played in Scriptural Reasoning by attempts to make sense of it, to *theorise* it, essayed from within each of the participating traditions.

Scriptural Reasoning as a Christian Discipline?

It has often been said that Scriptural Reasoning is a practice before it is a theory, and that whilst it is a stable and sustainable practice, its theorisation is piecemeal and secondary.[18] Obviously, this does not mean that practitioners don't have all sorts of thoughts about what they are doing, why they are

---

[18] Ford's essay in *The Promise of Scriptural Reasoning* is, for instance, "offered as only one portrayal of something that has already evoked many other descriptions and is constantly producing more" ("An Interfaith Wisdom: Scriptural Reasoning between Jews, Christians and Muslims" in Ford and Pecknold (eds), *The Promise of Scriptural Reasoning*, p. 2).

doing it, and what are its limits; nor does it mean that they don't share and discuss those thoughts. Equally, it does not mean that the practice is not organised in part by means of more or less detailed instructions and descriptions, nor that in some circumstances those might include quite detailed explanations and justifications. A theory of Scriptural Reasoning, in the sense intended here, would be some well-articulated account of the nature, purpose and limits of this practice, offered to and broadly accepted by the majority of the community of practitioners, and used by them to regulate and explain the practice, such that the practice and some version of this account would thenceforth tend to come packaged together. Furthermore, to count as a theory, the account will need to go beyond practical guidelines for organising the practice and descriptions of its typical progress, and will offer reasons for the shape of the practice that are not themselves couched in terms of the practice. So, if someone says, "We find that keeping the focus of the discussion firmly on the text in front of you helps the conversation flow", that is not in this sense theoretical. If, however, someone says, "A focus on the texts keeps the conversation flowing because scriptural texts are inexhaustible", that *is* theoretical—though unless it becomes part of a more comprehensive and well-articulated account of the practice, and is broadly accepted by the community of practitioners, so as to tend to come packaged with the practice, it still will not count as a theory of Scriptural Reasoning in the required sense.

The absence of this kind of theory of Scriptural Reasoning can, in part, be traced to the process of Scriptural Reasoning's emergence. It emerged through happenstance and friendship,[19] and only then did the practice that had emerged prompt a restless and ongoing task of theoretical reflection; theorisation was from the start playing catch up, trying to make sense of a practice whose evolution and spread outstripped it.

The absence of a full theory of Scriptural Reasoning is not, however, simply a matter of delay, as if there were a widespread acceptance amongst practitioners that some of them were working towards such a theory, but that the theoretical work had not yet caught up with the practice. Nor is it a matter of a simple refusal to theorise, as if Scriptural Reasoning practitioners were reticent before a mystery—though there has certainly been discussion in the past amongst Scriptural Reasoning practitioners about the difficulty of capturing Scriptural Reasoning conversations in theoretical terms without flattening them into unrecognisable dullness.

Far more fundamentally, the lack of a theory is due to the fact that Scriptural Reasoning is an inter-faith practice in which participants are welcomed to take part *as* faithful and committed members of their own

---

[19] See the works cited in note 5, amongst others. In this, too, Scriptural Reasoning resembles Comparative Theology: Clooney says that he does not "theorize inclusion" but prefers "the act of including" (*Comparative Theology*, p. 16).

religious traditions; it does not require those participants to speak in a different voice for the sake of this practice. Indeed, one practical discipline that has shaped the practice has been an insistence upon subjecting any purportedly religiously neutral account of Scriptural Reasoning to the scrutiny of practitioners from the three participating traditions, and to encourage each of them to question that account from the standpoint of their own tradition. In such a context, the hope for a single theoretical account offered to and broadly accepted by the majority of the community of practitioners, and used by them to regulate and explain the practice, looks like a chimera, unless one has confidence in the existence of a generic Abrahamic voice (and little in the practice of Scriptural Reasoning encourages such confidence).

Simply put, then, Scriptural Reasoning is a practice that calls forth not one account of itself, but three: Jewish, Christian, and Muslim (or, rather, *at least* three, since disagreements within traditions have often been as prominent as disagreements between them). The theorising of Scriptural Reasoning has therefore tended to be a conversation between multiple theorisations— multiple forms of account-giving, accountable to different traditions, interrupting and questioning one another, without any stable consensus emerging.[20] The practice of Scriptural Reasoning does not wait for the resolution of this conversation, nor do most practitioners seem to be expecting such resolution.[21]

An account of Scriptural Reasoning in relation to the discipline of Christian doctrine is a move in this multiplayer game of account-giving. It is resolutely *not* a generic account of Scriptural Reasoning, equally usable by Jewish and Islamic participants, or the increasing numbers of participants from other traditions. It will not even be an account that is generically acceptable to all Christian participants; it will be an account that makes sense of Scriptural Reasoning in relation to one of the primary discourses of a certain kind of Christianity. It is, however, *only* from such irreducibly one-sided accounts that the ongoing theorisation of Scriptural Reasoning is woven.

To say that, from the point of view of a certain kind of doctrinal Christianity, Scriptural Reasoning can be seen as a discipline within the discipline of Christian doctrine is not to exclude the possibility that very different Jewish, Islamic and other accounts might be given. It is, rather, to *invite* such alternative accounts—and the existence and sustainability of the practice does not rest upon our ability to settle the differences between

---

[20] More neutral accounts have been offered from time to time, but they have tended to become sparser, more plainly descriptive or heuristic as time has gone by, and none of them has become by consensus a handbook for Scriptural Reasoning.

[21] Compare, once again, Clooney in *Comparative Theology*. It is clear that Comparative Theology is, for him, a Christian discipline, but one with "close analogues in other traditions" (p. 80). On the other hand, he does also insist that "there is nothing essentially Christian about comparative theology as I describe it" (p. 11).

them.[22] The practice of Scriptural Reasoning is not defined by a single account, but negotiated between accounts.

The forms of reading practised in Scriptural Reasoning are not invented and sustained purely for the purpose of this conversation; nor are they simply forms of "reading in general", independent of any specific religious tradition. They are formed in the overlap and interaction between the practices of religious reading (and the accounts of those practices) brought to the process by the participants. Of course, as a sustained practice, Scriptural Reasoning inevitably forms its participants in certain recognisable habits that are specific to Scriptural Reasoning, but those habits are formed in the context of a mutual hospitality. I, as a Christian reader of Christian scripture, ask how I can invite others to share in my practice of reading, just as I am invited to share in theirs. I do not ask them to share my beliefs about the nature and authority of my scriptures, nor about the ground or purpose of reading, just as I am not asked to share theirs. We do, however, ask each other to share in the forms of attentiveness and exploration that are appropriate when we are faced by passages of our own scriptures and asked to focus on them as deeply as we are able.

I participate in Scriptural Reasoning as a Christian reader, just as the others around the table participate as Jewish or as Islamic or other kinds of religious readers: we bring into the discussion our own religious ways of construing the texts in front of us, and look for those construals to become part of a conversation in which multiple construals are offered, and each is tested against the words of the text.

In this process, I am not asked to treat the other readers as if they were Christian readers, subject to Christian doctrinal discipline. Doctrinally-tested *reception* of suggested readings is nevertheless mandatory for me—and if a new reading of one of my scriptural texts emerges in a Scriptural Reasoning session, there remains a task of establishing whether and how far I as a Christian reader can pursue that reading beyond the session (I read, after all, as someone accountable to a community and a tradition of reading, and doctrine is the form of that accountability). That does not mean, however, that I can only hear suggestions about this text from those who themselves acknowledge the same doctrinal discipline. My doctrinal discipline is supposed—as I have said—to drive me to the text, keep my nose to its difficulties and questions; it is not meant to allow me to dispense with attention to the text, nor sanitise the text for my consumption. It is an axiom of my doctrinal discipline that there is nothing to fear from looking again at the text—and to read with others who are differently disciplined, if our focus is on the

---

[22] It may be that such alternative accounts will also take the form of identifying Scriptural Reasoning as a particular discipline within a more basic Islamic or Jewish or other discipline, or it may be that this discipline-focused framing does not travel well across religious borders; that will be for other participants to determine.

scriptural texts in front of us and on the way their words run, is a natural accompaniment to that discipline.

Indeed, such reading with others can function as a proper accompaniment to my discipline precisely *because* those others differ from me. It is when another member of the group sees something in the text that I have not seen that their reading becomes a challenge to me to look again, to look more closely. It is the areas of unexamined agreement between us that make the words of the text difficult to see.[23] Someone who differs from me in their reading of this text, and who is willing to argue that difference on the basis of its words, becomes for me an agent of the way the words run—not because I am compelled to agree with them, but because I am compelled to look to see if I can see what they see, and to understand why it is that I differ.

Of course, participation in Scriptural Reasoning means that I devote time to reading the scriptures of others with them, just as they read mine with me. The Qur'an, for example, is not a text that I can read religiously, in the full sense, even if for the sake of this practice I try to read it seriously and attentively. It is not authoritative for me, and does not become authoritative in the course of this practice. Yet, reading this text shapes the way that I read my own scriptures; I see my scriptures differently when I see them alongside the Qur'an. This is, however, something more, and somewhat different, from simply reading the Qur'an for myself in a comparative frame of mind. I read with others who read this text religiously—who are serious about reading it more and more deeply, whose reading of this text shapes their lives, who seek to be exposed to the challenge of this text as they read, and who read to learn how their world is judged and blessed in the text. They are serious about the devotion that this kind of reading takes, the intensity, the time-taking discipline (even if our disciplines differ drastically); they are serious that this is a form of reading that requires prayer (even if our prayers differ, and we will not in most circumstances pray together). It is precisely because I read the Qur'an in company with others who read it as religiously as I hope to read the Bible that I am made to see echoes and contrasts, analogies and distinctions, challenges and attractions between their text in their hands and mine in mine. In other words, from the point of view of my doctrinal discipline, it is not simply the general difference of these others with whom I read that matters, but their specifically *religious* difference. Far from requiring me to assimilate the other participants to my own religious identity, offering an account of Scriptural Reasoning from the perspective of Christian doctrinal discipline requires that I attend to their unassimilability as religious others.

---

[23] Clooney, in *Comparative Theology*, pp. 76–77, explains his own decision to privilege similarities.

Coda: Deepening the Discipline of Christian Doctrine

Scriptural Reasoning, then, can make sense as a discipline within my discipline—a discipline of inter-faith engagement within my Christian discipline of doctrinally-governed scriptural reading; it drives me deeper into that Christian doctrinal discipline precisely by means of an engagement with those who live within different religious disciplines.[24]

This claim, however, only makes full sense if the "Christian discipline of doctrinally-governed scriptural reading" is flourishing, and if it provides the real practical context within which my participation in Scriptural Reasoning sits. I have spoken confidently above of a doctrinal theology that does not simply draw upon the results of biblical exegesis and criticism but is becoming inseparable from the kind of ruminative, contemplative steeping in scripture found in *lectio divina*; I have spoken of doctrines as claims that emerge from such reading and discipline its continuation. Such an approach to doctrinal theology is, however, a work in progress rather than an accomplished fact of the present theological scene.

The most urgent question that arises from a consideration of the relationship between Christian doctrine and Scriptural Reasoning is not, therefore, about the propriety of supplementing doctrinal reading with a practice of inter-faith reading; it is about the depth and resilience of the practice of doctrinally-disciplined reading itself. Am I, as a Christian doctrinal theologian who would expose my doctrinal understanding to the testing and purification made possible in this inter-faith encounter, deeply enough formed in practices of devout scriptural reading and in fine-grained attentiveness to the connection between doctrinal claims and those practices of reading? If I am not, then my doctrinal understanding will be inappropriately insulated from the challenges of reading with others; it will not be questioned and tested and cast into new light by their insistent differences, and neither will my religious difference from them be as fully present in the dialogue as it could and should be.

In order, then, to make sense of the practice of Scriptural Reasoning as a discipline within my Christian discipline of doctrinally-governed scriptural reading, I would need to attend to the practices within which doctrinally-governed scriptural reading is nurtured—and understand more fully what it means to take doctrine as a set of rules that have emerged from such practices and that shape their continuation. I might attend to the renewal in recent decades of *lectio divina* itself, or to the practice of exegetical preaching, or to catechesis, or to certain kinds of ecumenism, or to the Faith and Order deliberations of my denomination, or to many other contexts. Each of these practices can be a context within which doctrine makes sense, and within

---

[24] This is, of course, the sense it makes to me as a Christian participant; it may make very different sense from the perspective of other participants.

which the discipline of doctrine is learnt—and Scriptural Reasoning will make sense as a discipline within the discipline of doctrinally-governed reading just to the extent that it can take its place alongside these other practices, as one more context within which such reading is wrestled with, tested and explored.

Approaching such an account of doctrine from the direction of Scriptural Reasoning, however, raises one intriguing possibility. Of course, the existence of Scriptural Reasoning is not by any means the primary reason for providing the kind of account of Christian doctrine that I have sketched. Nor is this way of thinking about doctrine exhaustive: I said earlier that a fuller account of doctrine would need to consider Christian doctrine not only as a disciplining of reading, but also as a disciplining of worship and of ethical action, and possibly more. The existence of Scriptural Reasoning, and the desire to find a way in which it can impinge upon Christian doctrine, is but one additional and contingent impetus to the development of such an account. The existence of Scriptural Reasoning, and the possibility of its connection to doctrinal reading of scripture, does nevertheless suggest one additional way in which the deepening of doctrinal reading might proceed.

Unlike Comparative Theology, Scriptural Reasoning is insistently and irreducibly social. The journey deeper—into one's own faith, and into understanding of the faith of others—is driven by continually renewed encounter with the living and unpredictable otherness of multiple interlocutors: by all the things they say, and all the ways they read, that one could not have arrived at for oneself. This suggests that Scriptural Reasoning might cohere with a form of Christian doctrinal reading that was itself more insistently and ineradicably social than any account of "interior dialogue" as the primary form of doctrinal theology can allow.

Approaching the nature of Christian doctrine from the direction of Scriptural Reasoning therefore raises a question. Is it possible to envisage a form of Christian doctrinal theology one of whose fundamental practices would be group reading of scripture: small groups of differing Christians meeting for prayerful and argumentative reading of scripture together, exploring (and disagreeing about) how such reading is properly disciplined by doctrine— about what those doctrines mean as forms of such discipline, and about where such disciplined reading leads? Is it possible to imagine a form of Christian doctrinal theology which would involve extended engagement in something that looked a little like intensive *intra*-faith Scriptural Reasoning?

If some such form of corporate, doctrinally-disciplined reading were to be sustained, and if it were to have enough density as a practice to become habitual, it could become another source of a deep doctrinal patterning in its participants' reading of their scriptures, in this case a patterning established and explored by means of lively argumentative conversation over scripture— and so it could shape very directly the ways in which its participants went on to read in the similarly lively dialogues of Scriptural Reasoning, as well as providing a context in which readings proposed in Scriptural Reasoning could be appropriately tested, and their doctrinal implications explored. Such a development would, I think, provide (more directly and intensively than has been possible hitherto) a bridge between the other Christian practices within which the discipline of Christian doctrine lives and the lively sociality of Scriptural Reasoning conversations—and it would give new practical form to my claim that, for Christian readers, Scriptural Reasoning is an inter-faith discipline within their Christian discipline of devout doctrinal reading.

Modern Theology 29:4 October 2013
ISSN 0266-7177 (Print)
ISSN 1468-0025 (Online)

DOI: 10.1111/moth.12066

INTERRELIGIOUS READING IN THE CONTEXT OF DIALOGUE: WHEN INTERRELIGIOUS READING "FAILS"

TRACY SAYUKI TIEMEIER

Introduction

Although nineteenth-century intellectuals, such as the American Transcendentalists, were fascinated with Asian thought, it would be the World's Parliament of Religions in 1893 that would initiate the modern American dialogue movement. Legal restrictions on immigration and widespread religious, ethnic, and racial discrimination through the mid-twentieth century prevented positive interreligious contact and dialogue on a large scale. This changed with the rise of civil rights and other American social movements interested in justice and with the passing of the landmark Immigration and Nationality Act of 1965 which loosened prejudicial immigration restrictions in the United States and opened the doors to a flood of Asian immigrants and their religions. Despite continuing prejudice in America, the visibility of religions other than Christianity grew as the numbers of non-Christians grew, and as their leaders and followers gained in popularity. This popularization of religions other than Christianity and their practices led to wider interest in interreligious dialogue.

Religious communities became more interested in formal dialogues in order to foster positive inter-faith relations and collaborate on social issues of mutual concern. For minoritized religious communities, dialogue was a matter of survival in America. For dominant communities, dialogue was seen as an important part of growing religious interest in the emerging social movements and work for justice. This collaboration on formal, institutional

Tracy Sayuki Tiemeier
Department of Theological Studies, Loyola Marymount University, 1 LMU Drive, Los Angeles, CA 90045-2659, USA
Email: tracy.tiemeier@lmu.edu

dialogues coincided with the promulgation of *Nostra Aetate* (in 1965) at the Second Vatican Council. It was a watershed moment for Catholic ecumenical and interreligious relations. While the call to engage with other religious traditions and persons worked its way slowly into wider American life, it was embraced particularly in big cities like Los Angeles that had long histories of interreligious encounter. Official Catholic participation in Los Angeles interreligious dialogue efforts began in earnest after Vatican II with Archdiocesan participation in the formation of the Interreligious Council of Southern California in 1969.[1] While the Archdiocese of Los Angeles participated in the Council, it would not be until significantly later that it would initiate its own formal bilateral dialogues.

This article examines the history and practice of the Los Angeles Hindu-Catholic Dialogue (a dialogue group that I currently co-chair). A common feature of the monthly dialogue meetings is the reading of texts from both traditions on a chosen topic. While the group has had many "successes" in interreligious reading over the Dialogue's twenty-five year existence, it has also had many "failures". My focus here is on some of those examples of interreligious reading that simply failed to be productive for our dialogue. I also interrogate Comparative Theology's own practice of interreligious reading in light of dialogical interreligious reading. Ultimately, I argue that examples of "failed" interreligious reading done in the context of this dialogue help to highlight important elements of comparative reading that comparative theologians ought to consider more thoroughly in their work.

Creating a Bilateral Dialogue: Participation, Parity, and Friendship

The Reverend Monsignor Royale M. Vadakin, of the Archdiocese of Los Angeles Commission on Ecumenical and Interreligious Affairs, conceived of the Los Angeles Hindu-Catholic Dialogue in 1989. Monsignor Vadakin asked a Hindu friend, Brother David ("Jnana") Stump of the Vedanta Society of Southern California, to help him with the dialogue. In his letter to Stump, Vadakin says, "I would like to explore something with you. Due to a long and nourished friendship, I would like to begin this exploration by an informal private meeting with you".[2] After the meeting, Monsignor Vadakin wrote to Swami Swahananda (Vedanta Society of Southern California), saying:

> As you know I met with Bro. David Stump today. The purpose of that brief and informal meeting was to raise the possibility of a Catholic/ Hindu bilateral dialogue here in Los Angeles. The Archdiocese has a

---

[1] See the website of The Interreligious Council of Southern California: http://irc-socal.org/ faith; last accessed 12 October 2012.

[2] Royale M. Vadakin to David Stump, 18 December 1989, Los Angeles Hindu-Catholic Dialogue Archive, Tracy Tiemeier's personal collection, Loyola Marymount University, Los Angeles.

distinct bilateral dialogue with the other three religions mentioned in Nostra Aetate (Judaism, Islamic [*sic*], Buddhism).

With this correspondence may I formally and officially propose the establishment in early 1990 of the Catholic/Hindu bilateral dialogue . . .

May I add that Nostra Aetate—and Roman Catholic interreligious dialogue here in Los Angeles—seems incomplete without the richness, moral vigor and antiquity which Hinduism brings to the world. For me personally, it would be a great sense of completeness to begin and develop such a dialogue.[3]

Creating an "equal" field of dialogue when history and a hulking hierarchical institution loom was more than a challenge. Hindu participants in the Dialogue have remarked over the years that, then and now, they were warned not to participate in a Catholic-Hindu dialogue because Catholics have a covert agenda of conversion. Indeed, the history of colonialism and conversion in India, and associations of Catholics with other Christians practising aggressive proselytization tactics in India (and elsewhere) create an unbalanced dynamic for any Hindu-Catholic dialogue, and even more so for an official dialogue sponsored by the Roman Catholic Church. Vadakin sought to mitigate these problems by firmly grounding the dialogue in friendship and including equal numbers of Hindus and Christians.

Vadakin explicitly tied the Dialogue to Vatican II and the twenty-fifth anniversary of the promulgation of *Nostra Aetate*. The purpose of the Hindu-Catholic Dialogue was explained in the press release announcement (28 March 1990):

The Los Angeles Catholic Archdiocese and representatives of Los Angeles' Hindu community have established an "ongoing and official dialogue"—a significant Southern California development in relationships between the Catholic Church and the world's four great non-Christian religions in Southern California.

Announcement of the 16-member Roman Catholic/Hindu Dialogue was made jointly by the Archdiocese's Office of Ecumenical and Interreligious Affairs, the Hindu Temple Society of Southern California, and the Vedanta Society of Southern California.

Serving as co-chairs of the Dialogue are Swami Swahananda of the Vedanta Society, Dr. S. K. Durairaj of the Hindu Temple Society, and Msgr. Royale Vadakin, archdiocesan director of Ecumenical and Interreligious Affairs.

---

[3] Royale M. Vadakin to Swami Swahananda, 29 December 1989, Los Angeles Hindu-Catholic Dialogue Archive, Tracy Tiemeier's personal collection, Loyola Marymount University, Los Angeles.

Already existing are separate dialogue groups with the Jewish, Muslim and Buddhist communities.

"The beginning of a Catholic/Hindu bilateral is a significant development in local dialogue with four great religions of the world, so richly present here in Los Angeles", Msgr. Vadakin stated.

"Inauguration of the Roman Catholic/Hindu dialogue this year is particularly appropriate, as 1990 is the 25th anniversary year of the Vatican II decree on Non-Christian Religions (Nostra Aetate)", he added.

The Dialogue will consist of eight Catholic participants and eight Hindu participants, with its purposes being the following:

— Establish a formal and ongoing dialogue.
— Encourage and promote contacts between Los Angeles' Hindu and Catholic communities.
— Become more aware of the historical developments of both religious communities.
— Identify areas where there are mutual concerns.
— Develop language and conceptual frameworks for the joint exploration of religious topics and themes.

The Vedanta Society and the Archdiocese's Office of Ecumenical and Interreligious Affairs have worked together since the early 1970s on a number of ad hoc events and through the Interreligious Council of Southern California.

Two of these events included the 1986 Assisi Peace Day Observance and the visit of Pope John Paul II to Los Angeles in 1987.

Now with the inclusion of the Hindu Temple Society, the dialogue has a wider and more inclusive religious and cultural dimension.

Swami Swahananda, reflecting on the Vedanta Society's "friendly relationship with the local Roman Catholic community for a number of years", added that "it is only appropriate that we meet together and examine some of the areas in which there might not be a complete understanding".

He expressed appreciation to Msgr. Vadakin and Archbishop Roger Mahony for the initiative "they have taken to establish this dialogue" and stated it is "another welcome development in the remarkable outreach that has occurred since the Vatican II Council".

Dr. Durairaj said the Hindu Temple Society "welcomes the idea of having an ongoing dialogue" among the various religious communities and "will extend its full assistance and cooperation in the true tradition of Hinduism, ('Sanatana Dharma'—Universal Religion, in the Sanskrit language)."

"We are sure that such a dialogue will go a long way to remove the many misconceptions in the proper understanding of the different religions and their practices", he added.

Msgr. Vadakin explained that he had no idea—when the Interreligious Council of Southern California was started in 1969—that the dialogue would grow and widen to what it has become in 1990.

"Twenty-one years later, I can only marvel and give thanks for the marvelous religious understanding and cooperation which our communities enjoy. It is a gifted moment of religious cooperation", he said.

"However, that window of opportunity has to be valued and struggled with", he cautioned. "What has so marvelously opened can so quickly close, without effort, vision, and vigilance."

"I see this beginning of the Roman Catholic/Hindu dialogue—which now enjoins the four great world religions mentioned in 'Nostra Aetate' bilaterally with the Catholic community—as marking a capstone moment in my own personal 21 years of ecumenical-interreligious ministry here in Los Angeles", Msgr. Vadakin concluded.[4]

The Dialogue was mindful of the diversity within Hinduism and had three co-chairs, one Catholic, one Hindu from the Vedanta Society of Southern California, and one Hindu from the Hindu Temple Society of Southern California.

Surviving Dominus Iesus

Over the course of the Dialogue, structures and dynamics shifted with different participants and different Archdiocesan directors. In a 1994 letter to his fellow dialogue partners that announced a move from the Commission on Ecumenical and Interreligious Affairs back into parish life, then Director Reverend Vivian Ben Lima noted that he left his office "having made so many friends and colleagues who have stretched and shaped my life and my ministry" and "armed with the conviction that dialogue is the only way to understanding and peace". He also announced a shift in the structuring of the Dialogue groups. The Archdiocesan Director would act as a kind of coordinator, but the Catholic co-chairs of the individual Dialogue groups would come from the engaged participants within the groups themselves. This assures "the enthusiastic continuation of each group" and enables "a wider participation in leadership from the Catholic community at large".[5]

In a 1998 letter to Reverend Gilbert Romero, the new Director of the Los Angeles Archdiocesan Office of Ecumenical and Interreligious Affairs, Brother Stump says:

---

[4] Press Release by Archdiocese of Los Angeles, 28 March 1990, Los Angeles Hindu-Catholic Dialogue Archive, Tracy Tiemeier's personal collection, Loyola Marymount University, Los Angeles.
[5] Vivian Ben Lima to Colleagues in Dialogue, 6 June 1994, Los Angeles Hindu-Catholic Dialogue Archive, Tracy Tiemeier's personal collection, Loyola Marymount University, Los Angeles.

Since its inception in February of 1990, the Hindu/Roman Catholic dialogue's three directors have brought their unique skills and different approaches to organizing the agenda and special projects. No doubt, your office records and the previous directors have been very helpful to you.

Under Msgr. Vadakin, there was a greater involvement of Catholic clergy and there was an examination of particular subjects, documents, articles, etc. I believe Msgr. Vadakin envisioned some kind of joint publication resulting as a fruit of the dialogue, but it never came to be. Beginning in the Fall of 1991, Rev. Ben Lima took over and developed some themes, started a plan of discussions designed (yet unfulfilled) to lead to a publication, arranged for guest speakers, and organized a conference, with plans for another. When he stepped down, Fr. Burnham [the next director] requested Fr. Sean [Cronin] to conduct the meetings and only attended once or twice. By then, the only priest was Fr. Sean joined by Sister Gregory. The Hindu faith has been represented by several monastics from the beginning, including, for the last several years, our Assistant Minister, Swami Sarvadevananda. Lay people from both traditions have also contributed significantly.

For the last couple of years, the idea to publish seems to have been set aside.[6] We have followed some general themes and outlines with presentations from participants and we've had a lot of enriching spontaneous discussion, which was also true under the previous directors.[7]

Thus, the withdrawal of the Director from formal chairing of the group allowed the groups to develop their own initiatives and expand lay participation and leadership. But it also disconnected the group somewhat from the Archdiocese.

Father Romero was in office when the Congregation for the Doctrine of the Faith promulgated the controversial document *Dominus Iesus* (2000). The promulgation of *Dominus Iesus* was a disaster for Catholic dialogue groups everywhere. Dialogue groups around the world scrambled to understand the context of the document, respond, and keep their dialogues afloat. The Los Angeles Hindu-Catholic Dialogue was no exception, managing renewed suspicions from many in local Hindu communities. Members of the Dialogue felt it important to register a clear statement with the Archdiocese, addressing the Archbishop, Roger Cardinal Mahony.

---

[6] Although the group set aside its publication aspirations some time ago, two of the participants at the Dialogue's 2010 event "Teaching Hinduism in Catholic Schools: A Workshop and Dialogue" co-authored an article based on their presentations: Pravrajika Saradeshaprana and Tracy Sayuki Tiemeier, "Viewpoint: Teaching Hinduism in Catholic High Schools", *Journal of Hindu-Christian Studies*, 24 (2011), pp. 46–50.

[7] David Stump to Gilbert Romero, 3 April 1998, Los Angeles Hindu-Catholic Dialogue Archive, Tracy Tiemeier's personal collection, Loyola Marymount University, Los Angeles.

The Hindu-Roman Catholic Dialogue met today, September 13, 2000. We discussed and responded to the document *Dominus Iesus* and your editorial statement in the Los Angeles Times on September 10, 2000. The non-Roman Catholics among us resist any attempt to be converted to the Roman Catholic faith. We take issue with the characterizations of our faiths as deficient and/or defective. We understand the need for faiths to hold firm within their own belief systems but find contradictory the notion in *Dominus Iesus* that there can be equality of persons but no equality of doctrinal content. The deepest and best parts of our personhood derive from our faith including its doctrines. Dialogue by nature allows faiths to learn from one another, which implies that no one faith possesses the totality of truth.

We appreciate your concern for the tone of *Dominus Iesus* and its apparent implications. Many of us in this group come from parts of the world where *Dominus Iesus* will have very harmful effects on the relationship between Hindus and Roman Catholics. In our dialogue here in Los Angeles we respect one another as friends. We intend to continue with our dialogue, in a spirit of mutual search and sharing.[8]

Although *Dominus Iesus* may not have been out of line with Vatican II's teaching on other religions, many experienced the document as profoundly out of line with the spirit of Vatican II. Certainly, the document lacked any sense of the years of deep inter-faith dialogues that had developed in the thirty-five years after *Nostra Aetate*. For some non-Catholics suspicious of dialogue with Catholics, their fears were confirmed: "dialogue" is really about conversion. The Los Angeles Hindu-Catholic Dialogue's public efforts were challenged, but the deep friendships that had developed within the Dialogue prevented a rupture.

"Failures" in Interreligious Reading

In recent years, the Dialogue has followed a particular practice along with enthusiastic and invaluable participation by the Archdiocese's Ecumenical and Interreligious Officer, the Right Reverend Alexei Smith. There are two co-chairs, one Catholic and one Hindu. The overall format generally follows a four-fold dialogue of life, action, theological exchange, and religious experience.[9] We meet once a month, rotating between our "home" bases, and share a meal over light chitchat and personal updates (dialogue of life). At the

---

[8] John Casey, Christopher Key Chapple, Rada Krishna, Sumitra Menon, Joseph Prabhu, and David Stump to Roger Mahony, 13 September 2000, Los Angeles Hindu-Catholic Dialogue Archive, Tracy Tiemeier's personal collection, Loyola Marymount University, Los Angeles.

[9] The Pontifical Council for Inter-religious Dialogue, *Dialogue and Proclamation* (19 May 1991), 42, available at: http://www.vatican.va/roman_curia/pontifical_councils/interelg/documents/rc_pc_interelg_doc_19051991_dialogue-and-proclamatio_en.html

first meeting of the year, we will choose a theme for discussion throughout the year (dialogue of theological exchange). We will make suggestions for readings and start thinking of a public event based on the theme. Over the course of the year, we will have readings each month, talk about the readings, slowly plan a public event, and collaborate on community projects of mutual concern (dialogue of action). Over the course of the year, and at the event itself, the group also shares in meditation or prayer (dialogue of religious experience). At the end of the year, the Dialogue hosts a large event—a conference, workshop, or celebration. Themes have included Women and Spirituality (1999), Social Service and Spirituality (2000), Spiritual Practice (2001), Sacred Celibacy (2004), Ecological Spirituality (2005), Human Rights (2006), Teaching Hinduism in Catholic Schools: A Workshop and Dialogue (2010), and Death and Dying (2011).[10]

Although the group has engaged in many efforts in interreligious reading that were mutually enriching, challenging, and sustaining (lasting numerous sessions and often culminating in a public event), I focus here on two inter-religious reading efforts by the Dialogue that simply went nowhere. Because the texts or combination of texts did not inspire lasting conversation, mutual insights, or further interest, I call them "failures". However, experimental "failures" are often as instructive as experimental "successes". I explore here what insights can be drawn from our "failures".

The first effort began in a very interesting and promising way. One of the members of the Dialogue suggested reading a Christian commentary on the Bhagavad Gita. Hindu participants did not object to a Christian reading of a Hindu sacred text; instead, they disagreed among themselves on focusing on the Bhagavad Gita. While the Gita is a very popular text, it is far from being universally normative among the many and vastly diverse Hindu traditions. Indeed, one Hindu participant wondered if the Dialogue's selection of the Gita reinforced both Western attempts to find one single book that could easily define Hinduism and some Hindu attempts to create a seamless Hinduism that simply did not exist. Nevertheless, the group ultimately decided to proceed and went on to select a set of Christian commentaries in order to get a diversity of reflections on the text.

In the first meeting, Christian participants discussed how reading the Gita opened up their own understanding, and how Christian readers of the Gita broke open spaces for new ways of thinking and praying. Trying to stay focused on the broader question of insight through interreligious reading, we avoided the "minor" errors we noticed in the commentaries. When a Hindu participant noted the errors, we readily agreed and spoke out against them. I even showed my marginal comments noting the problems! We Christians wanted to smooth things over and maintain a positive exchange. A Hindu

---

[10] Event programs and posters, Los Angeles Hindu-Catholic Dialogue Archive, Tracy Tiemeier's personal collection, Loyola Marymount University, Los Angeles.

participant noted that Hindu readings of Christian texts were hardly the model of representation and scholarly textual interpretation. And yet, someone asked: do not interreligious readers have a responsibility to understand the "other" first and read the text as it is embedded in its own religious tradition?

While these exchanges offered the impetus in another piece to reflect on the importance of grounding interreligious reading in the texts' communities and in deep interreligious engagement,[11] I was not then in the position to reflect on how our interreligious reading developed thereafter. What happened was . . . nothing. The series of commentaries was essentially forgotten. Some participants simply did not bring the book to subsequent meetings. Others did not have time or make time to read. Other topics became far more interesting to discuss at our meetings. Efforts by myself to refocus the conversation back on our readings went nowhere. I always dutifully emailed participants with instructions, reminders, and a note of the meeting's readings. But we simply never made it around to the readings at the meetings. Or the comments on the readings were brief and unenthusiastic. The commentaries became uninteresting to both Hindu and Christian participants.

Another "failure" was of great surprise to me. To celebrate the one-hundred and fiftieth anniversary of Swami Vivekananda's birth and the fiftieth anniversary of the opening of Vatican II in 2012, the group tried for months to read Vivekananda's teachings and the texts of Vatican II together. Frankly, I thought it would be a wonderfully productive year of interreligious reading, as the majority of the Hindu participants in the Dialogue are members of the Vedanta Society of Southern California and the spirit of Vatican II continues to inspire the Dialogue. But other matters always seemed more interesting or important than the texts themselves.

In order to salvage our year of "dialogue about dialogue", we recently read the Gospel of John (Chapter 14) along with the Rig Veda (1.164) in order to think about the relationship between one and many, and about Christian and Hindu inclusivisms. To begin and contextualize the discussion, the reading also included Harvey Cox's "Many Mansions or One Way? The Crisis in Interfaith Dialogue".[12] The article holds together the "inclusivist" approach of John 14:2 ("In my Father's house there are many dwelling-places", NRSV) and the "exclusivist" approach of John 14:6 ("I am the way, and the truth, and the life", NRSV).

At the meeting, Hindu participants wanted to know right away why I had chosen the Rig Veda passage, for although the Rig Veda is highly authoritative

---

[11] Tracy Sayuki Tiemeier, "Comparative Theology as a Theology of Liberation", in Francis X. Clooney (ed), *The New Comparative Theology: Interreligious Insights from the Next Generation* (London: T & T Clark, 2010), pp. 129–149.

[12] Harvey Cox, "Many Mansions or One Way? The Crisis in Interfaith Dialogue", *The Christian Century*, 17–24 August 1988, pp. 731–735.

among most Hindus, it is complicated and hard to understand; moreover, it is not a text that is often read or discussed on its own. Indeed, the Rig Veda may be considered even more sacred than the Bible, but it is not something as widely read as the Bible, even among Hindu adepts. In our dialogue, we looked at the brief verses that were familiar to Hindus and the short passage that is often referred to when discussing Hindu "inclusivism" (1.164.46). But the discussion ended there.

The passage of John, on the other hand, was very interesting to the group. One Hindu member likened the exchange between Jesus and Philip to the relationship between Krishna and Arjuna in the Bhagavad Gita. Christian participants found this both surprising and interesting. Conversation followed this comparison and lasted quite some time. The parallels between Philip and Arjuna, Jesus and Krishna, made the seemingly exclusivist verses in John 14 take on a holistic, integrative, and cosmic tone. In a sense, then, the discussion was a "success". The interreligious conversation on John 14 was indeed fascinating. But since the initial juxtaposition of Hindu and Christian texts on a parallel theme did not really "work", I want to explore it more fully.

Factors that contributed to these less than ideal results included (but certainly were not limited to): 1) the decision to proceed with commentaries on a text that at least one participant thought was overemphasized; 2) the decision to try to keep reading commentaries some found objectionable in their misrepresentation of the Gita and its traditions of interpretation; 3) the decision to juxtapose Vivekananda's teachings, which are offered to a broad audience, with Vatican II's texts, which have a less conversational tone and target an "insider" audience; 4) juxtaposing an accessible biblical narrative with an esoteric hymn; and 5) including a "bridge" reading that considers one reading but not the other. These issues are largely related to textual selection, a process that varies for the Los Angeles Hindu-Catholic Dialogue from individual selection to group brainstorming. But issues related to the selection of texts do not explain everything. The group has read a wide variety of texts together, with sometimes gross misrepresentations of Hinduism and Christianity, in a wide variety of genres, often unbalanced, and with various target audiences. That the readings ended up being less than ideal does not necessarily, then, explain fully the "failure". It would therefore seem that sometimes texts or their juxtapositions just failed to inspire the group. After some initial remarks, the commentaries and the juxtapositions simply led to a collective indifference. Other topics, or only an individual text in the juxtaposition, became the material for dialogue. In the context of dialogue, the conditions for productive interreligious reading are not always obvious.

Interreligious Reading, Dialogue, and Comparative Theology

The interreligious reading in the Comparative Theology of Francis X. Clooney is characterized by reading religious texts together in order to produce new insights and perspectives for theology. For him, comparative reading aims "to inscribe within the Christian theological tradition theological texts from outside it, and to (begin to) write Christian theology only out of that newly composed context".[13] The goal of this (re)inscription of texts is the production of a "comparative intertext".[14] Clooney is influenced by Western postmodern scholarship, mimicking the "collage effect" of Jacques Derrida's experimental work and juxtaposing texts in columns.[15] He writes:

> Comparative theological reading shares features with this strategy of collage, as the constructive comparativist unsettles two (or more) traditions by excising important and familiar materials from their "legitimate" contexts in order to use them together newly, necessarily without prior warrant. The traditional interpretations woven around both texts, though recognized, are bracketed and rendered momentarily inarticulate. The reader, a member of either tradition who chooses to become a comparativist, is compelled to interact with the materials in a way that neither tradition would recognize as "its own way". She or he must work very hard with the newly aligned materials, each subjected momentarily to the disorienting power of temporary acts of decontextualization and recontextualization. The procedure is effective and productive, in part because there is no established, approved set of margins within which the reading can be contained; nor is there any entirely adequate summation, before or after the reading, of what the juxtaposition is supposed to mean.[16]

The juxtaposition destabilizes texts from their traditions and produces new insights neither controlled by, nor necessarily recognized by, the texts' home traditions. Yet even as Clooney plays with the subversive nature of interreligious reading, he expends a large portion (even a majority) of his energy contextualizing texts, particularly in light of commentarial traditions.

Even as dialogue and comparison grounds texts in their communities and traditions, both recognize the limits of reader control. In *Seeing Through Texts*, Clooney offers the Srivaisnava practice of prapatti (surrender) as a model for interreligious reading.[17] Later, Clooney would emphasize the affective, loving, dimension of surrender in *Beyond Compare*.[18] In focusing on surrender to the text, Clooney highlights the ways in which texts construct readers (and

---

[13] Francis X. Clooney, *Theology After Vedanta: An Experiment in Comparative Theology* (Albany, NY: State University of New York Press, 1993), p. 7.

[14] Francis X. Clooney, *Seeing Through Texts: Doing Theology among the Srivaisnavas of South India* (Albany, NY: State University of New York Press, 1996), p. 297.

[15] *Ibid.*, p. 257.

[16] Clooney, *Theology After Vedanta*, p. 174.

[17] Clooney, *Seeing Through Texts*, pp. 310–311.

[18] Francis X. Clooney, *Beyond Compare: St. Francis de Sales and Sri Vedanta Desika on Loving Surrender to God* (Washington DC: Georgetown University Press, 2008).

not the other way around). But there is another surrender that becomes clear through "failures" in interreligious reading in the context of dialogue: the surrender of individuals to the back and forth flow of the group. Dialogue, even when "successful" (whatever that means), is often tedious, boring, circuitous, meandering, and frustrating. Actual conversations cannot be scripted or clearly structured. The ebb and flow of a dialogue moves forward, backward, sideways, and every which way in between. Particularly for those persons looking to "accomplish something", dialogue is bound to be an exercise in madness. When readings simply do not "work", on their own or together, there is nothing that can be done to redirect the conversation or to produce results.

In this respect, the interreligious reading done by Comparative Theology is deceptively productive. Some texts resist comparison. Not every text or juxtaposition can be integrated into (or even held in tension in illuminative ways for) a Comparative Theology. More attention needs to be paid to the process of Comparative Theology in the selection of texts and the exploration of how and why some comparisons "work" and some do not. To take this into account is to recognize that the comparative theologian cannot squeeze meaning out of any arbitrary juxtaposition. And sometimes a comparison that seems obvious just does not yield any profound insight. To include reflection on "failures" in the comparative "experiment" is a more honest approach to Comparative Theology that recognizes the limits of the theologian to control and produce insight in cross-religious reading.

Moreover, although Clooney notes the ways in which comparative reading dislodges (temporarily) texts and theologians from their traditions, it is clear that the backgrounds (social, psychological, religious, etc.) of texts, readers, and contexts of traditions do not fall away when reading. Indeed, in *Divine Mother, Blessed Mother*, Clooney draws on Julia Kristeva's insight into how the autobiographical "text" interacts with texts in order to discuss the interaction of multiple religious texts.[19] But he does not explore fully the role of the autobiographical text in interreligious reading. For any number of reasons (personal and otherwise), certain texts and certain combinations of texts will "speak" (or not) to readers. This cannot always be anticipated, even when an individual knows her dialogue partners or her texts well. This autobiographical "text" is always present in interreligious and comparative reading. Thus, while some readings might be obvious choices to bring together, they may just not inspire insight. Moreover, even where readers try to keep an open mind and bracket out their preconceptions and assumptions, interreligious readers inevitably ask questions, choose topics, select texts, and privilege certain lines of discussion that fit with their own narratives. While insight is not scripted, and often leads to unexpected conclusions, personal and

---

[19] Francis X. Clooney, *Divine Mother, Blessed Mother: Hindu Goddesses and the Virgin Mary* (Oxford: Oxford University Press, 2005).

interpersonal realities are always at play. The personal issues of interreligious readers can plague dialogues and inhibit theologies. They can also bring dialogue partners together and provide unique approaches that would not have otherwise been considered.

Concluding Reflections

In interreligious and comparative reading, everything from the selection of texts in dialogues to the purpose of the comparison is an act of power that can be questioned.[20] Albertina Nugteren, for example, points out that:

> In colonial times, adventurous and greedy men sailed off to distant places, especially the Orient, in search for spices with which they could preserve and season their bland food at home. Now, can the same mistake be avoided here, i.e. that of interfering thoughtlessly with far-away people and their socio-economic infrastructures in this age for the sake of adding non-Christian spices to a Christian dish that may have become too bland? . . . Many are now well aware of the blind spots in the colonial enterprise, such as blatant cultural assumptions and dramatically uneven power relations. Yet many are still guilty of being mindless consumers on today's markets.[21]

When "failures" occur in dialogical reading, dialogue participants can question the person who suggested particular texts and topics. Particularly when the group has developed deep relationships, members are comfortable raising difficult questions of representation in texts, unbalanced texts, possible bias, or colonizing tendencies in the interpretation of texts. When Comparative Theology is done in isolation from others, there is no group to call the theologian to task and challenge her interpretation of texts.

Therefore, I have argued elsewhere that interreligious friendships and a deeply engaged dialogue community are essential spaces for comparative theologians:

> Through [dialogue], the theologian is held accountable to the concerns, interests, and goals of her dialogue partners. Even if a theologian publishes or speaks on a classic text seeming to have little present-day relevance, she serves her friends (and not just the academy) by contributing to mutual understanding and by allowing the overall body of her work to

---

[20] See Helene Egnell, "Scriptural Reasoning: A Feminist Response", in David Cheetham, Ulrich Winkler, Oddbjørn Leirvik, and Judith Gruber (eds), *Interreligious Hermeneutics in Pluralistic Europe: Between Texts and People* (Amsterdam: Rodopi, 2011), pp. 79–82.

[21] Albertina Nugteren, "Entitled to Understand: A Critical Look at Comparative Theology", in Cheetham *et al.* (eds), *Interreligious Hermeneutics in Pluralistic Europe*, pp. 156–157.

emerge from and serve the needs of the wider community. In this sense, then, the comparative theologian remains embedded in the real-life concerns of religious believers.[22]

The emphasis on interreligious solidarity and friendship [in dialogue] is essential for addressing the question of imperialism in comparative theology . . . That is, I need friends to be myself fully; however, true friends are ends in and of themselves, to be treated so. By extension, a comparative theologian needs a community of interreligious friends. But if they are truly friends, they are not important just because they improve my theology. Rather, they are persons with their own goals, interests, and needs.[23]

In the context of a diverse and multivocal dialogue where friends can call each other to task, problems of power can be raised, discussed, and addressed in ways that (hopefully) lead to more successful practices of interreligious reading in the future. Friends also can change the subject and dictate lines of discussion that may or may not be where we had hoped to go, shifting the power dynamics and offering more parity in the discussion. In this way, a comparative theologian who surrenders herself to a group of interreligious friends can be changed and challenged by her friends in significant ways that will factor into the focus of her work.

To be fair, for all of his celebration of the destabilizing nature of Comparative Theology, Clooney's careful approach to texts actually functions in ways similar to a dialogue group, investing texts and their traditions with an integrity that must be honored:

Skilled authors compose in such a way as to transform their intended attentive readers, to bring their lives into conformity with the realities and values their texts describe. Step by step, such texts draw the well-disposed person into a religious reading that is richly multidimensional and productive of affects irreducible to reasons offered in justification. Religious writing itself becomes the locus for further theological reflection: if openings for spiritual commitment and practice are written into a text, and if the text is read across religious boundaries to good effect, then intellectual and spiritual formation may be deepening and intensifying, as it were, line by line.[24]

Thus, as much as the comparative theologian sets up a particular project, texts are transformative wholes with a prior integrity that affects readers in ways

---

[22] Tracy Sayuki Tiemeier, "Comparative Theology and the Dialogue of Life", *The Japan Mission Journal*, 65:2 (2011), p. 130.

[23] *Ibid.*, p. 129.

[24] Francis X. Clooney, "Passionate Comparison: The Intensification of Affect in Interreligious Reading of Hindu and Christian Texts", *Harvard Theological Review*, 98:4 (2005), p. 368.

they cannot control. Texts in dialogue with the comparative theologian are friends in dialogue, whose difference, otherness, and integrity must be maintained.

In *Bridge to Wonder*, Cecilia González-Andrieu draws on the notion of "interlacing" as a way to understand the complex relationship between religion and the arts:

> [A] braid—the geometric representation of interlacing—incorporates difference as beautiful. As we picture a braid, it is possible to appreciate that the uniqueness of each thread is precisely what contributes to the dynamism and complexity of a multistranded rope, and it is the action of intricate weaving that makes this possible. The different strands of a rope have a definite sense of openness and ongoing engagement, never moving swiftly apart as intersecting lines do, but rather continuing to come together.[25]

Interlacing preserves difference, valuing the inherent beauty of each strand, yet noting the ongoing richness of bringing together the sacred and the beautiful. As practices of interlacing, Comparative Theology and interreligious reading done in the context of dialogue do not (should not) erase differences, but rather hold onto and value them, even as the process of reading together creates something entirely new.

The practice of interlacing also highlights more precisely the problem of power in interreligious reading. The image of interlacing calls to mind an outside and unfettered theologian who weaves texts and traditions together for her own "greater" purpose. Even if the integrity of texts is maintained as texts are embedded in their own long "strands" of communities of belief and practice, a "higher" (Christian imperial) authority is able to transcend, "bracket out", her own tradition and claim expertise enough to manipulate materials from both traditions—and in the service of the often privileged home tradition of the theologian. The image lays bare the reality that Clooney's confidence in the careful and "well-disposed" reader to truly surrender herself to an original authorial intention, interweaving texts where there are invited openings, is perhaps overly optimistic. Even when checked by an open group of interreligious friends or a deep care toward texts, the fundamental problem of the theologian's power in interlacing texts remains.

For her part, González-Andrieu is acutely aware of the ways in which the notion of interlacing demonstrates clearly the problem of power in scholarship, religion, and culture. Thus, her theological aesthetics is particularly interested in the conflicts over who controls the production and display of "religious art". Even more, her work has a distinctly liberationist edge. Thus,

---

[25] Cecilia González-Andrieu, *Bridge to Wonder: Art as a Gospel of Beauty* (Waco, TX: Baylor University Press, 2012), p. 88.

it becomes clear that the problem of power is less about theologians' positions of power and their entanglement in intellectual traditions of co-optation —this is inevitable—as it is about scholars failing to recognize situations of privilege in explicitly anti-colonial ways.

Not every comparison "works". Not every practice in interreligious reading is productive. "Failures" in interreligious reading done in the context of the Los Angeles Hindu-Catholic Dialogue highlight the limits of readers' capacity always to produce meaning through textual comparison and the extent to which readers' backgrounds and contexts inform the reading process. Exploring examples of "failures" can assist the theologian as she attempts to construct a comparative theology that honors the "other", attentive to the ways in which texts and traditions resist easy consumption. Constant self-examination and analysis of privilege allow the theologian to name how much she really is involved in the production of meaning. More sustained attention to both of these elements in comparative and interreligious reading is essential, if Comparative Theology is ever to shake the charge of hegemony.

Modern Theology 29:4 October 2013
ISSN 0266-7177 (Print)
ISSN 1468-0025 (Online)

DOI: 10.1111/moth.12067

LONG-TERM DISAGREEMENT: PHILOSOPHICAL MODELS IN SCRIPTURAL REASONING AND RECEPTIVE ECUMENISM

NICHOLAS ADAMS

This article will explore points of contact between two practices of encounter between different traditions: Scriptural Reasoning and Receptive Ecumenism. It will focus on shared philosophical shapes. This is not an area that has been explored much, and the findings of this inquiry should be treated as provisional. Scriptural Reasoning and Receptive Ecumenism will be characterised as strategies for dealing with long-term disagreement, that is, as strategies that do not seek to preserve or promote such disagreement, but which face it in a non-utopian manner and seek to maintain a concern with truth while taking questions of tradition seriously. The significance of Scriptural Reasoning and Receptive Ecumenism lies in their mediation of a sophisticated anti-foundationalism and a rejection of secular universalism in practices whose participants are not experts in philosophy. This is significant, I shall argue, because the philosophical habits of participants in inter-faith engagement and ecumenical dialogue often display signs of foundationalism and secular universalism: Scriptural Reasoning and Receptive Ecumenism explicitly aim to change these habits. Their significance lies not in any new insights into philosophical method so much as in their capacity to embed certain philosophical developments, especially within pragmatism, in institutions, in such a way as to shape everyday practices.

Nicholas Adams
School of Divinity, University of Edinburgh, New College, Mound Place, Edinburgh, EH1 2LX, UK
Email: n.adams@ed.ac.uk

There is a body of literature, from a variety of practitioners, about both Scriptural Reasoning and Receptive Ecumenism.[1] I shall comment on two short pieces, one by Peter Ochs, "Rules for Scriptural Reasoning", and one by Paul Murray, "Receptive Ecumenism and Catholic Learning: Establishing the Agenda".[2] Each is an introduction to their respective practices, naming the philosophical approaches that characterise them. These are named "pragmatism", which for Ochs derives from the study of C. S. Peirce and for Murray from the study of Nicholas Rescher.[3] This article focuses on the significance of the philosophical methods they advocate in relation to Scriptural Reasoning and Receptive Ecumenism.

Both Scriptural Reasoning and Receptive Ecumenism are explicitly reparative practices.[4] They identify particular problems in existing practices, resolving them through diagnosis and presenting alternatives. Receptive Ecumenism is concerned with existing practices of ecumenism that display failure of various kinds. Scriptural Reasoning is concerned with existing practices of the study of religious life (and the errant philosophical methods they rely on). Where Receptive Ecumenism is described by Murray explicitly as an alternative to existing failed ecumenical strategies, Ochs is less interested in inter-faith encounter, and more concerned with problems in the academy. Receptive Ecumenism is oriented to the Church, Scriptural Reasoning to the University. (I shall ignore more recent developments in Scriptural Reasoning, in which its practices are extended outside the university. These merit further investigation requiring detailed fieldwork.)

There are significant differences between Scriptural Reasoning and Receptive Ecumenism: for reasons of space I consider only their shared philosophical orientation. Ochs and Murray suggest that everyday problems in universities and churches are expressed in and exacerbated by errant philosophical methods. These are not a matter for philosophers alone: they

---

[1] On Scriptural Reasoning see various issues of the *Journal of Scriptural Reasoning* (http:// etext.lib.virginia.edu/journals/ssr; last accessed 31 December 2012) from 2001 to the present; see also David Ford and C. C. Pecknold (eds), *The Promise of Scriptural Reasoning* (Malden, MA: Blackwell, 2006), which contains 12 essays. On Receptive Ecumenism see Paul Murray (ed), *Receptive Ecumenism and the Call to Catholic Learning* (Oxford: Oxford University Press, 2008), which contains 32 essays. See also the website for the project, https://www.dur.ac.uk/ theology.religion/ccs/projects/receptiveecumenism/, whose documents extend up to the end of 2011; last accessed 31 December 2012: at that date, the site had a number of broken links.

[2] Peter Ochs, "The Rules of Scriptural Reasoning", *Journal of Scriptural Reasoning*, 2:1 (2002), available at: http://tinyurl.com/ochs-rules-2002; last accessed 9 December 2012, my emphasis. Paul Murray "Receptive Ecumenism and Catholic Learning: Establishing the Agenda" in Murray (ed), *Receptive Ecumenism*, pp. 5–25.

[3] See Peter Ochs, *Peirce, Pragmatism and the Logic of Scripture* (Cambridge: Cambridge University Press, 1998); Paul Murray, *Reason, Truth and Theology in Pragmatist Perspective* (Leuven: Peeters, 2004), especially pp. 91–162. Murray's introductory chapter to the Receptive Ecumenism volume rehearses, in an abbreviated form, many of the arguments in the opening chapter of his book on pragmatism, which is also entitled "Establishing the Agenda".

[4] For a brief overview of this approach to philosophy see Nicholas Adams, "Reparative Reasoning", *Modern Theology*, 24:3 (July 2008), pp. 447–457.

concern all those who study religious traditions and all those who engage in ecumenical dialogue. In the accounts by Ochs and Murray philosophical problems are treated alongside more local problems in the study of religious traditions and the practices of ecumenism.

Scholars of religious traditions and participants in ecumenical dialogue rely (whether implicitly or explicitly) on particular philosophical methods. Where these methods are problematic, Ochs and Murray recommend alternatives. The two most prominent errant philosophical methods identified in the study of religious traditions and in ecumenical dialogue are rationalist in character. Ochs and Murray do not mean that scholars of religious traditions or participants in ecumenical dialogue are advocates of such methods. Rather, certain philosophical habits can be discerned in their practices and their specific problematic features can be identified. These problematic features can arguably be traced back to Descartes and Kant, but it is the problematic features that are of concern rather than their intellectual heritage. These problematic features are named by Murray "foundationalism" and "the pursuit of neutral ground" and by Ochs "Cartesianism" and "Secular Universalism".

Foundationalism

Foundationalism has three key features: its orientation to previous philosophical methods, its way of handling doubt and certainty, and its approach to starting points. These can be elaborated briefly in turn.

Foundationalism rejects the methods of its predecessors. Cartesian philosophy grew out of a dissatisfaction with Aristotelian Scholastic practices.[5] Instead of diagnosing problems in those practices and repairing them piece by piece, the entire nexus of practices was taken to be in error and a new method was developed to replace it *in toto.* The root problem was dependence on venerable authorities. In the various scholastic practices of both Catholic and Protestant thinkers appeals were made to authorities in support of arguments. Such authorities included pagan sources (especially Aristotle), Biblical sources (especially Psalms or the letters of St Paul), and ecclesiastical sources including Church Fathers (especially Augustine). Many debates between Catholic and Protestant leaders were resolvable, at least in principle, so long as there was agreement on what counted as an authority. Aquinas had already shown in his *Summa Theologiae* that the principal authorities did not agree on certain doctrinal points, and it was central to his presentation of arguments that these opposing views were identified at the start, in the form of *"objectiones"* and *"sed contra"* summaries. It was

---

[5] See Jorge Secada, *Cartesian Metaphysics: The Scholastic Origins of Modern Philosophy* (Cambridge: Cambridge University Press, 2000); Roger Ariew, *Descartes and the Last Scholastics* (Ithaca, NY: Cornell University Press, 1999). The sketch that follows is my own.

then the task of the theologian, in a *"respondeo"* section, to work through these oppositions and offer a reasoned provisional judgement that resolved them. By the time of the seventeenth century, however, there was disagreement not only about such provisional judgements but disagreement on what counted as an authority. The Protestant principle of *sola scriptura* tended to undermine appeals to pagan authorities, to the doctors of the Church, to conciliar settlements or (most emphatically) to papal judgements *ex cathedra*. The scholastic methods of argumentation were unable to resolve these disagreements about authorities, because they relied on prior agreement at this level, and arguments thus began to display a tendency towards interminable debate. Cartesian philosophy thus commended a method that refused appeals to *any* authority. Rather than develop a philosophical method that took into account different authorities, Cartesian philosophy rejected methods which appealed to authority and instead promoted a method which appealed to demonstrable truths. This method was intended wholly to replace its predecessors.

Foundationalism pits unlimited doubt against absolute certainty. Cartesian method rejects the provisional judgements of the theological "I reply that": their starting points can be doubted. In their place, the method takes absolute certainty as the only rational starting point, in the expectation that a secure starting point will deliver more secure arguments. The uncertain conflict of competing authorities is replaced by the clarity of mathematical deduction. Only that which cannot be doubted counts as a starting point, and only that which can be deduced counts as a valid argument. The uncertainties surrounding the interpretation of authorities are removed. Doubt and certainty are no longer matters of "more or less"; they become matters of "yes or no". Beliefs are no longer more or less doubtful or more or less certain. They are either doubtful (because they cannot be demonstrated) or certain (because they can).

Foundationalism starts with doubt and ends in certainty. It is a distinctive mark of Cartesian thought that the initial orientation of the thinker is one of doubt. This doubt is pervasive and unrestricted: any proposition offered at the outset is automatically placed in doubt, regardless of its content. Only those propositions that survive such a test are admitted. They are not merely accepted provisionally, as axioms, but absolutely, as certainties. For Descartes himself such certainties are clear and distinct ideas, given by God, but for any foundationalism there must be some certainties of this kind. Once they are secured, a process of deduction can get underway: its purpose is to build on these certainties in a quest for further certainties.

The pragmatism commended by Ochs and Murray is intended to repair the deficiencies that characterise foundationalism along three corresponding axes. It seeks to recover a concern with authorities, especially those that are scriptural (Ochs) or doctrinal (Murray). It attempts to soften doubts and certainties. It reverses the priority of doubt and certainty.

The first repair begins with an acknowledgement that different traditions privilege different authorities. The pragmatic repair readily acknowledges that there is a problem to be addressed but sees the rejection of philosophies that admit authorities into trains of argument as an over-correction. It is genuinely a problem if a member of one tradition attempts to argue against a member of another tradition through appeal to authorities if each participant privileges different authorities. This is, however, the normal state of affairs in inter-faith encounter and in ecumenical dialogue. The pragmatic repair acknowledges that to understand another person's argument is to understand which authorities they privilege. The problem with the foundationalist method is its exclusion of authorities and thus of traditions themselves (because a tradition is the transmission of authorities). Foundationalism correctly diagnoses the problem: there are different authorities in play. But its repair is ruinously excessive: it refuses to admit authorities into argumentation. The pragmatic repair accepts the diagnosis, but commends investigation into authorities rather than the pursuit of demonstrable truths. Foundationalism fails partly because its demonstrable truths tend to be trivial. The interesting doctrinal questions are excluded from philosophy because few demonstrable truths can be found in theology from which to begin; but the whole point of the exercise was to debate doctrinal questions.

The second repair softens doubts and certainties. Instead of unlimited doubts and absolute certainties, the pragmatic repair deals in occasional doubts and provisional certainties. To those afflicted by a residual Cartesianism to speak of something as certain is to strip it of its provisionality. To be certain is not to be provisional. The pragmatic repair denies this. To be certain is merely to be undoubted. It might be placed in doubt at some point in the future, and it might survive or be defeated by such doubt. Something is certain because, for the time being, it is not doubted. Its certainty is provisional. Such provisionality may be long-term; if that is so, it is because it tends, as a matter of fact, not to be doubted. This is not because it is indubitable; it is because there is no good reason to doubt it. The pragmatic repair refuses unlimited doubt. *Doubts need reasons.* In the absence of reasons, there is an absence of doubt. A philosopher who says, "well I just doubt it" is not a serious thinker for a pragmatist. A philosopher is entitled to doubt if a reason for doubting can be given. A thinker who says, "well it can be doubted" utters a triviality for a pragmatist. Anything can be doubted; the question is whether anything stimulates such doubt. A foundationalist is committed to a method of saying "well it can be doubted" until something is found that cannot be doubted. Few of the things it finds are of much interest, theologically, because the important doctrinal questions tend to be provisional (if long-term) certainties. The pragmatist is thus "certain" of a great deal more than the foundationalist, but is more provisional about this certainty. The pragmatist also doubts a great deal less than the foundationalist, because she requires reasons for doubting. The pragmatist may also be indifferent to a range of claims: they are neither provisionally certain nor rationally doubted. One might say that they are trivially hypothetical.

The third repair reverses the priority of doubt and certainty. The foundationalist begins with doubt and labours until certainty is found. Once this basis is secured, a deductive method builds further certainties. The pragmatist begins with a web of provisional certainties bearing complex relations to each other. From time to time one or more of these certainties is placed in doubt, because a reason to doubt them arises, and this stimulates various investigations. An axiom (a certainty) becomes an hypothesis (it is doubted) which is then tested (by investigations). The hypothesis either survives such testing, in which case it becomes an axiom once again, or it fails to survive it, in which case its denial becomes certain (provisionally). The key question for the pragmatist is when to convert an axiom into an hypothesis. The thinker who says "any axiom can be converted into an hypothesis" utters a triviality for the pragmatist. The pragmatist begins with axioms, with a complex of provisional certainties, and introduces doubts only when good reasons stimulate a shift of orientation. Whereas for the foundationalist everything starts out as an hypothesis requiring investigation, for the pragmatist everything starts out either as an axiom or as trivially hypothetical: neither requires investigation until a reason presents itself.

Ochs and Murray make explicit the ways in which the pragmatist repairs of foundationalism inform inter-faith and ecumenical encounter. Foundationalism is likely to be corrosive not only of the claims of other traditions, but of one's own tradition. The need for the pragmatic repair persists so long as foundationalist habits are widespread. These are audible whenever one hears, "well I doubt that" without good reason, or "that can be doubted" or other variants. But it is also audible whenever one hears "I will only be satisfied by absolute certainty" or "unless you can demonstrate it, I will not believe it". These are widespread intellectual tendencies, and they are particularly ruinous when members of different traditions encounter each other. If both sides agree that only absolute certainty is satisfactory, then they will be doomed to fix their gaze on trivial certainties, and to relegate the things that matter most to them to the realm of irrational "blind" belief.

Secular Universalism

Like foundationalism, secular universalism (or the pursuit of neutral ground) is a pervasive intellectual habit which calls for repair.[6] Like foundationalism it rejects tradition. Where foundationalism seeks absolute certainty in the place of the provisional certainties of tradition, the pursuit of neutral ground explicitly refuses appeals to authorities and instead

---

[6] Ochs, "Rules", §4; Murray, "Establishing the Agenda", p. 7.

recommends "neutral" appeals to reason. The main assumption that underlies the pursuit of neutral ground is that the criteria for judgement are innate and invariant. This is a development of the Cartesian notion of the "natural light" which itself is a very late development of the Augustinian topos of divine illumination which accompanies his epistemology.[7] Its implications for philosophical method, especially in relation to questions of disagreement between members of different traditions, are serious. Because criteria for judgement are considered innate, they are taken to be necessary. An opponent in debate thus does not merely deny something that I affirm; my opponent denies reason itself.

To argue in a way that is contrary to reason is not just to be mistaken. It is to be grievously in the wrong. One's utterances do not merely require correction: they call for a particularly strong repudiation. Someone who teaches things that are contrary to reason does not merely provoke disagreement. They have no business teaching at all, and do not belong in a university devoted to the pursuit of reason.

In the realm of inter-faith engagement and ecumenical dialogue, such secular universalism, such pursuit of neutral ground—of criteria that are true *a priori*—is particularly toxic. It displays a tendency to treat opponents as irrational. Your arguments, in such a framework, are not just products of a different tradition: they are expressions of a refusal to think. I am liable not just to reject your arguments, but you yourself as a serious partner in discussion. Instead of disagreeing, we become engaged in mutual dismissal.

The pragmatic repair of the pursuit of neutral ground is to refuse to attribute criteria for judgement to neutral reason, but to identify them as reasons located in traditions of thought. Some criteria—trivial ones, from a theological perspective—are so widespread as not to need any such explicit attribution. There is no "Muslim" periodic table of the elements and no "Lutheran" trigonometry. By contrast, it is obvious that different traditions interpret texts in a distinctive way. Interpretations of the Talmud, of the New Testament and of medieval Islamic legal texts are not covered by a single discipline of "hermeneutics" which specifies a single set of interpretive rules applied to a range of different materials. Different traditions treat different texts differently. The nineteenth-century fantasy of a unified hermeneutic theory, which typically attempted to harmonise methods for interpreting Classical and Biblical texts, produced some fascinating insights and clarified a number of previously obscure questions. But it attempted to regulate the interpretation

---

[7] John Rist, "Faith and Reason", in Eleonore Stump and Norman Kretzmann (eds), *The Cambridge Companion to Augustine* (Cambridge: Cambridge University Press, 2001), pp. 26–39. This is a classic example of a concept whose meaning changes radically as it is transmitted. See Lydia Schumacher, *Divine Illumination: The History and Future of Augustine's Theory of Knowledge* (Malden, MA: Wiley-Blackwell, 2011).

of texts—to specify the rules an interpreter *must* follow—rather than to describe, in a more ethnographically attentive way, how texts are actually interpreted. It was strong on theory but weak on case studies.[8] It described reasonably well the practices of university scholarship but failed to do justice to the practices of ecclesial reading (and ignored the Jewish sages and Muslim jurists). The pragmatic repair of secular universalism, of the pursuit of neutral ground, is also a repair of the over-generalisations found in nineteenth-century hermeneutics. This does not take the form of a more adequate universal hermeneutics. It notices that there are, and attends to, different traditions of interpretation. Participants in Scriptural Reasoning and Receptive Ecumenism are stimulated to make small-scale investigations into another's practices of reading.[9] This does not yield a hermeneutic theory; it produces something analogous to ethnography: a description of something observed combined with an attempt to understand it.

The refusal of foundationalist method and of the pursuit of neutral ground in philosophy is a familiar topos in the discipline of philosophy in the university: such refusals are commonplace in German Idealism, in French Phenomenology, in English Analytic Philosophy or in American Pragmatism. Their significance for Scriptural Reasoning and Receptive Ecumenism is that such refusals are not only for disciplinary specialists. Their significance is their gradual institutionalisation into the practices of theologians whose training is in doctrine, biblical interpretation, Talmud, Da'wah, and other non-philosophical disciplines. Scriptural Reasoning and Receptive Ecumenism embed the fruits of specialised philosophical investigation—in this case those of pragmatist philosophy—in everyday practices of inter-faith and ecumenical engagement. One of the most regrettable failures of modern philosophy in the twentieth century is the limited scope of its application outside a small guild of philosophers. Scriptural Reasoning and Receptive Ecumenism show a capacity to mediate the later repair of these traditions, whether in idealist, analytic or pragmatist variants, in popular practices.

Having cast the discussion as one of repair—in this case the repair of rationalist method in philosophy—we can now turn to the fruits of this repair and attempt to discern the shapes of thinking displayed in Scriptural Reasoning and Receptive Ecumenism. Our concern here is with the shapes of thinking rather than their genesis and transmission.

The shapes of thinking in Scriptural Reasoning and Receptive Ecumenism display two notable features: a willingness to consider triadic as well as binary forms, and a privileging of positive over negative truth claims.

---

[8] See Nicholas Adams, "The Bible", in Nicholas Adams, George Pattison and Graham Ward (eds), *The Oxford Handbook of Theology and Modern European Thought* (Oxford: Oxford University Press, 2013), pp. 545–566.

[9] Ochs, "Rules", §6E.

Triadic Forms

Everyday forms of judgement tend, quite properly, to be binary. Words have meanings, claims are right or wrong, beliefs are axiomatic or hypothetical. A binary form assigns a value to a variable. As Descartes and Spinoza grasped so well, the most easily demonstrated examples are mathematical. A triangle is a polygon with three corners or vertices and three sides or edges which are line segments; the area of a circle is expressed as π multiplied by the square of the radius; we can treat as axiomatic the belief that a submerged object will displace its own volume whereas a floating object will displace its own mass, and so forth. In the realm of mathematics judgements quite properly take a binary form. The same is true in the realm of theology, for the most part. The world is God's good creation; Jesus is fully human and fully divine; we can treat as axiomatic the belief that God is Trinity, and so forth. Systematic theology within any one tradition is rightly taught as a nexus of axiomatic claims which then permit the investigation of various hypotheses such as "God shares in human suffering" or "Capitalism is incompatible with the doctrine of creation".

As is well known, however, things are more complex in classic doctrinal arguments. "The Spirit proceeds from the Father and the Son". "Salvation comes by faith alone". A Catholic theologian affirms the *filioque*, whereas an Orthodox theologian affirms its absence. A Lutheran affirms the formula *sola fides*, whereas an Anglican may or may not affirm it. What is positively axiomatic for a Catholic theologian is negatively axiomatic for an Orthodox theologian. What is axiomatic for a Lutheran is hypothetical for an Anglican. In a binary form of judgement, questions of truth are decided in a yes/no fashion. For a Catholic theologian, the Orthodox omission of the *filioque* is errant; for a Lutheran theologian the Anglican equivocation over *sola fides* is errant. I am right and you are wrong. This is a familiar shape of thinking with a bloody history. The nineteenth-century liberal Protestant approach to such questions was to recast "objective" dogmatic claims about God's being as "subjective" claims about human experience of the divine. This too is a binary shape of thinking: objective dogmatic claims are errant.

In ecumenical and inter-faith encounter, binary shapes of thinking are problematic. What I affirm, you deny. What is axiomatic for you is hypothetical for me. There are a number of strategies for addressing this problem, and these can be cast as ideal types. One is a conservative strategy of agreement. "We should focus on our shared affirmations and denials and should seek to minimise contrary cases." This strategy tends to produce documents with forms of words which both sides can affirm. Another is a liberal strategy of agreement. "We should assume that we approach a single truth in different ways: we are 'essentially' the same and only 'inessentially' different." This strategy, which over-generously permits the speaker to assume authority for identifying what is, and what is not, essential, tends to produce generalised truth claims and to avoid dogmatic forms that are particular to traditions. Both strategies preserve the binary shape of judgement. Where I affirm X and you affirm Y, an agreement can be forged where we affirm Z.

Scriptural Reasoning and Receptive Ecumenism offer alternatives to strategies of agreement. They furnish strategies for long-term disagreement. Instead of identifying the problem as one of substance, namely my affirmation of X versus your affirmation of Y, it identifies the problem as one of form. It is the binary shape that provokes conflict: I am right and you are wrong. In a binary shape, it is a problem that what I affirm you deny and that what is axiomatic for you is hypothetical for me. In a triadic shape, it is not a problem: it is merely a fact. Instead of confronting a triadic problem with a binary solution, it confronts a binary problem with a triadic solution. Instead of replacing the "for me" and the "for you" with a "for us", it preserves the "for me" and the "for you" structure. A binary form assigns a value to a variable. A triadic form describes how, or rather names for whom, a value is assigned to a variable.

This produces some significant changes to the form judgements take.

Consider the binary form: "X is true; Not-X is false."
A triadic form is quite different: "I affirm X; you deny X."
Consider another binary form: "X is axiomatic; Y is hypothetical."

The triadic form includes qualifications:

"X is axiomatic for me but hypothetical for you.
Y is hypothetical for me but axiomatic for you."

Truth claims do not disappear in triadic forms. They are preserved but qualified:

"I affirm 'X is true'; you deny 'X is true'."

It is worth considering the problematic claim: "X is true for me but false for you".

This last claim is confused. A binary claim assigns a value to a variable. A triadic claim describes for whom a value is assigned to a variable. The problematic claim assigns a value (indeed two contrary values) to a variable; it does not properly describe for whom (or how) a value is assigned to a variable. That is not the main problem, however. The deeper problem is that it misuses the word "true". X is either true or not true. A triadic form does not modify the assigning of a value to a variable. Triadic forms do not adjudicate truth claims at all. A triadic form preserves that act of assigning without modification. It adds a description: it specifies who assigns the value to the variable.

Scriptural Reasoning and Receptive Ecumenism are specialised forms of discourse which deal in a disciplined way in triadic forms. They avoid claims about what is "essential" and "inessential". They also avoid, in an interesting way, "we" or "for us" claims. Scriptural Reasoning and Receptive Ecumenism tend not to seek common ground in the face of difference. Instead they tend to produce forms of thought which describe difference in ways that preserve long-term disagreements.

This might appear a rather meagre benefit. After all, it is no great shock to those engaged in ecumenical dialogue to discover that Catholics affirm, but Orthodox deny, the *filioque*. Likewise it is no great surprise to those engaged in inter-faith encounter to learn that Muslims deny, but Christians affirm, the divinity of Jesus.

There are two benefits. The first is that Scriptural Reasoning and Receptive Ecumenism tend not to pursue strategies for agreement, whether of the "conservative" kind (through documents with approved forms of words) or the "liberal" (which aggressively identify a common "essential" core and treat differences as "inessential"). Instead they pursue strategies for long-term disagreement, in which binary claims are preserved in triadic forms. The second is that the triadic forms tend to stimulate new investigations. The claim "I am right and you are wrong" stimulates a rather limited investigation. I seek to demonstrate my rightness and your wrongness. The criteria for judging my rightness and your wrongness will most likely be uniform. If I adopt a triadic form, "I affirm, you deny" then this permits more sophisticated approaches. The binary form "X is true or false" requires X to be univocal. The claim "I affirm X; you deny X" normally indicates that X is univocal, but this is not necessarily so. I might mean something different by X from you. The case of the *filioque* is instructive. This appears to be a case in which Catholics affirm, but Orthodox deny, X. But as every student of theology knows, it is not straightforwardly true that what Catholics affirm, the Orthodox deny. Catholics affirm something about God's love in affirming "and the Son". The Spirit here is an expression of a relation of love. The Orthodox affirm something about the Father's authority when they affirm "from the Father". They do not take themselves to be denying something about God's love when omitting "and the Son". Catholics and Orthodox are affirming different things when they include or omit the *filioque*. This is a commonplace in the study of theology. To say "X is true or false" in this case is highly misleading. To say "C affirm X; O deny X" is misleading if X is taken univocally. But the triadic form permits equivocation in a way the binary form does not. A failure to equivocate over the *filioque* is arguably a failure to understand Catholic and Orthodox doctrine. *Triadic forms stimulate investigation into equivocation.*

A Christian-Muslim conversation can clarify some further benefits of this way of proceeding. Take the claims "Jesus is divine and human" and "Muhammad is a prophet". These are binary claims as they stand:

they assign a value to a variable. They can be easily rendered in triadic forms:

Christians affirm "Jesus is divine and human".
Muslims deny "Jesus is divine and human".

This case is fairly straightforward.

Muslims affirm "Muhammad is a prophet".
Christians do not affirm "Muhammad is a prophet".

This case is more complex, because "Muhammad is a prophet" is not a claim on which Christian doctrine typically takes a view. The two cases, about Jesus and about Muhammad, are thus not of the same kind. A further triadic clarification is needed.

It is axiomatic for Christians that Jesus is divine and human.
It is axiomatic for Muslims that Jesus is not divine and human.
It is axiomatic for Muslims that Muhammad is a prophet.
It is hypothetical for Christians that Muhammad is a prophet.

This triadic form does not stimulate investigation, for Muslims, into whether Jesus is divine: it shows that such investigation is not needed, because there is nothing introduced that might unsettle the axiom. But it does stimulate investigation, for Christians, into whether Muhammad is a prophet. Such investigation is, in this case, unlikely to lead to a consensus in Christian theology, although it might provoke some interesting sermons. The prophethood of Muhammad is likely to remain a hypothetical matter. That suggests that it is unlikely to become an axiom for Christians that Muhammad is not a prophet. This has very significant benefits for inter-faith engagement. It is not possible to achieve the same level of sophistication with binary claims. Consider the following four:

Muhammad is a prophet.
Muhammad is not a prophet.
Muhammad may be a prophet.
Muhammad may not be a prophet.

The second and fourth claims are not innocuous for Muslims. Any Christian who utters them is assigning a value to a variable in a way that will make conversation prickly, to say the least. Sometimes such prickliness is appropriate or at least unavoidable. But in this case it is eminently avoidable. To say, "it is hypothetical for Christians that Muhammad is a prophet" is to suspend the assigning of a value to a variable. It does not make any claim about Muhammad. The binary forms cannot avoid making such a claim, however optative its mood. The triadic form permits a theological investigation of a noticeably different kind.

An issue of trust underlies this difference. It will be difficult to sustain trust in conversation if it appears that a participant is not saying what he really believes. Many Muslims are taught, disastrously, that Christians deny that Muhammad is a prophet. This teaching is vague: it is not clear whether it is an empirical claim ("some Christians deny it") or a grammatical claim ("to be Christian is to deny it"). It is a dangerous teaching because it can insinuate the grammatical claim (which is false) by proving the empirical claim (which is true). If a Christian is asked a question in a binary form, "Is Muhammad a prophet?", any answer in a corresponding binary form is likely to be problematic. A Christian who affirms it may appear a liar; one who denies it is no friend; one who says "He may be" is making the best of a bad binary job (and probably sounds a bit shifty). By contrast, a triadic form offers a rather different complexion: "For Christians, this is a question that merits investigation". This is obviously not a lie; it is not unfriendly; and it is not shifty. It keeps the conversation going, which is no small matter, and in such a way that the participants are likely to learn more about each other's theologies. Triadic forms may promote peace, at the same time as they not only permit but require members of traditions to remain true to their traditions.

Positive and Negative Truth Claims

Scriptural Reasoning and Receptive Ecumenism are practices which tend to privilege positive truth claims and to be suspicious about negative ones. This might appear to be a sign of their lamentable wishy-washiness—an indication that they lack backbone in the face of difficult conversations. Perhaps participants are just too polite to speak plainly, and for this reason such practices just delay the inevitable and are best avoided. That is possible. But it may, more positively, be a consequence of attending to triadic forms. When judgements are offered in a binary form, an affirmation entails the denial of its negation. "Jesus is divine and human" entails denying "Jesus is not divine and human". This case is straightforward. When judgements are offered in a triadic form, however, entailment works differently. "Muslims affirm the prophethood of Muhammad" does not entail "Christians deny the prophethood of Muhammad". There is no entailment at all: triadic forms stimulate investigation rather than offering *a priori* judgements. "Jews privilege law" does not entail "Jews refuse grace". There is no entailment; there is only a possible investigation into Jewish understandings of law and grace.

This latter case is worth considering further. The Council of Trent articulates its canons on justification in a properly binary fashion:

> [Canon] 1. If anyone says that a person can be justified before God by his own works, done either by the resources of human nature or by the

teaching of the law, apart from divine grace through Jesus Christ: let him be anathema.[10]

This is properly binary because its function is to regulate theological claims; it quite properly assigns a value. Its explicit task is to clarify Catholic doctrine in the face of Protestant challenges. The first canon is interesting, in this regard, because it would be hard to find a Catholic or a Protestant who might contradict it. The important point is that claims made in such a binary fashion, such as this canon, make no claims about what people believe. This Catholic canon makes no claims about Protestants or indeed about Jews. Those who drafted it certainly intended that Jews be anathema. They were doubtless certain that Jews refused divine grace through Jesus Christ. Yet the canon itself makes no such claim: it is not a statement about what Jews do or do not believe. The canon can be cast in a triadic form: "For Catholics it is axiomatic that if anyone . . ." No further claims are entailed by it.

The problematic claim "Jews say a person can be justified . . . apart from divine grace through Jesus Christ" has a triadic form: it specifies for whom a statement holds true. This claim, however, is not entailed by the canon expressed in binary form. To cast that canon in triadic form can only yield a claim about what Catholics believe, because it is a Catholic canon. The only canon that could be cast in a triadic form to express a claim about what Jews believe would be a Jewish canon. A Catholic canon that said, God forbid, "Jews say a person can be justified . . . apart from divine grace through Jesus Christ" still has a binary form. It can be cast triadically, but this will be informative in a rather different way: "For Catholics it is axiomatic that Jews say a person can be justified . . . apart from divine grace through Jesus Christ." One is still unable to generate a triadic claim about Jewish belief: it can only produce a binary claim about Jews and a triadic claim about Catholics. Other essays in this collection, especially those by David Ford and Paul Murray, draw attention to the ways in which documents from the Second Vatican Council contrast with, if not contradict, the claims of previous documents, including those of the Council of Trent. It would be a travesty to attempt to generate triadic claims about contemporary Catholicism on the basis of those older documents. But my deeper point is that even those older documents offer resources for inter-faith and ecumenical encounter when one is equipped with intellectual tools relating to binary and triadic forms.

It is in this sense that Scriptural Reasoning and Receptive Ecumenism are reserved about negative claims. By negative I mean the identification of some shortcoming or deficiency. Triadic forms are typically generated by taking binary forms and specifying for whom the claims hold true or false. This

---

[10] Council of Trent—1545–1563: Session 6 (13 January 1547), Canons concerning justification, in Norman P. Tanner, SJ (ed), *Decrees of the Ecumenical Councils*, vol. II: *Trent to Vatican II* (London: Sheed & Ward and Washington, DC: Georgetown University Press, 1990), p. 679.

requires a statement made by someone; the triadic form specifies that someone. *Triadic forms that are not produced in this way are suspect for Scriptural Reasoning and Receptive Ecumenism.* Catholic claims about Protestants have a binary form; Christian claims about Muslims have a binary form: they assign a value to a variable. Catholic claims about what Protestants believe admittedly have a triadic form. But it is crucial how this is generated. If it is produced from a Protestant claim, it has the character of reported speech, and is likely to command Protestant assent: "Yes, we do believe that". But these are likely to be positive claims: "Only by faith. . . . only by scripture . . ." It is easy enough to produce negative claims, of the kind "Protestants have an inadequate account of sacraments". But this has a binary form. A triadic form is also relatively easy to produce: "It is axiomatic for Protestants that X". This will require some prior investigation, for sure. But it is a positive claim, not a negative one. Even the claim "It is axiomatic for Protestants that not-X" is a positive claim in this sense. The attempt to produce, in a triadic form, a negative claim about another tradition, in the sense of specifying its deficiencies, is much more difficult. It is difficult to identify deficiencies in Jewish thinking, by producing triadic claims about what Jews believe about grace, without a great deal of investigation into Jewish claims about grace. This is rather rare.

Typically, Christian statements about Jewish belief will turn out to be statements of Christian belief. They are thus informative, but perhaps not in the way that those who make them intend. They are properly triadic. If they are produced by specifying the "for whom" of a binary statement made by Jews they will tend to be positive. If they are produced by specifying the "for whom" of a binary statement made by Christians, then their proper form will be "Christians believe that Jews believe that . . .". These may well be negative, in the sense specified above, but for practitioners of Scriptural Reasoning and Receptive Ecumenism, they will tend to be treated as guides to Christian rather than Jewish belief. It is for these reasons that Scriptural Reasoning and Receptive Ecumenism tend to privilege positive claims about other traditions: negative claims are easily produced but they are uninformative, or at least they are not informative in the way that those who utter them intend.

Three Grades of Long-Term Disagreement

Scriptural Reasoning and Receptive Ecumenism share a pragmatic repair of certain tendencies in modern philosophy. These tendencies have long been diagnosed and addressed in philosophy itself from the late eighteenth century onwards, but at a more popular level they are persistent and in the cases of inter-faith and ecumenical encounter they are damaging. This repair, in Scriptural Reasoning and Receptive Ecumenism, concerns the handling of doubt and certainty, a higher tolerance of provisionality, and a facility in handling triadic as well as binary forms. I want to end by elaborating three grades of long-term disagreement, focusing on the positive possibilities that accompany the pragmatic repair, in ascending order of sophistication.

The goals of Scriptural Reasoning and Receptive Ecumenism are not primarily those of agreement. They are practices which make deep reasonings public, and which foster understanding and collegiality in the face of enduring differences.[11] The possible forms of understanding and what Murray terms the "call" of learning are multiple, however, and extend to qualities of engagement that have hitherto proven rather rare.

The first grade of engagement might be named simply "claims". In practices of engagement, this level is reached when a member of one tradition can rehearse the claims made by a member of another tradition. The Baptist minister who rehearses the contours of Catholic Eucharistic theology engages at this level. The Muslim who rehearses what Christians mean by "I believe in one God" does the same. This is a significant raising of the level of discussion and mutual understanding between traditions; it has tended hitherto to be confined to those who have undergone formal study of a tradition other than one's own. One of the potential benefits of practices like Scriptural Reasoning and Receptive Ecumenism is that they enable participants to express this form of learning even when their expertise tends to lie (as it does for most theologians, most of the time) in their own traditions. It is no great surprise when a Christian scholar of rabbinical texts displays an understanding of Jewish interpretation of Genesis 22. When a Christian theologian shows such understanding, as a result of the experience of reading Genesis 22 with Jewish interpreters, something rather different has occurred. It is not just a display of learning; indeed it is a rather meagre and unreliable display because it is not rooted in thorough study of the relevant scholarship. It is a decidedly limited display of learning; but it is also an act of collegiality which expresses a changed relation between members of traditions. Part of the promise of Scriptural Reasoning and Receptive Ecumenism is their provision of occasions where members of one tradition learn to rehearse the claims of members of other traditions. As I suggested above, these will often be claims expressed quite properly in binary forms, which can then generate triadic forms in which various small-scale investigations can be launched.

The second grade of engagement might be named "conflicts". In practices like Scriptural Reasoning and Receptive Ecumenism, this level is reached when a member of one tradition can identify and rehearse disagreements within another tradition. A Catholic theologian who can rehearse disagreements within Reformed theology over the doctrine of election engages at this level. The Christian theologian who can rehearse rival accounts of Tawhid in

---

[11] See Nicholas Adams, "Making Deep Reasonings Public", *Modern Theology*, 22:3 (July 2006), pp. 385–401; *id.* "Scriptural Reasoning and Interfaith Hermeneutics", in David Cheetham, Ulrich Winkler and Oddbjørn Leirvik (eds), *Interreligious Hermeneutics in Pluralistic Europe: Between Texts and People* (Amsterdam: Rodopi, 2011), pp. 59–78.

medieval Islamic thought does the same. This is obviously a deeper and more sophisticated form of engagement, and it is also rather riskier. Forms of inter-faith and ecumenical engagement sometimes generate a temporary unity within denominations, for example, especially when there are more fundamental differences with other traditions in view. For a member of such another tradition to disrupt this temporary unity, by reintroducing the conflicts that have been suspended, can prove surprising and unsettling. It also deepens engagements in various ways. To know another tradition's conflicts is to be able to identify nuances that might permit more fruitful forms of collegiality. Engagements between Christians and Muslims which focus on the oneness of God have a different character if the Muslim participants are familiar with internal Christian conflicts over the Trinity and if the Christian participants are able to rehearse different and perhaps rival strands in the medieval Islamic traditions. Again this is a commonplace in scholarly discussions between experts. The promise of Scriptural Reasoning and Receptive Ecumenism is to introduce conversation at this level of sophistication between those whose primary focus of scholarship is their own tradition.

The third grade of engagement might be named "obscurities". Each tradition has its settled habits of speech and action, the beaten paths through familiar territory and the deep grammars on which one draws to negotiate the strange and the new. But each tradition also has its blind spots: those areas of expression where language is stretched to breaking point, zones of experimentation, paradox and wilful self-contradiction. These are found in the mystical traditions, in negative theology, in the more speculative regions of philosophy, in the areas of theology that, in those traditions that practise or have practised censorship, are considered too dangerous for popular teaching. Areas of obscurity show up where experience contradicts the deep grammars, and where mutating social forms stimulate descriptions that extend beyond the reach of settled categories. In these cases certain voices of authority may insist all the more strongly on the familiar categories, and refuse to acknowledge any reality that cannot be cast in the old language; but in the long run this rarely proves satisfactory. Languages change, in spite of those who refuse to let them. The latter turn out not to be conservatives but dangerous innovators who speak undead words, uttering incantations strangely frozen in a state of arrested development. At the same time human wickedness has shown itself agile and adaptable down the ages and it is often the deep grammars and the settled categories of religious traditions that act as a brake on their wild and destructive adventures. It is a matter of obscurity whether a tradition is facing a new and strange expression of the good or yet another cunning face of human sin. Theological debates over political forms, sexual practices, and medical interventions are often marked by conflicts between deep grammars and new words, and by categories being stretched and shrunk as they are pressed into unfamiliar use. The third grade of engagement is reached when a member of one tradition is able to identify and rehearse the obscurities that mark another tradition. This is not a simple matter of rehearsing a tradition's claims, or even of tracing the course of its conflicts. It is to give voice to its obscure utterances, to participate as a stranger in its attempts to say the unsayable. This is an experience found most commonly in literary historians who learn to inhabit the poetry of the past. It is as yet a largely untapped potential of Scriptural Reasoning and Receptive Ecumenism: mutual engagements between the mystical traditions are nonetheless on the horizon and it will be interesting to see how they develop.

In conclusion, the philosophical shapes displayed in Scriptural Reasoning and Receptive Ecumenism have a reparative character, at least initially, as they work to re-tool a new generation of ecumenical and inter-faith practitioners. Old habits of foundationalist method and a leaden pursuit of neutral ground pose deep problems for encounter between traditions, and Scriptural Reasoning and Receptive Ecumenism offer better pragmatic models to facilitate engagement. Those philosophical shapes, which foster a facility in handling binary and triadic forms, harbour other more-than-reparative possibilities, however. They hold out a range of new modes of interaction, including the three grades of engagement elaborated here. Time will tell how generative they prove to be as the world's religious traditions learn new ways of living with their long-term disagreements.

Modern Theology 29:4 October 2013
ISSN 0266-7177 (Print)
ISSN 1468-0025 (Online)

DOI: 10.1111/moth.12068

IN THE BALANCE: INTERIOR AND SHARED ACTS OF READING

FRANCIS X. CLOONEY, SJ

I recently completed a book entitled, *His Hiding Place Is Darkness*.[1] In it, I read the *Song of Songs*, along with some Hindu mystical poetry from South India, each guided by medieval commentators of its tradition. By way of an introduction to these reflections on Comparative Theology in relation to Scriptural Reasoning and Receptive Ecumenism, I take my book as a reference point as to where we find ourselves with respect to the questions raised in this volume about interreligious learning, text and conversation, and responsibility in Catholic and other Christian communities.

It is first of all a book about the Biblical *Song of Songs*, that most beautiful book of the Bible, love poetry that tells, indeed enacts, the story of this young woman and her beloved, their moments of intense union, their separations and her several searches for him. It shows us human love in all its frailty, the fragility of being together and being apart, seeking one another, having moments of unity and then it falling apart. It is all the more remarkable because it is a sublime religious text in which God is never mentioned. Yet, throughout the traditions of Jewish and Christian commentary from the early centuries of the church, it has been understood as the story of God and the soul. God, mentioned nowhere, is found to be everywhere: in their desire, in her words and those of her lover, in their separations and moments of union. If you want to know what it is like to love God, turn to the *Song*. The drama of love and its interruptions heighten the reader's awareness of God's presence even in absence. The scenes of absence and longing in the *Song* captivate me also because, as poetry and drama, they open an imaginative space we

Francis X. Clooney, SJ
Harvard Divinity School, 45 Francis Avenue, Cambridge, MA, 02138, USA
Email: fclooney@hds.harvard.edu

[1] Forthcoming, Stanford University Press.

ourselves must fill. Read theologically, hers is an account of a God who comes and goes, a lover who, near and present, is also absent, hiding. To be faithful and loving is not simply to possess God all the time, but rather to be in the presence of a great mystery: God is also like the lover who comes in the night—or, when expected, fails to appear. This has also fascinated me as a theme for commentary in the Christian tradition, and so I have been reading the *Song* with the commentary/sermons of St Bernard of Clairvaux, Gilbert of Hoyland, and John of Ford.

All this is just part of my book. I have recognized that I need to make interreligious openness central to my writing, inscribing the religious other inside my thinking as a Christian theologian, during a project and not just as a passing moment or at the end, after refined reflection on Christian tradition. For this, I need to cross the seemingly stark, even closed borders between religions, by also studying another tradition as I would study my own tradition. From early on in my scholarly career I have found it best to enter upon the careful reading of texts of Hindu religious traditions, with an openness, reverence, and critical attention analogous to how I treat the treasures of my own tradition.

In recent years and in the writing of *His Hiding Place is Darkness*, I have in particular been reading great texts of the Srivaishnava Hindu community, which worships Vishnu as the supreme deity and Shri as his eternal divine consort. Beginning in the seventh century, we find a proliferation of beautiful poetry, written in the Tamil language, about Vishnu, and about a natural and human world entirely focused on him. The greatest of these poets was Shatakopan, known for his poetry and particularly for *Tiruvaymoli* (the *Holy Word of Mouth*, henceforth the *Holy Word*). That work is comprised of 1102 verses in praise of Vishnu and Shri, one hundred songs that offer praise, explore the divine nature, rework mythological themes, celebrate specific temples, and retell the story of human love. He dedicates nearly thirty of those hundred songs to a voice of the young woman in love. Like the woman in the *Song*, she too has no proper name and her entire life is given over to this passionate love for God. The beloved may be the transcendent Vishnu or the incarnate Rama or Krishna, but in all this the young woman herself is distinguished by her longing for God. In almost all of these three hundred verses in the voice of this young woman, her beloved is deeply loved and remembered—and absent. Never quite united and at rest with her beloved, she embarks on a long search for him, suffering confusion and distress at his absence. Even at the end of the songs in her voice, she is still distressed. And yet, the poetry is beautiful, and the rendering of her pain in separation is a testimony to the intensity and purity of her love. Here too I am reluctant to read alone, and so I am also reading Shatakopan with the great commentators of the Srivaishnava Hindu tradition of the thirteenth and fourteenth centuries, Tirukurukkai Piran Pillan and Nanjiyar, his student Nampillai, and so too his, Periyavaccan Pillai and Vatakkutiruviti Pillai.

The task I set myself then is to respect my own Catholic tradition and this Hindu tradition together, without settling for a generalization or a theme larger than them both, and without, in our reading, diminishing either merely to glorify the other. The same crisis of love erupts in both traditions, traced in the Jewish and Christian traditions of the *Song* and the Srivaishnava Hindu tradition of the *Holy Word*. In both, the drama of absence is counter to how the tradition's theology predicts things should work out, if God is ever faithful, true, and present. Neither faith nor rational affirmation adequately accounts for this perceived absence of God. Reading these texts together intensifies the experience of longing and confusion, now that one has memories and commitments in one's own tradition and the other as well. This is a practical chemistry, not a theoretical claim about religions. Theorizing, worrying into existence a theology of religions, is in principle a worthy venture, but here it also stands in the way of this particular, close-up learning, engaged *in* and not *about* the other religion. Such an approach allows us, in the free space where the two traditions meet poetically and dramatically, to contemplate the possibility that God is missing and in hiding, the lover hiding amidst today's pluralism.

In carrying out my project and wanting to make evident its theological grounding and relevance for Catholic theology, I appealed in the opening and concluding sections to the theology of Hans Urs von Balthasar. In the seven volumes of *Herrlichkeit*—what we might now call a Theo-Poetics—he explores poetic and literary apprehensions of the beauty by which we apprehend the infusion of divine glory into human experience, imperfectly, eventfully caught in human words. In the five-volume *Theo-Drama*, Balthasar sees the theo-dramatic as distinct from but not contradictory to the theo-logical. Here he cultivates a dramatic understanding of God in the world, attuned to the events of salvation in which our participation is required. God interacts in particular and never entirely predicted ways with the human race. The work of salvation is a drama that must be allowed to play itself out. Would-be spectators are inevitably drawn in, to participate in a drama that becomes their own story as well. Only after these theo-poetic and theo-dramatic practices does one turn (back) to theology *per se*, the *Theo-Logic* in its three volumes.

I take my book to be an instance of religious and interreligious reading guided by Balthasar's insights, a venture on the level of the theo-poetic and theo-dramatic; the woman seeking her beloved is not entirely bound to either tradition, and the theologian cannot neatly separate her or his own plight from hers; caught in the midst of two traditions, it is her job to find her way out, back to the more familiar world of theology as familiarly understood. It is, in other words, a Catholic theology that is a Comparative Theology, indebted to the work of interreligious learning and understanding. Yet in truth it is not clear where such work leads. Its reverence for tradition and traditions notwithstanding, the best comparative theological work is by definition on the edge, written at the margins, on the fault line where two texts of two traditions come to share a proximity that is difficult to decipher, insofar as neither text is to be allowed to dominate the other, neither tradition's mode of reading given absolute priority, and no higher academic perspective permitted to decide what counts in the reading. As the reading deepens, the tension grows, especially when members of the other tradition reinterpret and re-read for us the scriptures of our own tradition—and when a growing understanding of and affinity for the "other" text changes our own relationship to a more familiar text of our own tradition, and thus begins to create a new community among those willing to engage in this reading.

Questions therefore arise. How do I connect this relatively rarified research back to the mainstream of Christian theology? What kinds of reading practices and interreligious engagement across differences, enacted by whom, can count as Catholic theology? Where is there room for the back and forth of ideas and reactions among believers in the Christian and (in this case) Hindu traditions? How does it relate to lived interreligious exchange, and the back and forth possible when people of two traditions sit down together?[2]

As I understand it, this issue of Modern Theology is itself a step toward an answer, since it seems now that Comparative Theology cannot fight the battle for theological legitimacy on its own. Let us now find our way through the essays, and how they help us deal with the several issues I raise in mentioning my book and the particular, intense problems it raises regarding what counts as theology in any of its particular denominational forms. The best place to start is David Ford's essay, which gives an artful overview of the interconnections of reading practices, Scriptural Reasoning included, in the context of the aftermath of Vatican II, and brings Comparative Theology into the conversation. Lindbeck's dour judgment, cited by Ford but worth citing again here, reminds us of what had been left undone after the Council, and at what cost:

> With the disbandment of the Council, there were no environments in which its reading practices could propagate . . . Those skills were present in abundance, but their existence as identifiable, rule-governed and deliberately transmissible behaviour was unknown . . . Recognition, contrary to modern biases, that theory must grow out of practice, not the other way around, is a key to this progress.[3]

---

[2] See also my "Comparative Theology and Inter-Religious Dialogue", in Catherine Cornille (ed), *The Wiley-Blackwell Companion to Inter-Religious Dialogue* (Malden, MA: Wiley-Blackwell, 2013), pp. 51–63.

[3] George Lindbeck, "Progress in Textual Reasoning: From Vatican II to the Conference at Drew", in Peter Ochs and Nancy Levene (eds), *Textual Reasonings: Jewish Philosophy and Text Study at the End of the Twentieth Century* (London: SCM Press, 2002), p. 257; Cited in Ford, p. 96.

We are still in a position of needing to learn how to read properly, and for the communities to which we belong.[4]

While there are Catholic practitioners of Scriptural Reasoning, it seems that Anglican and Protestant Christians are still more likely to be participants in Scriptural Reasoning. Reflection on why this is the case has served to uncover complexities that underlie even the seemingly self-evident value of coming together in the reading of scripture. Readers know that we Catholics have our own complicated relation to the Bible, including old instincts to prefer Bible histories, and other secondary summaries of Biblical texts, catechisms and ecclesial documents, and modern challenges in trying to respect Biblical scholarship while yet not divorcing theology from its responsibilities to the Bible. Catholics, self-conscious as a community with its own long, long habits of doing certain things in certain ways, tend also to a sense of Catholic difference and exception—as in standing at the edge of the World Council of Churches, for instance, and not joining as a regular member. It is not surprising that a Catholic view of Scriptural Reasoning will raise questions about what (else) is included in Scriptural Reasoning or in the broader work we might call "reasoning together religiously". How do tradition and doctrine matter, when a first-hand conversation about scripture is the project of the day? While Ford makes the case for the positive contribution of participants with Catholic ecclesial and theological sensitivities to Scriptural Reasoning, he does also offer this caution:

> Scriptural Reasoning does not have a Vatican-like official consensus; it is a varied practice that embraces many arguments, debates and ongoing disagreements. It creates a space for relating across such differences in ways that allow participants to be true to their own traditions. This continually raises awkward, often irresolvable, questions, and, whilst there is no pressure for them to be resolved consensually, integrity requires that the questions be faced.[5]

David Dault, though sympathetic with the goals of close and shared reading, helpfully brings a certain skepticism to the conversation, wondering aloud whether Catholic theology can comfortably accommodate practices of

---

[4] Ford overgeneralizes in assuming that Scriptural Reasoning and Comparative Theology had to grow up outside tradition-specific institutions: "it is no accident that Scriptural Reasoning and Comparative Theology have, as mentioned above, been nurtured in settings not controlled by one tradition, where there is both theology and religious studies, and students and staff come from many religions and none. These are quite rare niches in the academic world, and in fact contain many Catholic students and academics" (Ford, p. 113). My own work in Comparative Theology is deeply indebted to more than my two decades of teaching in the Theology Department at Boston College, a Roman Catholic institution. My Comparative Theology developed there, nowhere else. My eight years at Harvard have mattered much less to my theology, its academic environment less conducive to a truly interreligious theology, and indeed to all matters theological.

[5] Ford, p. 117.

reading the sacred text "by itself". Attention to scripture, as laudable as it is, must in the Catholic context still be connected with due respect for learning from tradition, the Magisterium, and doctrine. Dault is concerned that Scriptural Reasoning not be too closely linked to a (Protestant) *sola scriptura* remedy that puts aside values essential in the Catholic context. One cannot put doctrine aside, nor read scripture apart from the church and its rules for where reading begins and ends. He is likewise uneasy with any simple differentiation of the Jew-Christian-Muslim, as if each, or any of the three, is a single simple reality. He urges us to remember that there are problems inside Christianity that require us to keep using words such as Protestant and Catholic, even in Scriptural Reasoning, until the mending within the church takes place.

In the end, Dault holds out for an analogous "Catholic Reasoning":

All of these experiments in Catholic preparatory reasoning are text-based, but the documents that form the texts of study are not necessarily scripture. Where scripture is studied, this study occurs with tools like the New Jerome Commentary and the documents on Biblical interpretation. In all cases, then, these experiments in Catholic Reasoning take seriously the desire expressed through the Council that exegesis and catechesis occur within the clear framework of the Magisterium of the Church.[6]

Dault also cautions against too general an apprehension of the tradition where doctrines arise:

This form of preparatory reasoning has cognates in Textual and Qur'anic Reasoning, but cannot simply be collapsed into "Christian" reasoning. In an attempt to think through this difficulty, I have suggested that the proper starting point for any praxis of Catholic Reasoning must be in the reparative hope of deep healing/*tikkun olam* shared by Catholicism and Scriptural Reasoning, rather than in a specific text or textual methodology.[7]

This sound advice notwithstanding, it seems to me that a characteristically Catholic Reasoning need not be imagined as so very different from Comparative Theology and Scriptural Reasoning, as if these disciplines can and should operate independently, apart from Catholic theology. The price would surely be too high. A "Catholic Reasoning", were it entirely distinctive, would not of itself be adequate to conversations with Anglicans and Protestants, Jews and Muslims, and so we must ask where else Catholics would hope to find the hospitable ground for interreligious and ecumenical

---

[6] Dault, p. 60.
[7] *Ibid.*, pp. 60–61.

conversations "outside" the Catholic Church. Since we are now talking about ways of reading, appeals to natural theology and apologetics, both traditional ways to mark off common ground, here will not suffice. The goal is to seek out ways in which Scriptural Reasoning and Comparative Theology will flourish as Catholic ways of learning. It is here perhaps that Receptive Ecumenism plays an added role, enabling Christians of various backgrounds to talk among themselves regarding the implications of ways of learning more at home in one Christian tradition than another, and yet still, clearly, Christian.

Where then do reading, doctrine, and tradition connect, for Catholics? Kevin Hughes steps back and offers historical background, a view to the long lead-up to Vatican II and the rediscovery of exegesis in a Catholic way. He emphasizes the practice of interpretation as it has occurred in the church, but also, in recent decades, with the same dearth of detail noted by Lindbeck. Hughes writes that

> while the Second Vatican Council's clarion call to engage the wider world in *Gaudium et Spes* and *Nostra Aetate* opened the doors for Catholics to engage other religious communions in dialogue, the call itself did not present Catholics with any particular models or rules for engagement. However, when this invitation is taken together with the deep scriptural logic recovered for the Catholic Church through the tireless work of de Lubac and Daniélou, Catholics can recover the internal resources, the "deep reasonings", that allow them to come to the Abrahamic tent of meeting with fitting gifts.[8]

He continues: "That is, it is not only that the fruits of *ressourcement* have given Catholics a way of joining the conversation; even more, they may bring particular gifts that help to advance the work of Scriptural Reasoning in a productive way"[9]—and a Catholic way. The reader of scripture is an active interpreter, yet works within the living community of the church. Even if one cannot discount appropriate cautions about what counts as the Bible that is to be shared by Jews and Christians, the very fact of such debates, as well as Catholic and Protestant debates on the same topic, suggest that differences here are not insurmountable obstacles. The text lives in community, and the text by itself is never the sole factor to take into account. Even the most dedicated practitioners of Scriptural Reasoning bring more than the scripture to the conversation.

Michael Barnes too notes the important work done before the Council leading up to its very important change in the style of Catholic conversation. He also offers a masterful review of Vatican II's rich legacy, stressing the

---

[8] Hughes, p. 33.
[9] *Ibid.*

Council's fresh insight into the centrality of the Word of God for the lived reality of the church—ever and already God's dialogue with God's people. In this situation, tradition aids us to read better. Reading within the heart of the church can and should affect directly the practice of dialogue, and support an appreciation of Scriptural Reasoning and Comparative Theology in its text-grounded form. The values proposed in *Nostra Aetate* become practical in accord with *Dei Verbum*, which insists that reading, tradition, and insight go together:

> Tradition, and the Magisterium which serves that tradition, are not inde-
> pendent sources of truth but intrinsically related to the revealing power
> of the "sacred page" as it is read, prayed, studied and celebrated in the
> life of the church. In these terms *DV* is not so much a new theological
> synthesis of the sources of revelation for a new age as it is a meditation
> on the church's experience of being formed and transformed through
> the Word of God which goes on speaking in the world of human
> experience.[10]

We witness here a great conversation extending itself outward, Catholicism's "catholic" instinct at work. Comparative Theology makes a useful contribution here, I can add, since its work is never limited to scripture, nor is it supportive of any theology or doctrine cut off from the literary dimensions of the texts in question.

Mike Higton deepens still further the reflection on doctrine pursued by Hughes and Barnes, and with an acute sense of the inner requirements of Catholic tradition. He emphasizes the Catholic tolerance for the necessary creativity and fluidity of imagination intrinsic to how that reading takes place, as in the tradition of *lectio divina*. He also helps us to unknot concerns about doctrine, lest doctrine seem, for better or worse, to stand outside the realm where the practices of reading occur. Indeed,

> doctrinal theology [can] itself be envisaged as a practice of devout scrip-
> tural reading. Renewed engagement with scripture since Vatican II has,
> after all, deeply shaped Catholic doctrinal or dogmatic theology—not
> simply in the sense that such theology now draws more intensively on the
> results of Biblical exegesis and criticism, but in the sense that the practice
> of such theology is (for some, at least) becoming inseparable from the kind
> of ruminative, contemplative steeping in scripture found in *lectio divina*.[11]

It is here that doctrinal claims find their rightful place, from and for the sake of reading: "they emerge from [the *lectio*] and discipline its continuation, and

---

[10] Barnes, p. 18.
[11] Higton, p. 121.

they are properly understood by tracing that emergence and participating in that continuation."[12] Accordingly for a reading to be truly dialogical, we need "Christian doctrinal theologians steeped in the practices of scriptural reading that constitute their discipline" and ready to devote "attention to the way the words run in particular scriptural texts".[13] It is here that good theology and Scriptural Reasoning—and Comparative Theology—meet.

Higton finds that Comparative Theology shows the way here, for its reflective nature makes possible its "relatively greater ability to treat matters of doctrine, in comparison to Scriptural Reasoning". Here the individual and distinctive intentions of the comparativist become assets in the reading and in the retrieval of doctrine:

> The individual theologian, who intuits an intriguing resemblance that might be worth pursuing can set his own agenda; he can organise the ruminative reading that is the heartbeat of Comparative Theology's method around his perception of resemblance, and explore assiduously whatever texts allow him to probe it more deeply. It is this freedom to explore wherever the resemblance leads that makes possible the achievements of Comparative Theology—and where the resemblances intuited are doctrinal, it is this freedom that makes possible its fresh insights into doctrinal claims.[14]

Doctrine is valuably intertwined with the purifying practices of dialogue: "The most urgent question that arises from a consideration of the relationship between Christian doctrine and Scriptural Reasoning is not, therefore, about the propriety of supplementing doctrinal reading with a practice of interfaith reading". Rather,

> it is about the depth and resilience of the practice of doctrinally-disciplined reading itself. Am I, as a Christian doctrinal theologian who would expose my doctrinal understanding to the testing and purification made possible in this inter-faith encounter, deeply enough formed in practices of devout scriptural reading and in fine-grained attentiveness to the connection between doctrinal claims and those practices of reading? If I am not, then my doctrinal understanding will be inappropriately insulated from the challenges of reading with others; it will not be questioned and tested and cast into new light by their insistent differences, and neither will my religious difference from them be as fully present in the dialogue as it could and should be.[15]

---

[12] *Ibid.*
[13] *Ibid.*
[14] *Ibid.*, p. 125.
[15] *Ibid.*, p. 135.

These several perspectives and insights pay off in the fact that distinctively Catholic traditions of reading already have within them resources for honoring authority and doctrine in the church, yet in a way that does not betray the obligations and fruits of reading. Indeed, attention to tradition makes for better reading—as I discovered in writing my book, as I learned to complicate my encounter with the *Song* and the *Holy Word*, by reading with Bernard, Nanjiyar and their heirs. So there is no reason to insist that a Catholic participant in Scriptural Reasoning cannot benefit from *both* a Catholic sensitivity *and* the creativity and openness necessary for a constructive reading. Higton aids us in sorting out the relation of Scriptural Reasoning and Comparative Theology, two practices that are neither identical—just as neither of them is identical with interreligious dialogue—nor in competition, as if a preference for one of them entirely rules out attention to the other.

However strong a case may be made for a Catholic appreciation of reading and study, such as would support Comparative Theology and Scriptural Reasoning, one has also to confront the issue of the variety of Christian views of what should count as theology and the resources of theology. Catholics are among a larger group of Christians who ponder these issues. At a deep level, Scriptural Reasoning and a comparative theological project such as the one with which I began this response both expect and instigate an intra-Christian conversation around the differences that surely become evident when real learning from other religious traditions begins to occur. Paul Murray makes explicit the beneficial links between Scriptural Reasoning, Comparative Theology, and Receptive Ecumenism, eloquently arguing for the common ground among these three disciplines, and ways they can complement one another. He points us to the interplay between shared reading and shared Eucharist, the former enhancing the possibility of the latter. Our present context is "one in which some Christian traditions find themselves incapable of breaking the bread of Eucharist together", and it is here that a recognition of our ability to break

> the nourishing word of hallowed scripture across and between such divisions is highly significant. Alongside the opportunities this affords for real learning in the here and now, it can act as counterbalance to any unintended possibility there might be of Receptive Ecumenism focusing narrowly on the purely structural and pragmatic without due attention being given both to the primary context of spiritual and religious life such structures serve and to the forms of sustenance already available *in via*.[16]

The practice of reading both needs and enhances the still richer possibilities of Eucharistic sharing.

---

[16] Murray, p. 89.

Murray rightly notes the elite nature of Comparative Theology as a discipline with higher demands on its practitioners, and he helpfully notes ways in which this theology might be opened up to a more dialogical and less restrictive mode of proceeding. It strikes me that one reason for the solitary nature of Comparative Theology is that so few Catholics engage in it, and among those who do, the chosen examples are so diverse that collaborative work is rare: one may be reading Srivaishnava Hindu material; another, medieval Islamic texts; and a third, something from Japanese Zen. Indeed, some of those who talk critically or positively about Comparative Theology in a more accessible fashion do not actually study any tradition other than their own. Such talking-about Comparative Theology misses the point of the discipline, since it occurs and can be understood only in the course of the actual study of two traditions read together. My sense is that Scriptural Reasoning and Receptive Ecumenism too are hard to understand for those who look upon them from afar.[17]

Nicholas Adams, drawing on Murray, argues on more strictly philosophical grounds the value, in both Scriptural Reasoning and Receptive Ecumenism, of the respect for differences. Both disciplines notice, respect, and preserve differences without permitting them to be used to divide or create antagonistic oppositions. Scriptural Reasoning and Receptive Ecumenism "avoid claims about what is 'essential' and 'inessential' ".[18] Scriptural Reasoning and Receptive Ecumenism also avoid, in a fruitful way, "we" or "for us" claims. Scriptural Reasoning and Receptive Ecumenism do not merely seek common ground in the face of difference. Instead they cultivate forms of thought that describe difference in ways that preserve long-term disagreements. Indeed, "they pursue strategies for long-term disagreement, in which binary claims are preserved in triadic forms", which "do not adjudicate truth claims at all" but preserve the "act of assigning without modification", adding only the specification that identifies "who assigns the value to the variable".[19] These modest interpretive forms "tend to stimulate new investigations".[20] Adams recognizes the need for a new way forward, since "[o]ld habits of foundationalist method and a leaden pursuit of neutral ground pose deep problems for encounter between traditions", while "Scriptural Reasoning and Receptive Ecumenism offer better pragmatic models to facilitate engagement".[21]

---

[17] I likewise welcome Murray's emphasis the healing work of "repair"—akin to Dault's "deep healing". Even if Comparative Theology has not stressed this social responsibility as much as it might, there is no reason why comparative theological study cannot be more explicit in its social responsibility, as long as it keeps its theological edge and is not held to a higher standard than other theological disciplines.

[18] Adams, p. 164.

[19] *Ibid.*, p. 163.

[20] *Ibid.*, p. 164.

[21] *Ibid.*, p. 171.

The pragmatism common to Scriptural Reasoning and Receptive Ecumenism seems also to fit Comparative Theology and even, I would add, a broader array of practical Catholic theologies. Most of the essays collected here testify that Comparative Theology, Scriptural Reasoning, and Receptive Ecumenism also involve personal change; even noticing differences and refining attitudes toward such differences also changes those who have noticed and honored the differences. Learning to live with the fact of other claims, negotiated differently, leads quickly to changes in how one relates to one's own work as well, even when one has "gone back to" an "ordinary" theological project that has no noticeable interreligious dimension to it.

Working with more practical instances, Tracy Tiemeier reminds us that every kind of study benefits from accountability and response; Comparative Theology needs counterparts such as interreligious dialogue and Scriptural Reasoning, as correctives to comparisons that are too comfortable. When Tiemeier speaks to the practical limits of Scriptural Reasoning and Comparative Theology, she does so in the context of pointing out dangers and limits inherent even in efforts at dialogue. Her essay lifts up failures familiar to all of us, when (in class, in writing, in dialogue) seemingly sound choices about what to study are found objectionable or simply uninteresting. Many dialogues fall short because interest and vitality are not where one expects them to be, but somewhere else. The failed dialogues she notes serve as a caution for theologians in any specialization; study and conversation often fall short when bereft of controls and without the opportunity for the negative feedback arising in honest and open dialogues. Tiemeier may therefore be seen as supportive of the dialogical nature of Scriptural Reasoning, actually sitting together and actually learning from one another where correction and question are likely. I agree with her cautions regarding any theology that has no such safeguards built in, including any comparative theological project that touches upon another tradition lightly and from afar and has no place in it for correction. Reading, interpreting, and theologizing must always have written into them occasions for correction.

Tiemeier warns against too much emphasis on similarity and, if similarities are the goal, the temptation to deceptive productivity:

> Some texts resist comparison. Not every text or juxtaposition can be integrated into (or even held in tension in illuminative ways for) a Comparative Theology. More attention needs to be paid to the process of Comparative Theology in the selection of texts and the exploration of how and why some comparisons 'work' and some do not. To take this into account is to recognize that the comparative theologian cannot squeeze meaning out of any arbitrary juxtaposition. And sometimes a comparison that seems obvious just does not yield any profound insight. To include reflection on 'failures' in the comparative 'experiment' is a more honest approach to Comparative Theology that recognizes the

limits of the theologian to control and produce insight in cross-religious reading.[22]

Of course this is right, but part of the problem may be in the expectation that "comparison" favors similarities, just as it would be misleading to assume that all dialogues must aim at consensus. The reader of texts outside her own tradition will need to attend to the stubborn facts of a text, its meanings, and its refusal to be at the service of a theme alien to what it is really about and how it speaks. Careful reading does indeed have abundant opportunities for correction built into it; it is hard to imagine a comparative theologian who studies texts closely leaving a comparative project with an initial expectation regarding similarities intact. Persons in dialogue may quickly find differences as well as similarities among themselves, and that some topics work better than others; no two texts, studied carefully, merely confirm similarities on a predetermined issue.

All of this is perhaps about the need for a community that draws the reader out of her own small world and settled expectations. Ford speaks well to the value of a community of learning:

> One of the distinctive features of Scriptural Reasoning is that, at its best, it enables participants to go deeper into their own texts, deeper into the texts of others and deeper into the common good of our world. These deepenings can be correlated with *ressourcement, conversazione* and *aggiornamento* respectively, and so can also be found in Vatican II and its legacy. What this might mean and how it might happen more fully is perhaps the core challenge for both Scriptural Reasoning and the Catholic Church today.[23]

This then is a matter of community too, as Ford adds:

> There is also a fourth deepening: the deepening of relationships among those who come together in the first three deepenings. What is true of interreligious learning can also be true of these relationships. Just as awareness and learning can be intensified through the dynamic between oneself, the other and the wider society, so love, friendship and delight in each other can also intensify.[24]

Barnes too notes the intersection of interpretation, the formation of community, and a spiritual appreciation of reading:

> as Chenu reminds us, the prayerful reading of familiar texts makes possible a "look of trust". Philosophical reasoning, a sense of history,

---

[22] Tiemeier, p. 149.
[23] Ford, p. 119.
[24] *Ibid.*

scholarship and learning, preaching and catechesis, and—Paul VI would, no doubt, want to add—the generosity of a never-ending *colloquium* with the wider world: all have a part to play in the theological enterprise.[25]

He rightly adds that what makes these practices cohere as *doctrina sacra* is

not a set of summary propositions, however well-crafted, but the divine pedagogy which enables the community of faith to reconnect with the most vital and formative of memories *and* to be taken forward into further imaginative explorations of the depths of God's providential purposes.[26]

Perhaps we can add that out of the shared reading, "the community" and its counterparts also begin to share in a richer, wider community comprised of some readers from both. The ideal outcome of a book such as *His Hiding Place Is Darkness* is, after all, also the convening of a conversation indebted to two scriptural texts, two traditions of readers, and two bodies of doctrine. Since the community of scholars and students leading up to comparative study is only the beginning and not the end of the communicative process, there is the question of what to do with what one has written; finding readers for comparative theological work, or an audience to hear about scriptural reasons, is of course always an additional challenge.

Anna Bonta Moreland's contribution invites us actually to read together. She prepares us for the actual doing of comparative theological work, as a dialogue that might then open into Scriptural Reasoning and Receptive Ecumenism. She gives us a specific example that might be thought of as the fruits of her own reading back and forth between the Bible and Catholic tradition on the one side, and the Qur'an on the other—or perhaps, Biblical notions of prophecy and the prospect of honoring Muhammad as a prophet. Her essay is more the groundwork of constructive theologian, rather than Comparative Theology, but it is a close relative, making it possible to turn to the Qur'an with more specific questions in mind. Her suggestion is cautious:

The pattern of discussion here is analogical—and I have witnessed it in action in the practice of Scriptural Reasoning. When Muslims revere Jesus as a prophet, they are not revering him as Christians do, and they are not equating this prophetic role with Muhammad's singular one. I suggest that Christians can revere Muhammad as a prophet in a limited and relative sense, not one that Muslims would embrace, but one that Christians nevertheless should consider.[27]

---

[25] Barnes, p. 31.
[26] *Ibid.*
[27] Moreland, p. 73.

Moreland gives us the theological ground, a thesis, with which to look deeper into Islamic sources in relation to the Qur'an.

That is to say, her essay invites us into a comparative theological experiment (by studying Qur'anic texts on prophet and prophecy), the prospect of a case for Scriptural Reasoning (by reading the Christian texts Moreland cites with Jewish and Muslim counterparts, along with prophetic texts of their choosing), and even Receptive Ecumenism (by then bringing fresh insights back to Christian theological conversations on prophecy, in and beyond and after Biblical sources). For any of this, it is necessary next to examine in some detail the *content* of prophetic texts of Muhammad that would speak to a Christian audience, and how this content, honored as prophecy, enables a deeper learning that is still authentically Christian. Moreland admits that she has only begun the project:

> This article is admittedly offered as a prolegomena to an extended Christian analysis of Muhammad's prophecy. And questions linger that need to be addressed: how do we analyze those passages in the Qur'an that contradict the narratives of the Bible?; do Catholics simply accept what coheres with their predetermined beliefs and reject the rest?; what relationship does Muhammad have to prophets in the Hebrew Scriptures? The analogical argument about Muhammad's prophecy developed in this essay opens into these questions. These would pose a way forward in the trajectory of Comparative Theology.[28]

Certainly we can be grateful that these essays have made explicit a whole set of questions regarding how Catholics read the Bible, how the individual reader and community relate, and how Magisterium and community play their role in the consciousness of the individual Catholic who participates in Scriptural Reasoning. As with any issue in interreligious matters, the answer will not lie in a prior, entirely intra-Catholic conversation such as might be wrapped up among Catholics before turning to Scriptural Reasoning or Receptive Ecumenism. As in Comparative Theology, the next steps for the Catholic participant lie in the greater conversations, which should be able both to respect and change how Catholics, among other Christians, think about the Bible and our reading of it.

As for *His Hiding Place is Darkness*, the book with which I began this response: it is clear now that as a work of Comparative Theology it will have its own logic and cogency, in obedience to the texts I was reading throughout its preparation. I sought to root my reading of the *Song* in the medieval Catholic tradition and then to return to Catholic theology by drawing on Balthasar. This was a process that confirms at least the possibility of positive and mutually beneficial transitions from text to tradition, and from tradition

---

[28] *Ibid.*, pp. 74–75.

to explicitly Catholic contemporary theological reflection. At every ste
though, much of the work keeps requiring that one step outside the ordinary
range of Catholic texts and conversations, to read, and read with believers in
other traditions. I do think that my study of the *Song*, a Jewish text before it is
a Christian text, along with a Hindu text to which I do not have any proprietary
rights, is quite possible as a project undertaken by a single reader of both sets
of texts together. But even this reader needs to be mindful of all the ways in
which such a project might stumble and fall short. Nothing is gained by
reading entirely at a distance from the richer dialogical context provided by
Scriptural Reasoning. A particular form of Receptive Ecumenism will also
have to play its role in this work of the reception of the work of the
comparativist, in this instance a Catholic theologian deeply immersed in the
study of Hinduism. The dialogues inherent in Scriptural Reasoning and
Receptive Ecumenism serve to purify and maximize what might be of value in
my comparative theological search into the absence and presence of God in
two traditions. In turn, my work should, at its best, complexify expectations
regarding the participants in Scriptural Reasoning and Receptive Ecumenism,
since they will never today be simply "pure and uncomplicated instances" of
the traditions to which they belong, as if knowing only their own tradition and
nothing else.

October 2013 DOI: 10.1111/moth.12069

e)

⟩ WORD IS AS A GOOD TREE: A MUSLIM RESPONSE TO THE INTERFAITH CHALLENGES OF VATICAN II

MARIA MASSI DAKAKE

Hast thou not considered how God sets forth a parable?
A good word is as a good tree: its roots firm and its branches in the sky.
It brings forth fruit in every season, by the leave of its Lord.
And God sets forth parables for mankind that haply they may remember.
And the parable of a bad word is a bad tree:
uprooted from the face of the earth, it has no stability.
Qur'an 14:24–26

Reading through the many thoughtful pieces in this volume, the image put forth in the Qur'anic verse above continues to come to mind. The authors' collective expositions of Vatican II documents encouraging the Church to plunge its roots more deeply into scripture (*Dei Verbum*), and at the same time expand its branches outward to touch, if not fully embrace, what is sacred in other religious traditions (*Nostra Aetate*), suggest to me that these doctrinal pronouncements can be thought of as examples of the "good word" in the Qur'anic parable. Like a good tree, they have the potential to "bring forth fruit in every season"; and while some of the theological fruits of this double movement deeper into scripture and outward toward wider dialogue are only beginning to be realized through practices like Scriptural Reasoning, Comparative Theology, and Receptive Ecumenism, if the parable is correct, then there are more fruits yet to be enjoyed as we move through the seasons.

Maria Massi Dakake
Department of Religious Studies, College of Humanities and Social Sciences, George Mason University, 4400 University Drive, 3F1, Fairfax, VA, 22030, USA
Email: mdakakem@gmu.edu

Vatican II as a broad set of changes to Roman Catholic doctrine and practice has had its critics as well, of course, including those unhappy with its apparent break with the Magisterial tradition, as well as its liturgical changes. The concerns of the contributors to this volume are more theological than liturgical, yet some raise important issues about the way in which the authority of the Magisterial tradition is challenged, and potentially compromised, by reading scripture too independently of Christian or specifically Catholic theology, and about the need to develop terminologies that allow for a fuller and more fruitful engagement with other religious traditions without a loss of doctrinal integrity. These seem to me to be very legitimate concerns. Moreover, they are concerns that roughly parallel those of Muslim participants in inter-faith reading engagements, such as Scriptural Reasoning, who have to struggle with a less official, but nonetheless weighty and authoritative, tradition of scriptural commentary in their inter-faith reading encounters.

In this response, I will attempt to examine both the encouraging and the cautionary views of the authors in this volume regarding Vatican II's opening toward scripture and toward the religious other, as well as the various inter-faith reading practices it has inspired, against the background of my own experience with inter-faith reading, and my hopes for a scripturally-rooted theological deepening of my own Islamic tradition. Ultimately I will argue that the openings in *Dei Verbum* and *Nostra Aetate* as understood by the authors in this volume constitute an organic and dynamic model for religious thinking and thriving in light of contemporary challenges. Like the metaphorical tree in the parable above, it is a model that allows for stability and change, for rootedness and growth.

David Ford and other authors in this volume have mentioned the three defining characteristics of the legacy of the Second Vatican Council: *ressourcement*, the re-sourcing of theology in the Biblical tradition; *aggiornamento*, which Michael Barnes describes as "bringing the church into the world of today"[1] and David Ford defines more openly as a "response to the modern world"[2]; and *conversazione*, dialogue and engagement with other religious traditions. I think that it is fair to say that the first and the third elements of this legacy are the key constituents of the second: that is, the effort to renew theology through a "depth-ward" turning toward scripture and an opening outward toward the religious other are two opposite, but profoundly complementary, movements that constitute the heart of Vatican II's "response" to the contemporary world. Together, they represent a more organic model of religious thinking and living within the Roman Catholic tradition, premised on openness toward various forms of spiritual nourishment and a healthy integration of these diverse sources, and designed for growth rather than limitation. I prefer to speak of these developments as

---

[1] Barnes, p. 14.
[2] Ford, p. 93.

having moved the church toward a more "organic" rather than a more "modern" approach to its own tradition, and to think of them as constituting a "response" to modernity rather than a "modernization", for these are terminologies that are less potentially binary or divisive in nature, that do not overdetermine the outcome of these developments. A "response" to modernity might mean an embrace of modes of thinking encouraged by contemporary developments outside the religious world *per se*, a rejection of these modes of thinking entirely, a selective embrace or rejection, or else a new trajectory defined by the dialectical tension between the two.

Perhaps the most important element contributing to Vatican II's more "organic" construction of religious thinking and living comes through the principle of *ressourcement*—the attempt to renew theological thinking by allowing for more direct inspiration from scripture. The notion of scripture as "saturated with signification" to use Kevin Hughes' terminology[3], and as the life-giving and inexhaustible source of all religious understanding[4] encourages all scripturally-based traditions to sink their roots deeper into the fertile soil of the divine word. The essays of Kevin Hughes and Michael Barnes suggest that for Roman Catholics the scriptural basis of theology and doctrine had become somewhat attenuated under the weight of the scholastic theological tradition. Vatican II, especially in *Dei Verbum*, addressed this by allowing for a reinvigoration of Roman Catholic theology through renewed engagement with its own scriptural tradition.

Barnes notes that Vatican II's insistence that the church re-engage its scriptural roots inspired a movement away from deductive modes of theological reasoning toward more open-ended and inductive ways of doing theology. It encouraged the substitution of Biblical for scholastic concepts in theological thinking, and a more contemplative attention to scripture focused on the " 'logic of signs' "[5] rather than on the formulation of demonstrative proofs. The emphasis in such a construction is on a conception of God that can be "pointed to" and "indicated" from innumerable vantage points, rather than one that can be universally and rationally demonstrated (on the basis of scripture or anything else). The twentieth-century Islamic scholar Fazlur Rahman argued that the Qur'an encourages a similar way of thinking about God as a reality that cannot be "proven" but only "found"—infinitely discovered and uncovered in the signs and reflections of God around us.[6] Such conceptions of the nature of God in relation to human knowledge allow for a theology oriented toward indefinite growth, rather than delimitation.

---

[3] Hughes, p. 40.

[4] *Dei Verbum*, for example, describes scripture as "the church's support and strength, affording her children sturdiness in faith, food for the soul and a pure and unfailing fount of spiritual life" (*DV*, 21).

[5] Barnes, p. 31.

[6] Fazlur Rahman, *Major Themes of the Qur'an*, second edition (Chicago, IL: University of Chicago Press, 2009), p. 2.

This movement that Vatican II inspired toward a deeper rooting in scripture is complemented by an outward movement toward dialogue with other religious traditions. As Paul Murray notes, the spirit of openness to other embodiments of truth contained in *Nostra Aetate* stands in direct contrast to the previous ways in which the church tended to address ecumenical issues, that is by seeking to "neutralise and overcome difference as efficiently as possible".[7] Indeed, this document encouraged broadening rather than narrowing the religious conversation by allowing for a deeper engagement with a wider range of conversation partners, and recognized the need to live with "un-reconciled divisions" among religious communities.[8] It favored extending the metaphorical branches of the church in such a way as to allow them to intermingle with those of other religious traditions through conversation and dialogue over attempts at pruning its own branches in the interests of maintaining doctrinal purity.

Scriptural Reasoning as a Practical Application of the Spirit of Vatican II

Various practices of interfaith reading of scripture can be understood as fruitful, practical applications of the ideas of *ressourcement* and *conversazione* found in the Vatican II documents. In his essay David Ford presents Scriptural Reasoning as the practical embodiment of the principles of renewed scriptural focus and interfaith engagement established in doctrine by the Vatican II pronouncements, and gives us an historical overview of the development of Scriptural Reasoning in relation to these principles. Scriptural Reasoning combines the conviction that scripture is an endlessly rich resource for religious renewal and theological deepening, with a commitment to engagement with the religious other and the possibility, as Paul Murray describes it, of "learning *from* and *across* long-term [religious] difference".[9] Scriptural Reasoning's practices of interfaith reading are guided by a stance described by Murray as that of "*committed pluralism*", which seeks not to overcome religious difference but to "live it well".[10] As Nicholas Adams also points out in his essay, it is guided by the commitment to avoid the errors of a secular humanism that seeks an artificially constructed "neutral ground" or a "view from nowhere" in the pursuit of objective truth.

In Scriptural Reasoning each participant comes to the table both as an individual and as a representative of their own tradition. They may have left their respective confessional "houses" to read with others in a temporary "tent" of the interfaith meeting,[11] but the way in which their confessional

---

[7] Murray, p. 78.
[8] *Ibid.*
[9] *Ibid.*
[10] *Ibid.*
[11] The Biblically inspired metaphor of the interfaith gathering as a "tent" or "tent of meeting" has been used repeatedly by the founders and participants in Scriptural Reasoning. See, e.g.,

houses have shaped their thinking is brought implicitly, if not explicitly, to the table. A recognition of the fallacy of the "view from nowhere" and the barrenness of a misplaced pursuit of "objectivity", however, does not necessarily make negotiating multiple doctrinal and faith commitments in Scriptural Reasoning a straightforward or easy task, and I will address this issue in the following section.

In addition to providing a model of interfaith encounter through reading scripture, Scriptural Reasoning also practices a mode of reading that is contemplative and ruminative in nature, lingering on short passages for extended periods of time. Such a method of reading pushes against deceptively simple, univocal, or obvious interpretations, refusing to turn away from difficult or problematic expressions or passages in scripture, or to abandon sustained contemplation of what makes us unsure or uncomfortable in our own scriptures or those of others. In some Scriptural Reasoning meetings, such as those held at the Center of Theological Inquiry at Princeton from 2003 to 2006, this contemplative mode of inter-faith reading is accompanied by regular moments of prayer, embodying the ideal of prayerful and reflective reading encouraged in *lectio divina*.

Nicholas Adams further discusses the way in which Scriptural Reasoning reading practices seek to avoid the error of foundationalism, a conception of religious knowledge production that largely dismisses the importance of authoritative religious propositions in arriving at religious truth. It is premised upon the confident attitude that the application of purely rational modes of analysis applied to scripture or other sources can and should inevitably lead one from a position of conceptual or religious doubt to one of certainty. In Scriptural Reasoning, the importance of traditional authorities— although in this case a plurality of authorities—is recognized, and the discussion tends to move in another direction: it begins with scriptural texts whose meaning may initially seem clear and certain for those accustomed to reading them in the context of their own faith tradition, but whose understanding often becomes temporarily destabilized in the context of sustained, inter-faith reading. The questions, even informational questions, posed by the outside reader (i.e. the reader reading texts from outside her own religious tradition) frequently force the inside reader to rethink what he thought he knew, sending him, as Mike Higton notes, "back again to the text, to look more deeply".[12] This stress exerted on the texts by the pressures of sustained inter-faith reading do not result in the texts metaphorically "breaking", nor does their meaning descend into doubt and confusion. Rather it is only the simple or simplistic understandings of those texts that sometimes "break" or

---

David F. Ford, *Christian Wisdom: Desiring God and Learning in Love* (Cambridge: Cambridge University Press, 2007), pp. 282–293.

[12] Higton, p. 130.

crumble, often revealing deeper, richer, or even more "stable" meanings that would not be uncovered otherwise.

This is not unlike a mode of Qur'anic interpretative practice described by the medieval Islamic theologian and exegete, al-Māturīdī, who argued that certain elements of Qur'anic understanding—e.g. the linguistic meaning of its Arabic terms and idioms, the historical contexts of its various revealed verses, and the Prophet's explication of the verses when it has been recorded—could only be known through the transmitted tradition of the Prophet's companions and immediate successors. But he went on to indicate that such "traditional" sources do not exhaust the many spiritual meanings latent in the scripture, but merely give them a basis and a touchstone. Further explorations of the meaning of Qur'anic verses can be done by any Muslim capable of understanding the text, but while such "individual" processes of reading and interpretation can result in potentially endless new meanings, they can never result in meanings that are "certain" —that is, as speculative explorations they can never reach a definitive closing point, but indeed can go on indefinitely. They are exercises in seeking meaning, not certainty.[13]

As a Muslim participant in Scriptural Reasoning, I have found its procedure for inter-faith reading has not only afforded me the opportunity to access deep meanings from Jewish and Christian scriptures in a way not possible without knowledgeable and religiously committed Jewish and Christian reading partners, but has also refocused my attention on the Qur'an as the fount of religious meaning and truth in my own tradition. The Catholic conception of *lectio divina*, and the practical embodiment of this model in Scriptural Reasoning reading practices, is profoundly compatible with the mode of religious reading the Qur'an itself demands of its readers, as it asks them to contemplate (*tadabbur*)[14] its verses, to reflect and think deeply about its metaphors, its imagery, and its "signs".[15] Inspired by the productivity of deep, sustained, and contemplative reading practices in Scriptural Reasoning, I recently organized, in March of this year, an inaugural, (largely) intra-faith conference entitled *Tadabbur al-Qur'an* (Contemplating the Qur'an). This conference brought Qur'anic scholars, Muslim community leaders and clerics, and ordinary Muslims together to listen to a series of presentations arguing for a return to deep and contemplative readings of the Qur'an as a means of rediscovering the importance of properly theological thinking based on the Qur'an.

But like Roman Catholics, Muslims are relative "late-comers" to the Scriptural Reasoning table, whose initial participants were predominantly Jewish and Protestant; and Muslims share with Catholics some of the problems and

---

[13] See the introduction in Abū Mansūr al-Māturīdī (d. 944), *Kitāb Ta'wīlāt Ahl al-Sunnah*, 10 vols. (Beirut: Dār al-Kutub al-`Ilmiyyah).

[14] See Qur'an 38:29; 47:24.

[15] See, e.g., Qur'an 2:266; 59:21.

issues that Scriptural Reasoning poses for those with different conceptions of the relationship between scripture on the one hand, and authority and established tradition on the other. While there is no Magisterium in Islam, no single, orthodox theological school, and no universally recognized doctrinal authority, Muslim participants come to Scriptural Reasoning with the more internally diverse but collectively authoritative weight of traditional commentaries on the Qur'an. This legacy of classical Islamic Qur'anic interpretation is also particularly difficult for Muslim participants to embrace, negotiate, or challenge in the context of Scriptural Reasoning, since it is so large and diverse in nature. Recognizing the deep multivalence of the Qur'an, Muslim scholars were unwilling to canonize any single authoritative commentary or set of commentaries upon the Qur'an, as was done for collections of *ḥadīth*. Yet Muslim tradition regularly invokes this variegated and imprecisely defined tradition of classical commentary as a safeguard against the danger of independent interpretation—an idea clearly formulated in the *ḥadīth* of the Prophet warning that anyone who interprets the Qur'an according to his own opinion has erred, even if he is correct in his opinion.[16]

Despite this particularity, the problem Muslims is not entirely different from the problem faced by Catholics, or even Protestants who wish to be doctrinally guided in their interfaith reading: how does one allow and engage in free and open discussion of religious texts to which one is committed, as well as religious texts that challenge those commitments, while honoring one's own doctrinal truth claims and the inevitable limitations they impose? David Ford addresses this central problem from several angles in the list of questions he poses regarding Scriptural Reasoning toward the end of his essay, asking what role tradition-specific commentaries have to play in Scriptural Reasoning, what it means to take a text outside of its traditional "home", and what status new "experiments" in meaning or new interpretations arising out of inter-faith reading should have.

Authority, Doctrine, and Tradition

Several of the authors in this volume address the ways in which doctrinal commitments and orientations may be maintained in the context of interfaith scriptural reading without closing off possible avenues of discussion and dialogue. Mike Higton acknowledges the difficulty of bringing doctrinal commitments to the Scriptural Reasoning table, noting that explicitly addressing doctrinal questions in the course of a Scriptural Reasoning discussion tends to "kill" it. In order to address this, Higton offers us a dynamic conceptualization of Christian doctrine that allows it to be very much present at the Scriptural Reasoning table without impeding the flow of discussion.

---

[16] Abū Dāwūd, *Sunan*, b. 24, h. 3644, available at: http://www.usc.edu/org/cmje/religious-texts/hadith/abudawud

He describes this conception of Christian doctrine "not as a summarising and organising of the yield of scriptural reading, but as a guiding and impelling of an ongoing practice of delving into scripture".[17] This dynamically-conceived understanding of doctrine is capable, he argues, not only of disciplining the Christian participant's own reading of the scriptural texts, but also of shaping the manner in which the readings of other participants are "received".

Higton's conception of doctrine in the context of Scriptural Reasoning provides us with a partial answer to David Ford's question regarding the status of new interpretations and insights that emerge from the Scriptural Reasoning discussion. At the table, these new readings and interpretations remain hypothetical and experimental, with their ultimate status being determined only after they have been reflected upon and tested within the context of the doctrinal and communal commitments of each participant. This is to say that the status of these experimental interpretations will differ for each of the participants in relation to their faith commitments and the extent to which these new readings can be accommodated within their particular confessional "houses". Higton's essay helpfully offers a dynamic conception of doctrine that can move with and guide (for the Christian participant) the flow of Scriptural Reasoning discussions.

David Dault attempts to tackle the arguably more difficult question of how Catholic doctrinal commitments—which include Magisterial authority over the interpretation of scripture and the impossibility of meaningful scriptural exegesis "apart from the Apostolic community"—can be honored in the context of Scriptural Reasoning inter-faith reading practices.[18] Dault makes the important observation that for traditions such as Protestant Christianity, the reading of scripture, whether in inter-faith gatherings or individually, often entails a struggle or negotiation between a fundamentalist acceptance of the literal meaning of the text and the liberalist notion of the autonomy of individual experience or reason. But as Dault makes clear, for Catholics "there is never a bargain to be made between the 'authority of the text' and the "authority of reason' ".[19] For Catholics, neither the text nor individual reason can ever stand alone as sources of authority; their authority is always mediated by the Magisterial tradition, making the experience of a Catholic participant at the Scriptural Reasoning table distinct even from that of other Christians.

Yet Dault argues that for all her distinctiveness the Catholic participant nonetheless comes to the Scriptural Reasoning table first and foremost in the spirit of *tikkun olam*, a shared sense that the world is in need of healing. He suggests that this shared end justifies the otherwise non-traditional practice

---

[17] Higton, p. 127.
[18] Dault, p. 52.
[19] *Ibid.*

of Catholics reading scripture in the explicit presence of the religious other, which necessarily entails a temporary suspension or partial "occultation" of the Magisterial tradition in the approach to scripture. Yet in a manner distinct from, but ultimately analogous to, Higton's conception of the role of Christian doctrine in the Scriptural Reasoning encounter, Dault argues that the Catholic participant in Scriptural Reasoning can fruitfully bring her religious specificity to the table by taking steps to ensure that she is sufficiently grounded in her own tradition of reading. To this end, Dault recommends that Catholic participants engage in preparatory "Catholic Reasoning" sessions, in which exclusively Catholic participants come together to discuss primarily Magisterial texts, and only secondarily scriptural texts read through the medium of traditional Catholic commentaries.

Both Higton and Dault present useful methods by which Christian and Catholic doctrinal commitments may be honored in the context of Scriptural Reasoning, but these methods require not only faith commitments, but also substantial time commitments, as participants need to develop a grounding in their own tradition that is deep enough to allow it to remain stable and guide their contributions to and reception of interfaith discussions of scriptural texts. This brings us to question, raised by Paul Murray, of whether or not Scriptural Reasoning is inherently an "elitist" practice—one that can only meaningfully and productively engage those with extensive knowledge and deep understanding of their own traditions acquired over years of committed study and steeping in the sources of their own tradition.

What kind of promise does Scriptural Reasoning hold for those who have had not had the opportunity or the inclination to devote so much time and intellectual energy to the study of their own traditions? I would suggest that for some Scriptural Reasoning participants—including Catholic and Muslim participants for whom access to scriptural meaning in their own tradition requires, to some extent, familiarity with an esoteric and authoritative tradition of commentary and extra-scriptural sources—a certain level of more or less "elite" training may be particularly helpful. Catholic or Muslim participants without extensive knowledge of these sources may want or need the presence of a fellow Catholic or Muslim with such training in order to feel comfortable proceeding. For a Muslim, the Qur'anic text seems to speak in direct and unmediated fashion to its audience. Yet this apparent accessibility and the open, even universal, and at times personal and intimate ways in which the Qur'an addresses its audience is tempered for most Muslims by an awareness of the text's semantic difficulties and its lack of an intrinsic and sometimes necessary context for its verses. Accessing meaning through these difficulties is something for which Muslims have typically relied on scholars (*"ulama"*) capable of teaching the text through the medium of a rich extra-scriptural tradition.

It is to this concept of tradition that I now wish to turn in the final part of this section. In his essay, Kevin Hughes explores the role of "tradition" in the context of Scriptural Reasoning, and argues that it is possible for Catholic participants to conceive of their tradition in a way that would not only allow them to come to "the Abrahamic tent of meeting", but to do so with "fitting gifts".[20] This conception of tradition, Hughes argues, is not one based upon a "scriptural sensibility" possessed exclusively by the church's "spiritual and intellectual elite", but rather one that manifests itself in the "collective action of the church community" based as it is upon the legacy of "the moral and spiritual lives of the apostles".[21] It is not a set of static concepts and propositions formulated in the past and transmitted to the present, but a lived reality that guides one (much like Higton's conception of Christian doctrine) toward conceptual truths, rather than the other way round. Like Higton's conceptualization of Christian doctrine, Hughes' "tradition" is dynamic in orientation, allowing it to move with the Catholic community as it seeks to live faithfully according to the apostolic tradition in changing circumstances. Hughes gives us the metaphor of tradition as a river that never that flows back to its source.[22] The river both is and is not the same at every moment, and thus provides a metaphorical model of renewal within the context of tradition as advocated by Pope Emeritus Benedict XVI.

Perhaps most importantly, Hughes argues for the importance of tradition as a mediating force between theologians and critical scholars of scripture, between the demands of history and dogma, and as a buffer against the "sovereign activity of the solitary *cogito*", or singular reading of scripture.[23] If we return to the tree as a metaphor for religious living and thinking, with its roots in the soil of scripture, and its branches reaching upward toward the spirit and outward toward the religious other, we might say that the trunk of this tree represents tradition. It is the medium through which life-giving nourishment is conveyed between the roots that keep it firmly anchored and the branches that allow for growth. As the roots and branches grow, the trunk of the tree also grows and thickens without moving from its established place. It remains firmly situated, even as it grows and widens in concentric circles around its life-giving core. Nothing of the trunk is ever lost or replaced, it is merely built and expanded upon, with the core of the trunk continuing to define the shape of the concentric circles that grow around it. Indeed, this central core, this "tradition", must remain strong and alive, lest the tree rot from within and collapse from the competing pressures of roots and branches, which it can no longer sustain; and it must remain an open and vital pathway whereby the nourishing water of the divine word can be conveyed to its limbs.

---

[20] Hughes, p. 33.
[21] *Ibid.*
[22] *Ibid.*
[23] *Ibid.*

Vatican II, Scriptural Reasoning, and Non-Biblical Traditions

In some ways, it is easier for the Catholic Church to define its relationship to other Christian denominations and to the Jewish community through the medium of scripture and interfaith readings of scripture, since these traditions share at least some scriptural texts in common. Interfaith encounters require more complex "mapping" and more selective modes of engagement when non-Biblical traditions, such as Islam or Hinduism, are involved.

Tracy Tiemeier's piece offers us several cautionary tales about interfaith reading either among lay or partly lay groups (specifically the Hindu-Catholic Dialogue Group in Los Angeles) or in the more individual, scholarly context of Comparative Theology. She warns us above all to be aware of the way in which uneven power relations between the religious communities engaged in the dialogue (either real or perceived) can affect the dialogue. She reminds us that some minority religious communities may view interreligious dialogue as "a matter of survival in America"[24], while for some dialogue partners who are members of the dominant religious tradition, it may merely be a matter of curiosity or interest. The situation may be likened to that of an ethnic restaurant owner who desperately needs to alter his native cuisine to make it simultaneously exotic and familiar and thus palatable for the American patrons who support his business, while the American patrons may well not even realize the compromises to the integrity of his cuisine that he has made to suit their tastes.

In my experience with Scriptural Reasoning at a more academic level, it seems clear that its various participants are driven to the table neither by the sense of a need for survival, nor by a trivial intellectual curiosity, but rather by a serious interest in interreligious understanding and healing. But at the level of lay participation in such interfaith reading encounters, such motivations cannot necessarily be easily excluded. Some of the problems in the group Tiemeier discusses were generated by the selection or suggestion by the Catholic participants of Hindu texts for discussion that the Hindu participants found for one reason or another inappropriate, or based upon shallow understandings of their tradition. These problems may well stem from a subtle dominance exercised by the Catholic participants in this dialogue, who seem to have been the initiators and "hosts" of this group; as such, the problems point back toward a concern with the subtle (and unintended) interplay of power relations between majority and minority religious participants in the interfaith encounter.

Anna Moreland's article presents perhaps the most direct challenge to Vatican II's understanding of its relationship to other religions, particularly Islam, as articulated in *Nostra Aetate*. She notes that while the document approves of Islam in its worship of the single Creator, its veneration of Jesus

---

[24] Tiemeier, p. 138.

and Mary, and its belief in resurrection and judgement, it pointedly excludes reference to the founder of Islam, the Prophet Muhammad. In some ways this is obvious and to be expected: Muhammad has no Biblical presence and no real counterpart in the Judeo-Christian tradition. Moreover, the legacy of Muhammad is one that cannot be fully appreciated even in the context of the Qur'an (which seems to be the primary reference point for the *Nostra Aetate* authors), where Muhammad's presence is ubiquitous but understated. His legacy is more fully found in the *ḥadīth* tradition (larger and in some ways more difficult to access than the Qur'an), and in the lived practices, values, and ethics of the Muslim community. Yet following Daniel Madigan, Moreland challenges her fellow Catholics to take Muhammad seriously, and argues that since Muhammad does not easily fit into existing Catholic theological categories, his position must be understood by way of analogy.

She mentions, in the very beginning, the increasingly well-known analogy that likens Christ to the Qur'an as the "Word of God" for Christians and Muslims respectively, and Mary to Muhammad as the pure bearers of that "Word" to humanity.[25] Moreland's essay does not dwell on this particular analogy, but rather asks us to consider another one, which would allow the Catholic religious thinker to accommodate Muhammad within an expanded conception of prophethood. It takes seriously the idea that Muhammad is a prophet, and makes use of terminology that Muslims would recognize, even if such a Catholic description of Muhammad as prophet would be significantly different from what Muslims mean by this term. In this exposition, Moreland shows us not only the importance of a careful and nuanced use of analogy in finding compatible, if not commensurate, terms to be used in dialogue across traditions, particularly the Abrahamic traditions, but also the value of the extra-scriptural religious tradition as a rich resource for such thinking. Moreland cannot find a clear way to discuss Muhammad as prophet within the strictly Biblical tradition, but finds that the Catholic conception of prophecy can be usefully broadened through an examination of the theological writing of Thomas Aquinas. Moreland's argument for a Catholic way to think of Muhammad as a prophet makes use of the Catholic theological tradition, and exemplifies one way in which such resources, in addition to scripture, may help us cross otherwise impassable divides in inter-faith encounters.

To conclude, I wish to return to the organic metaphor of individual religions or religious perspectives as trees, with their roots in the soil of scripture and their branches reaching ever upward and outward. This organic and dynamic metaphor may leave some questioning the role of tradition in such a formulation, especially if tradition is understood as a more or less static set of doctrinal propositions. Indeed, the movements of Vatican II depth-ward

---

[25] This was originally suggested by S.H. Nasr in *Ideals and Realities of Islam* (London: Aquarian Press, 1966), pp. 43–44.

toward scripture and outward toward the religious other seemed to some to threaten a break with the church's Magisterial tradition. The essays of this volume, however, tend to indicate otherwise. I suggested earlier that the accumulated and accumulating tradition of a religion—its commentaries, doctrines, theologies, and lived practices—can be conceived of as the "trunk" of this tree. The trunk mediates a religion's scriptural roots, and its ever expanding branches, keeping the tree stable and nourished. It stores the accumulated wisdom of the religion, and grows with it, as it radiates outward in concentric circles from its core. In the inter-faith encounter, it is perhaps the support against which we can lean our backs, as we dwell, temporarily, in the metaphorical shade of the entwined branches of our separate religions. We may appear to turn our back to it as we turn to face our interlocutors from other religions, but it remains our steady and unmoving support.

Modern Theology 29:4 October 2013
ISSN 0266-7177 (Print)
ISSN 1468-0025 (Online)

DOI: 10.1111/moth.12070

RE-SOCIALIZING SCHOLARS OF RELIGIOUS, THEOLOGICAL, AND THEO-PHILOSOPHICAL INQUIRY

PETER OCHS

This is a wise and elegantly articulated set of essays on two topics of urgency for scholars of religious, theological, and theo-philosophical inquiry. One is the topic of Catholic religious inquiry after Vatican II, in particular Catholic thinking in the context of other religious traditions. A second topic is the relative contributions of Comparative Theology, Scriptural Reasoning, and Receptive Ecumenism to this thinking and to religious inquiry in general. I compose this response essay just after reading Frank Clooney's comprehensive response to each of the essays and both of these topics. His incisive commentary frees me to devote my response to a narrower topic: the potential contribution of Scriptural Reasoning to both Comparative Theology and Receptive Ecumenism and to religious, theological, and theo-philosophical inquiry more broadly, in both seminaries and the academy.

In pursuing this topic, my first goal is to strengthen a lesson readers will already have learned from this volume: that Scriptural Reasoning, Comparative Theology, and Receptive Ecumenism are best read as three different and complementary new contributions to religious and theological inquiry, all of them applicable to different aspects of Catholic studies and, by analogy, to different aspects of inter-Abrahamic studies as well. The three approaches are best read as contributions to a division of labor in interreligious studies, so that, depending on our individual strengths and proclivities, we may each have reason to pursue some one of these, as complement to the others, or to pursue now one, now another, at different times in our work. Our experience in any one of these approaches should also enrich and expand the way we

Peter Ochs
University of Virginia, Department of Religious Studies, P.O. Box 400126, Charlottesville, VA
22094-4126, USA
Email: pwo3v@cms.mail.virginia.edu

pursue the others. My second goal in this essay is, by way of illustration only, to imagine how academic and seminary research and education could be influenced by Scriptural Reasoning's relational model of cognition (for lack of expertise, I comment much more briefly on the ways Comparative Theology and Receptive Ecumenism may complement this influence).

The Regionality of Scriptural Reasoning

Scriptural Reasoning is, for one, the trademarked name of a practice of study across differences: prototypically the study of scripture across the borders of Abrahamic traditions; more recently the study of scripture across the borders of Asian traditions as well; and, in ways that have varied and will continue to vary unpredictably, a host of complementary studies across difference (for example, different verses, different canons, different commentaries, different genres of literature, different ritual practices, different art forms, and so on). The character of these practices is not trademarked, only the name, owned by The Society for Scriptural Reasoning Inc. (SSR). The senior board of this Society has, so far, set up four regional boards: in the UK and Europe (with a center currently at the University of Cambridge), in North America (with a center currently at the University of Virginia), in the Middle East (with a center currently in the Sultanate of Oman in the offices of the *Tasomah Journal*), and in China (with a center currently at Minzu University).

I have begun with these institutional aspects of Scriptural Reasoning, because Scriptural Reasoning names a historically and institutionally embodied family of practices. These practices may spread outside the groups that initiate them and, in the spreading, they may change, reshaped to fit the needs and character of a given time and place. Like reading and ritual practices within each Abrahamic sub-tradition, Scriptural Reasoning practices will retain traces of their history of transmission; practitioners will disagree about how best to practice Scriptural Reasoning; and in various times and places, individual groups will institutionalize what they deem to be best practices. We have no reason to assume that other practices, "isms", or even natural laws have greater independence from their lived contexts. Scriptural Reasoning belongs to a twentieth/twenty-first-century genre of what Aristotle called "hylomorphism": disclaiming our knowledge of "forms" independent of embodied contexts or of "matter" independent of formed activities. One goal of emphasizing the institutional basis of Scriptural Reasoning is to encourage scholars to disclaim the independence of their favored models of theology or science or logic from their histories of transmission and institutionalization, just as here I am disclaiming the independence of Scriptural Reasoning from its institutional and historical contexts. As we will see, however, my claim is not mere historicism.

Consistent with what I just argued, the senior board of SSR eschews any single, top-down definition of Scriptural Reasoning. Its business is guided only by negative definitions of Scriptural Reasoning or exclusions: that Scriptural Reasoning excludes certain characteristics. Positive definitions of Scriptural Reasoning are provided only by regional boards, and there is no set limit to the number of regional boards that could be established. The "form" of Scriptural Reasoning is therefore displayed only in region-specific embodiments, but these embodiments display generalizable forms nonetheless. In Charles Peirce's helpful expression, such forms "spread" from one place to another and from less extensive to more extensive locations (or domains). In the vocabulary of Scriptural Reasoning, terms like "spread" should replace terms like "generality". The term "universality" should be dropped altogether, except as it measures how far something spreads within a given limit or location. Regions of the SSR will tend to nurture different forms of Scriptural Reasoning, as shaped by differing interests, assumptions, and challenges among the regions and by the way Scriptural Reasoning evolves locally. At the same time, interactions among the regions and their members, overlapping memberships, and activities of the senior board will tend to moderate Scriptural Reasoning's tendency to multiplicity.

One and Many: Divisions of Labor within Scriptural Reasoning

Attracted at once toward both the one and the many, Scriptural Reasoning tends to generate a variety of sub-practices that may be attracted once again toward each other, forming more or less organized societies of sub-practices. To take one set of examples: the original circle of Scriptural Reasoning scholars focused on "Formational Scriptural Reasoning" (see below) in the mid-nineteen-nineties; they formed an "additional meeting group" at the American Academy of Religion (AAR) to invite religious studies scholars to explore and expand Formational Scriptural Reasoning; they generated a Cambridge-and-AAR-based "Scriptural Reasoning Theory Group" to explore the hermeneutical and epistemological implications of Formational Scriptural Reasoning; in 2007 they renamed this "Scriptural Reasoning in the University" to signal their overall focus on Scriptural Reasoning in academia; in the meantime, from 2003 to 2006, the Scriptural Reasoning research group at the Center of Theological Inquiry in Princeton examined Scriptural Reasoning and the history of medieval scripture commentaries; after 2010, Professor Yang Huilin of Renmin University, Beijing, began writing and teaching about Scriptural Reasoning as a model for comparative literary theory, while Professor You Bin of Minzu University, Beijing, began writing and teaching about Scriptural Reasoning as a model for the comparative history of scriptural religions in China. So many different approaches to Scriptural Reasoning, yet all these scholars seek to maintain contact with one another and compare notes on their methods and findings. So it is that Scriptural Reasoning names a historically and institutionally embodied family of practices that may spread across a finite range of possible locations.

This oscillating movement toward one and toward many is central to the activity of Scriptural Reasoning and to its hylomorphism. Scriptural Reasoning tends toward form, but not in the either/or sense of "universal forms" that get embodied in the (mere) materiality of some space-time setting. Scriptural Reasoning exists, formally and materially, only where it is practiced, and the practice integrates formal and material elements that can be abstracted only for the sake of analysis: elements that can be examined as patterns or regulae and elements that can be examined as contexts and conditions. Any such patterns appear as patterns that could operate (and thus "spread") only within some range of conditions, and such conditions are discernible only with respect to certain patterns.

Across the regions of the SSR, Scriptural Reasoning should therefore manifest itself in a multitude of ways. The mode of Scriptural Reasoning that typifies a given region should also be embodied in a variety of different ways across the variety of different contexts of practice within the region. But in what characteristic way will the many manifest the one, or the one manifest the many? I devote much of this essay to answering this question, because I believe an answer would display a dimension of Scriptural Reasoning that remains as yet mostly absent from scholarly discussion, and because I believe discussion of this dimension would correct some unfortunate misunderstandings about Scriptural Reasoning.

Up until the last few years, Scriptural Reasoning scholars have tended to limit their Scriptural Reasoning theory (their efforts to examine abstracted patterns of Scriptural Reasoning) to the single context of small group study of scripture: the prototypical activity of "scripture study around a table", which we call *Formational Scriptural Reasoning.* The pattern of "one and many" is at play in such theory, since there are *many* religious traditions (or denominations of a tradition) represented by the individuals seated around a *single* table, the *many* individuals studying a *single set* of verses (one set at a time), and the *many* possible meanings entertained for each *single* textual item (word or verse or pericope). Theory about Formational Scriptural Reasoning has generated broad reflections in several areas, among them hermeneutics/semiotics (for example, on the relation of *sign* [*ayat* or verse] to *meaning* for some context of *interpretation* ["interpretant"]) and the philosophy or logic of relations (for example, on the correlative development of unexpected friendships and unexpected depths of inter-textual discussion). By itself, however, this theory cannot account for the multitude of ways that Scriptural Reasoning can be practiced or for how that multitude would also display the unity of Scriptural Reasoning.

While Scriptural Reasoning scholars have more recently begun to turn their attention to other contexts for Scriptural Reasoning study and to new domains of theory, there is as yet still insufficient data to provide an empirical answer to the question of how Scriptural Reasoning organizes the one and the many. I shall therefore devote this essay to imagining an answer rather than reporting one. I shall try to imagine a network of Scriptural Reasoning practices within which Scriptural Reasoning sub-groups might pursue different yet complementary and coordinated areas and levels of Scriptural Reasoning work. And I shall try to imagine how the network would be organized, so that its principles, purposes, and logistics would manifest the unity-in-multiplicity that will typify Scriptural Reasoning as a society-wide practice and not only a way of gathering different readers around tables. This is not mere speculation, but an effort to extend what we have observed for years about Formational Scriptural Reasoning into a theory about the broader societal purposes of Scriptural Reasoning. Moreover, even an empirical account of a network of Scriptural Reasoning practices would have to begin with suggestive hypotheses[1] that might be similar to these speculations. Finally, a network of Scriptural Reasoning practices will more likely be established intentionally, rather than by accident. The purpose of my speculations is to stimulate new practical plans as well as new theories.

Preliminaries: Elemental Purposes in Scriptural Reasoning[2]

For those who tend to identify Scriptural Reasoning only with Formational Scriptural Reasoning, the primary purpose of Scriptural Reasoning appears to be something like interreligious understanding or peacebuilding. For the founders of Scriptural Reasoning, the original purpose was to repair what they judged to be inadequate academic methods for teaching scripture and scripturally-based religions, such as the Abrahamic religions. From the start,

---

[1] Peirce names the processes that generate such hypotheses "abductions", contrasting abductive reasoning with both inductive and deductive modes of reasoning. The study of scripture is a particularly strong source of models for abductive reasoning, and Scriptural Reasoning is animated by these.

[2] What we call "Formational Scriptural Reasoning" represents the signature activity within the project of Scriptural Reasoning in the way that, for example, the Cartesian *cogito* represents the signature activity within the Enlightenment project of reasoning. To understand any of the goals of Scriptural Reasoning, one must first learn to practice Formational Scriptural Reasoning and, in the process, be socialized into the cognitive, relational, and interpretive skills and habits that are presupposed by all other levels and kinds of Scriptural Reasoning practice. This does not, of course, mean that scriptural reasoners no longer engage in the work of the *cogito*. It means only that they acquire visceral knowledge of the difference between the "I think" and other epistemic activities and, thereby, the capacity to recognize the appropriate settings for engaging in now one, now another of these activities. Individuals sitting at the Scriptural Reasoning table may often cogitate by way of the "I think", but they also recognize that the overall activity of their table fellowship is irreducible to the "I think" as the measure of what it means to reason and to know. If they are trained by modern academic disciplines, they may therefore have a bit of work to do to get over the habit of overusing the "I think" as such a measure and under-using other forms of thinking that are nurtured across the Scriptural Reasoning table. At the same time, Scriptural Reasoning participants who are trained outside of the Academy and within certain religious orthodoxies may find that they have a bit of work to do to get over the presumption that the "I think" has no place in scriptural interpretation. The reparative work of Scriptural Reasoning as a whole depends on the work of scriptural reasoners who have broad experience in several modes of thinking and have acquired at least minimal wisdom in knowing when and where to engage in a given mode.

this purpose was to be served both by intra- and inter-traditional study, that is, by both Textual Reasoning and Scriptural Reasoning. Textual Reasoning referred to ways of studying traditional, sacred texts across the kinds of difference that manifest themselves in both different denominations of a religion and different disciplines of scholarly study. The most developed example has been Jewish Textual Reasoning, which was formed in the mid-nineteen-eighties around the study of Talmud and Talmudic Biblical commentaries by members of all the various Jewish denominations and the various sub-specializations in Jewish Studies. As discussed by the founding members of the SSR, Textual Reasoning was a tradition- rather than scripture-based practice.[3] Over time, both Scriptural Reasoning and Textual Reasoning acquired new purposes as participants discovered additional consequences of these practices.

---

[3] *Pace* comments in this volume by David Dault and Francis Clooney, who reports that "David Dault, though sympathetic with the goals of close, shared readings, helpfully brings a certain skepticism to the conversation, wondering aloud whether Catholic theology can comfortably accommodate practices of reading the sacred text 'by itself' " (Clooney, 176). But as indicated in Peter Ochs and Nancy Levene (eds), *Textual Reasonings: Jewish Philosophy and Text Study at the End of the Twentieth Century* (Grand Rapids, MI: Wm. B. Eerdmans Publishing Company, 2002), Textual Reasoning focuses on the study of traditional commentaries, not scripture apart from tradition. Dault wonders if a Christian Textual Reasoning would be synonymous with "New Testament Reasoning" or something, against which he prefers something more like "Catholic Reasoning". But the latter is, in fact, the more appropriate analogue to Jewish Textual Reasoning. Depending on the memberships gathered, perhaps one group might be animated by "Baptist Reasoning", another—closer to Receptive Ecumenism—by "Christian Reasoning" in a broader sense. Whatever the character of an individual Textual Reasoning group, writings by both Textual Reasoning and Scriptural Reasoning scholars should make it clear enough that *both* Textual Reasoning and Scriptural Reasoning were promoted as urgent but *occasional* projects, never as substitutes for any denomination's primary practices of study.

The Textual Reasoning projects were considered urgent as exercises that might re-acquaint participants with patterns of traditional study that served deeper purposes than those of any individual academic discipline within the whole of religious scholarship (in that tradition) or of any individual denomination within the unity of the divine word and command (as received in that tradition). The Scriptural Reasoning projects were considered urgent as exercises that might repair modern and recent tendencies to "binarism" in both the academy and some of the religious denominations (see discussion of binarism below). Recalling a visit he made to a Scriptural Reasoning session at the University of Virginia, Dault recalls that "Slavica Jakelic, raised a concern. 'This is not the way I read the Bible,' she said plainly. I am a Roman Catholic, and we do not simply sit and read Scripture, bare Scripture. . . .' " (Dault, 50). This protest is, however, not unique to Roman Catholics. I have heard it voiced vociferously by Reform and Reconstructionist, as well Orthodox Jewish participants; by Muslims of every sub-tradition and legal school; and by scholars from Lutheran, Calvinist, Dutch Reformed and any number of other Protestant groups. The method of Scriptural Reasoning is, purposefully, to engage all its participants in forms of reading apart from their sub-traditions, in a manner and for purposes that are adequately discussed in many of the volume's essays. I will add that this method arose by trial-and-error, after we learned that the presence of commentaries tended to limit a group's capacities to move beyond either-or terms of engagement. Once having moved beyond such limits, several long-term groups have, indeed, introduced commentarial and other literatures without losing the spirit of inquiry that had been achieved. One such group met for three years at the Center of Theological Inquiry in Princeton, successfully alternating between Scriptural Reasoning study and the historical study of medieval scriptural commentaries. They produced the book: Peter Ochs and William Stacy

Purposes of Formational Scriptural Reasoning

Formational Scriptural Reasoning refers to the simplest practice of Scriptural Reasoning: symbolized by study around a small table, with three or more chairs, one small selection from each of the three Abrahamic scriptural canons, and three or more persons of any age eager to enter into a conversational fellowship with one another and, as it were, with these three text selections. This practice is the basis for all training in Scriptural Reasoning and it is also what we might call the "mode of welcome" that initiates all Scriptural Reasoning-related encounters.

One purpose of Formational Scriptural Reasoning is to provide a venue for members of different traditions or modes of inquiry to share their affection for scripture. This is an exercise for its own sake (*l'shma* in Hebrew) or, as David Ford puts it, "for God's sake". Unlike strictly academic study, this affective dimension of Scriptural Reasoning is welcomed alongside the cognitive dimensions. And it is the affect that appears to contribute most to *another purpose: raising unexpected friendships across the borders of religious traditions.* The most likely source of these friendships is that *the style of Formational Scriptural Reasoning tempts participants (often unawares) to reveal at least a bit of the warmth and ingenuousness they display in intimate settings of scripture study among coreligionists at home.* As a result, religious "others"—even members of groups in conflict—unintentionally share some signs of warmth, tempting them (again unawares) to share more signs. This happens in most groups that continue Scriptural Reasoning over several weeks and months; the unexpected displays of warmth to warmth (what I call "hearth to hearth dialogue") leads to what participants experience as "friendship".

Another purpose of Formational Scriptural Reasoning is to open unexpected levels of textual and hermeneutical discovery, again for its own sake. With inhibitions reduced by the friendships, participants often voice cognitive and affective responses that they would not usually share in such settings: responses to words and verses in their "own" scriptures as well as in those of the others. The exchange of responses stimulates further responses, resulting (as they later report to us) in insights and readings they had not previously considered. If Formational Scriptural Reasoning is facilitated correctly, participants understand that these are typically *not* new readings *of* the tradition, but only of mere words and verses, and these acquire *religious* meaning *per se* only if and when participants bring them (unawares) or test them (intentionally) in their home settings.

I shall take time to mention *one more purpose of Formational Scriptural Reasoning: to serve as a major resource for reparative reasoning*, as Nicholas Adams

---

Johnson (eds), *Crisis, Call, and Leadership in the Abrahamic Traditions* (New York: Palgrave Macmillan, 2009).

names it.[4] As I will argue at length, the reparative function of Scriptural Reasoning is fully displayed only in societal networks of Scriptural Reasoning and may be visible in Formational Scriptural Reasoning only for those who have seen how it works across a whole network. When contributing to broader networks, Formational Scriptural Reasoning is in fact like the cylinder inside the engine of Scriptural Reasoning repair. If you can tolerate this simile, I will extend it and call "scripture readings" the "pistons": activities in which the Spirit that is present to some participants gets ignited, generating *abductions*, or reasonings that open new hypotheses about whatever issue the Scriptural Reasoning group is examining within a reparative network. The engine's "drive wheel" is the highly focused line of reasoning that emerges in experienced groups that have taken on a reparative project: this reasoning reframes some reparative issue in terms that are meaningful to the group, directs the group's attention to scriptural texts and styles of reading that may illuminate the issue, receives reparative hypotheses that emerge from the group's reading, and delivers these hypotheses in ways that may prove useful to other groups that work on this issue. The "cylinder" as a whole is the collection of religious traditions that will serve as agents of these reparative hypotheses.

Repairing Binarisms

At times I describe the primary purpose of Scriptural Reasoning as repairing binarism in modern Western civilization and in religious groups that have, willy-nilly, adopted this binarism as if it were an engine of indigenous religious discourse and belief. My description overstates the case, since Scriptural Reasoning has a range of purposes. But it is still helpful to conceive of Scriptural Reasoning as having emerged in response to the dangers and inadequacies of both academic and intra-religious binarisms. All I mean by "binarism" is a strong tendency to overstate and over-generalize the usefulness of either/or distinctions.[5] I assume that we appropriately rely on such distinctions whenever we seek to communicate something clearly: when, for example, someone says "pass the salt", meaning "salt and not pepper".[6] But I also assume that such communications are appropriate only within groups

---

[4] See Nicholas Adams "Reparative Reasoning", *Modern Theology*, 24:3 (July 2008), pp. 447–457. Without using the term explicitly, Adams' essay in this volume offers a sophisticated account of reparative reasoning in Receptive Ecumenism and Scriptural Reasoning. He shows how "the philosophical shapes displayed in Scriptural Reasoning and Receptive Ecumenism have a reparative character, at least initially, as they work to re-tool a new generation of ecumenical and inter-faith practitioners" (Adams, 171).

[5] In Adams' terms, "The pragmatic repair of secular universalism, of the pursuit of neutral ground, is also a repair of the over-generalisations found in nineteenth-century hermeneutics" (Adams, 161).

[6] As Adams writes, "Everyday forms of judgement tend, quite properly, to be binary" (Adams, 162).

of language users who tend to share common understa
terms and only in settings where communication doe'
or judgements of probability. "Binarism" refers or
application of either-or distinctions to settings of irr
probability. Scriptural Reasoning is stimulated in part -
the modern Western university has an inveterate tendency
binarist modes of thinking, writing, and arguing. The goal of Su-
Reasoning is not to weaken the university's disciplines, but to propose test-
able means of repairing the tendency to binarism. Scriptural Reasoning is
stimulated by the perception, furthermore, that the religious institutions that
reside in the modern West have tended to assimilate these binarist tendencies
into their theological discourses. One result is that many movements labeled
"fundamentalist" display tendencies to a modern Western-style binarism that
has been rewritten into the tissue of traditional religious practices and discourses. This is not to say that the various religions lack their own indigenous
tendencies to nastiness, but only that binarist nastiness probably comes from
the West.

Scriptural Reasoning scholars worry about binarism because of its prob-
able consequences.[7] Among these are:

- *Misperception and misrepresentation:* The defining problem is that binarism
  leads to false knowledge claims. The binarist assumes, for example, that
  some term (X) names a given object in the world (O), that some clear
  proposition involving X (X is Y) is true because it corresponds directly to
  some claim about O (O is Y), and that any apparently contradictory claim
  about O (O is Z) contradicts the true proposition and is therefore false.[8] The
  binarist is wrong whenever O is adequately characterized only by ambiguous or probabilistic claims (for which the principle of non-contradiction
  does not apply). According to Scriptural Reasoning scholars, non-binarist
  religious belief claims often include ambiguous or probabilistic elements.
  When they do, binarist accounts of religion are particularly subject to error.
- *Failed efforts to repair wounds:* If the object (O) is some problematic situation, rupture, or wound, then binarist efforts to repair the situation may
  most likely fail. These efforts are particularly disruptive when applied to
  ruptures within religious groups. Binarist systems of knowledge tend to
  misdiagnose such failures, in which case the failures are repeated and the
  situations worsen.
- *Inter-group conflict:* When an intra-group wound festers, anxieties and
  fears are heightened, efforts to repair the situation intensify, and suspicions

---

[7] Adams' essay offers a sophisticated account of this critique of binarism, identifying it
helpfully with a critique of foundationalism ("The pragmatism commended by Ochs and Murray
is intended to repair the deficiencies that characterise foundationalism" (157)) and a critique of
"the pursuit of neutral ground" or "secular universalism" (156).

[8] The condition Wittgenstein portrayed in the *Tractatus*.

ut potentially false remedies grow stronger. One consequence is that narist tendencies grow, sometimes exponentially; suspicions generate divisions and then open conflicts within and among affected groups.

In such situations, the goals of Scriptural Reasoning are to diagnose the sources of binarism and to attract some members of opposing groups to search for and test alternative, reparative hypotheses. Scriptural study is one but by no means the only instrument for this search. It depends on the character and culture of the groups.

When applied to such situations, Scriptural Reasoning can be described as a family of methods for repairing sources of binarism. There is a division of labor within this family,[9] and for two reasons. First, a plurality of specializations will be needed to help diagnose and repair binarisms in a range of possible contexts. Second, repairing even a single case of binarism will require the cooperative efforts of a network of different but complementary nodes of inquiry.

Envisioning a Network of Complementary Nodes of Reparative Scriptural Reasoning

Here, then, I turn to imagine a Network of Scriptural Reasoning practices, organized so that its principles, purposes, and logistics would manifest the unity-in-multiplicity that typifies Scriptural Reasoning as a society-wide practice. In this vision, there are two interdependent streams of Scriptural Reasoning work, one that moves ground-up from local Scriptural Reasoning to reparative work in the academy, and one that moves ground-up to reparative work in the religious school (seminary, yeshiva, madrasah, monastery and so on). It is important both to name these as separate streams, while recognizing that the streams will overlap at most of their places of activity (or "nodes"). In practice, labeling the streams separately may help participants on occasion handle the politics of their relations to either purportedly secular institutions or religious ones.

Academic Stream

A1. Local Formational Scriptural Reasoning
As described above, all participants in Scriptural Reasoning engage in this kind of activity as a way of initiating every meeting. After establishing formational study for about a year, local groups direct their studies to reparative

---

[9] Events of binarism are observable only *in situ*, only within the concrete contexts of some earthly life. This means that occurrences of binarism can be observed only by those who participate in and have intimate acquaintance with the local context. A society of reparative reasoners must therefore include specialists in different regions of the world, in different types of context, in different tools of diagnosis and repair.

goals: identifying local problems or "wounds" that appear to be inadequately repaired by regional service institutions. Scriptural—and, if necessary, additional forms of study—should eventually generate reparative hypotheses that might conceivably be applied to repairing those institutions so that they can repair those wounds. No repairs are actually undertaken. The hypotheses are referred, instead, to SRS (node A3 below).

A2. House Textual Reasoning

As introduced above, Textual Reasoning is a practice of "House-specific" (tradition- or denomination-specific) study, gathering representatives of different sub-groups and sub-disciplines to examine what they consider primary commentarial texts in their shared tradition. This node of study contributes directly to both the academic and the seminary streams of Scriptural Reasoning. In the seminary stream, Textual Reasoning functions the way local Formational Scriptural Reasoning functions in the academic stream: setting the initial standard for all other levels of study, including efforts to identify cases where regional religious institutions have failed to help repair local wounds or ruptures. In the academic stream, Textual Reasoning prepares members of local congregations for future work in Scriptural Reasoning groups.[10] Even when a Scriptural Reasoning group is formed at a location, it may be good for each house Textual Reasoning group to continue its separate work.

A3. SRS: Scriptural Reasoning Society

Members of SRS would include one or two representatives from each region plus representatives from SRA (node A4 below) and from appropriate research agencies. The work of SRS is to generate hypotheses about how given societal problems could be repaired. Reviewing reports from each region of Formational Scriptural Reasoning, SRS reports to SRA about which institutions merit repair. Reviewing research material and recommendations it then receives from SRA, SRS prepares reparative hypotheses to be tested in appropriate local Formational Scriptural Reasoning.[11]

---

[10] In Manhattan, for example, Reverend Michael Bos has offered this recommendation: that he spend up to a year nurturing a Christian Textual Reasoning group in his church before we seek to grow a Manhattan Scriptural Reasoning group. A nearby synagogue and mosque would start groups at the same time, perhaps studying texts gathered under parallel themes. After a year or less, each of these three houses may then recommend which of its members are truly ready to join a Scriptural Reasoning group on the same theme.

[11] These groups test the recommendation of SRS by generating concrete blueprints of how specific service or oversight organizations could reform their practices in a way that would generate appropriate on-the-ground solutions to specific societal problems. Regional groups hold conferences with representatives of such organizations and of the communities in which these problems have been observed. The goal of each conference is to evaluate the potential effectiveness of a given set of blueprints. Each regional group concludes its "test" by reviewing this evaluation and drafting an account of the potential quality and reparative power of SRS's recommendations. A subject for future theoretical work in Scriptural Reasoning, such testing

A4. SRA: Scriptural Reasoning in the Academy

SRA is modeled on the work of the current society for Scriptural Reasoning in the University.[12] The work of SRA goes in two directions: (1) Its contribution to the reparative network is to receive reports from SRS, to examine academic resources available for helping SRS frame reparative hypotheses, and to send reparative recommendations back to SRS. (2) Its work within the academy is to recommend illustrative ways of repairing binarist tendencies in all academic disciplines. Comparable to recent projects of the Cambridge Inter-faith Programme, this work of SRA includes: (a) forming SRA teams whose training is within the discipline to be examined. Unlike current Scriptural Reasoning academic groups, therefore, there might be only a few generalists and theologians in an SRA team. If, for example, the team plans to examine practices in anthropology, then the majority of team members would have anthropology PhDs; (b) investigating binarist tendencies within such a discipline; (c) formulating hypotheses about how such binarisms might be repaired within a given discipline's elemental patterns of inquiry; (d) publishing and testing the results of its work.

A5. Elemental Reasoning

For those of us who have experimented with it, "Elemental Reasoning" refers to a Formational Scriptural Reasoning-like study fellowship that begins its typical sessions by studying scriptural selections but then addresses different genres of texts or non-texts. My first experience of Elemental Reasoning was with Gavin Flood and Emma Kwan, one wonderful night in Oxford. We studied a pericope from the Gospel of Mark, then turned to T.S. Eliot's *Four Quartets*, then to Emma Kwans's paintings of a white silver moon against a black sky. Our manner, pace, and spirit of study were generated out of the discussion of Mark. We read *Four Quartets* as if it were almost another set of pericopes and "read" the series of paintings in an unexpectedly similar way.

On another occasion of Elemental Reasoning, Oded Zehavi had composed and recorded a piece of Abrahamic classical music, each movement of which was stimulated by a different scriptural passage. The University of Virginia's graduate student Scriptural Reasoning group studied these passages after hearing a corresponding movement of the piece. On yet another occasion, we integrated studies of scripture, poetry and live music.[13] Elemental Reasoning

---

would require nurturing many kinds of relations: for example, political relations with the appropriate service-organization and community leaders, communities of inquiry with appropriate specialists in a given technology (such as engineering, medical research, social work and so on), and an effective fellowship of Scriptural Reasoning.

[12] Currently co-facilitated by Steven Kepnes and Mike Higton.

[13] The next summer, the graduate group and I, joined by Randi Rashkover and several University of Virginia colleagues, engaged in five sessions of Elemental Reasoning over a two-day period. The study "texts" of one session included scripture, paintings, and brief texts of fiction. Another session began with a carefully prepared Southern meal, after which our first text was our host's menu for the meal, examined in light of our experiences of eating it. We then

is playful, providing opportunities for us to experiment with reading practices and loosen any over-determined relations among Scriptural Reasoning, the academy, the religious houses, and a variety of cultural practices. The purpose of Elemental Reasoning is not, therefore, to play a predefined role in the Scriptural Reasoning Network, but to serve as the jester among the network of practices, generating unpredictable investigations and recommendations. It should also be fun: a source of humor in the leaven of the Scriptural Reasoning Network.

A6. Contemplative Reasoning and A7. Scriptural Reasoning-Mathematics

Both groups offer resources for generating elemental hypotheses about how to repair problematic features of any academic discipline. They (a) receive reports from SRA about where fresh hypotheses are needed; and (b) generate potentially useful hypotheses and communicate these to SRA. There are slight differences between these two nodes of the Scriptural Reasoning Network.

Members of Contemplative Reasoning groups spend a few days together every so often, meditating, praying, and practicing cognitive exercises. For now, the goals of each Contemplative Reasoning group are best stated briefly and from a few perspectives: (a) to develop a common elemental vocabulary among group members (comprised, for example, of icons, images, and patterns), which will empower them to visualize potential objects of repair more efficiently and effectively; (b) to prepare a space comparable to Descartes' cabin, except that the agent of inquiry in that cabin will not be a single *ego cogito* but a team of inquirers dedicated to uncovering mutually intelligible patterns of abductive reasoning; (c) to generate reparative hypotheses in answer to requests from SRA and SRS.

Members of Scriptural Reasoning-Mathematics teams will be mathematicians in either the academic sense or the Peircian sense (those who gaze at domains of elemental possibilities in any medium of inquiry). This node of activity is like Contemplative Reasoning, but more highly specialized. Its purpose is to recommend ways of repairing logics or other formal systems that appear to contribute binary tendencies to certain academic disciplines.

Seminary Stream

S1. Local Pastoral/Clerical Textual Reasoning

Textual Reasoning is the formational practice for the seminary stream of the Scriptural Reasoning Network. It is vital to foster many kinds of local Textual Reasoning in the seminary network, such as: (a) Pastoral Textual Reasoning: local pastors and chaplains who share in formational Textual Reasoning for

---

moved to a novella about the South, which we had read earlier and turned to one brief passage. Then came scriptural study and prayer.

its own sake, but also, eventually, to examine wounds or ruptures that appear to have arisen among local congregations; (b) Homiletical Textual Reasoning: focusing on sources for homiletics/preaching and on problems that may arise in local practices of homiletics; (c) Liturgical or Sacramental Textual Reasoning: focusing on sources for prayer and ritual and on problems that may arise in local practices[14]; (d) Doctrinal or Legal Textual Reasoning: focusing on sources for religious doctrine and law problems that may arise in local practices; (e) Textual Reasoning-social ethics: focusing on sources for social ethics and on problems that may arise in local practices.

S2. Regional Doctrinal Reasoning and Inter-Ecclesial Reasoning
Each regional group of this kind includes representatives from sets of local groups. The purpose of each regional group is to nurture environments of Textual Reasoning or Scriptural Reasoning study, within which the group can examine unrepaired wounds within the region and generate reparative hypotheses. As in the academic stream, such regional groups mediate between the work of local Textual Reasoning groups and the seminaries and research institutions whose teachings ought to provide reparative resources down the entire chain of religious institutions. Depending on local issues and needs, some nodes in this chain will remain house-specific; others will nurture interreligious practices of Scriptural Reasoning.

S3. Seminary Reasoning
The seminary stream places greatest responsibility for change on institutions among the religious houses that train ministers, priests, imams, rabbis, and other educators and leaders in the various denominations. According to the vision of the Scriptural Reasoning Network, binarist tendencies in these institutions significantly influence binarist behaviors within the various religious houses, on the ground and in the various religious bureaucracies. I hypothesize that, wherever the political influence lies in the traditions, the most economical route to repairing binarist tendencies in the houses is to repair such tendencies in the traditions' educational institutions. Corresponding to the work of SRA, the work of this node would be carried out by a decentralized number of research-and-study teams, some of which practiced Textual Reasoning as a resource for house-specific reparative work and some of which practiced Scriptural Reasoning as a resource for reparative work in polyglot institutions or on relational issues among Abrahamic institutions. Teams from this node would generate hypotheses about how to repair binarist tendencies within specific institutions. If the teams acquired

---

[14] Liturgical Reasoning represents a distinct node of Scriptural Reasoning, but I list it here for reasons of space. As introduced by Steven Kepnes, Liturgical Reasoning applies Textual Reasoning-like approaches to the study of liturgical texts. See his *Jewish Liturgical Reasoning* (New York: Oxford University Press, 2007).

political influence, these hypotheses could be tested within the seminaries. Until then, the teams would "test" their hypotheses by lending them to the lower-number nodes and seeking feedback on how useful these hypotheses were for guiding discussions within those nodes.

S4. National Theo-Political Scriptural Reasoning

This node serves functions analogous to those of SRS and SRA in the academic stream, but organized on a national or an international scale. Today, theo-political binarisms display themselves most acutely in national politics. I would therefore anticipate considerable interest in gathering interreligious Scriptural Reasoning fellowships on the subject of national, church-state issues. Such fellowships might best be peopled by representatives from node S2 or from an independent gathering of religious, seminary, political and academic leaders.

S5. Spiritual Reasoning

The purpose of this node is analogous to that of Contemplative Reasoning in the academic stream. Through practices of meditation, contemplation, prayer and Scriptural Reasoning, Spiritual Reasoning teams explore otherwise unpredictable patterns of imagination and reflection to fund resources for reparative reasoning.

Patterns of Organization-and-Purpose in the Scriptural Reasoning Network

I have just imagined for you what a "Scriptural Reasoning Network" might look like. Several pieces of this network are already being practiced, and my vision represents a reasonable extrapolation from tendencies evident in these practices. In conclusion, I shall illustrate some of the patterns of Scriptural Reasoning organization-and-purpose that are, I believe, exhibited in this extrapolation.

(A) Societal and Academic Reparative Reasoning[15]

Nicholas Adams' essay in this volume offers a sophisticated introduction to "reparative reasoning". Hopefully close to his usage, I shall employ the term here to refer to the primary, overall purpose of the Scriptural Reasoning Network, in service of which the Network acquires its organizational rules. This means that a kind of *repair* is the ultimate purpose of Scriptural Reasoning, not "the shared study of scripture" by itself. The latter—Formational Scriptural Reasoning—has so far proven to be the most reliable instrument of reparative reasoning but, for the sake of repair, Formational Scriptural Reasoning is not an end in itself. It can be modified or replaced by another, complementary practice when the need and context of repair demands it. If a

---

[15] These are two distinct patterns; I combine them for the sake of brevity.

Scriptural Reasoning scholar says, "Yes, but only because the word of scripture has commanded this activity of repair," I would reply "It is in service to this command that I must always examine which specific practice will best serve the occasion of a specific repair, and which teaching will best communicate and warrant this practice to a given community of potential repairers. The command does not speak in the finite and context-specific terms of human language." If the scholar replies, "But we have learned that Scriptural Reasoning study succeeds only if it is adopted as an end in itself," I would reply, "David Ford put it better: 'only if adopted for God's sake'. God is served in different worldly ways at different times. At the same time, I know what you mean, but we should add, '*When* the time comes to practice Scriptural Reasoning, practice it *as if* it were for its own sake'." This also applies to my understanding of the goal of repair: this cannot mean repair *as* I might understand it at a particular time; it must mean "repair for God's sake", even when I may not be able to understand this *as* repair.

Within the account I have constructed of a Scriptural Reasoning Network, repair has several objects. Local groups of Formational Scriptural Reasoning are not only studying scripture but also studying it for the sake of becoming reparative reasoners. The place of their repairs will be in their communities. To illustrate how this repair might contribute to society, I re-imagined all of our social institutions as if they were ordered according to levels of service:

- The ultimate objects of service are "wounds" (pains, sufferings, disturbances or, in John Dewey's language, "problematic situations") in the individual bodies and social or relational bodies that inhabit the everyday world or *Lebenswelt*. Human beings and social groups cannot survive if they cannot in basic ways repair themselves;
- Because individuals and groups cannot always repair themselves, societies provide service institutions to help with this repair when needed (for example, hospitals, police forces, local government);
- Because service institutions sometimes fail to repair certain wounds or problems, societies provide institutions to service them (for example, research, training, and educational institutions that diagnose such failures and recommend ways of repairing them);
- One can imagine a chain of service institutions, each one repairing another. I imagine that, in western societies like the USA, the academy is a prototype of the last line of repair;
- But what if the academy fails to fill this reparative role? American pragmatism emerged as a critique of this failing. Pragmatists like Peirce and Dewey argued that each discipline should provide resources for repairing failings in a given range of service institutions: philosophy should redirect its efforts to reforming any discipline that fails to play its part in the chain of societal repairs;

- But what if pragmatism fails to reform philosophy in this way? I b\
contemporary pragmatism does tend to fail in this way, in part because
pragmatists go the way of other contemporary philosophers (serving the
academy as an end itself rather than as an agent of societal repair), in part
because they lack Peirce's sense that the pragmatic logic of repair derives
from a scriptural logic of redemption and repair.[16] When pragmatism fails,
then I believe Scriptural Reasoning is obliged to take on the role of pragmatism in the academy: Scriptural Reasoning as reparative reasoning in
the academy for the sake of society.

The Scriptural Reasoning Network illustrates how Scriptural Reasoning
would do the effective work of pragmatism in both academy and seminary.
As a whole, the Scriptural Reasoning Network links together a chain of
reparative nodes. Each node of the Scriptural Reasoning Network contributes
to each vector of the chain: (a) *turning toward what needs repair*, each node
helps identify and examine failed service institutions and offers reports on
the kinds of repairs that are needed; (b) *turning toward the possible resources
and agents of repair*, each node contributes to the work of testing reparative
hypotheses.

(B) An Intentional, Transactional Network of Scriptural Reasoners
Here, my observation can be stated briefly. Considered independently of
some network like the Scriptural Reasoning Network, a Scriptural Reasoning
group may appear to pursue its goals only within the inner dynamics of that
group. Reconsidered in the context of the Scriptural Reasoning Network, a
Scriptural Reasoning group pursues goals both within the group (study that
must be pursued as if for its own sake) and across an entire chain of complementary groups (helping identify inadequate service institutions and test
possible ways of repairing them). Within this broader context, each scriptural
reasoner contributes to a transactional network of fellow reasoners.

(C) "Hearth to Hearth" Engagements
Whatever the Scriptural Reasoning Network achieves as a whole depends on
the transformational activity that is made possible by Scriptural Reasoning
within each Scriptural Reasoning Network node and group. When applying
Scriptural Reasoning to projects of peacebuilding, I have found it useful to

---

[16] In "Pragmatism", Peirce writes: "All pragmatists will further agree that their method
of ascertaining the meanings of words and concepts is no other than that experimental method
by which all the successful sciences . . . have reached the degrees of certainty that are severally
proper to them today, this experimental method being itself but a particular application of
an older logical rule, 'By their fruits ye shall know them' [Matthew 7:16]." The Gospel of
Christ, Peirce adds, is the rule of love. (Charles Sanders Peirce, "Pragmatism" (MS 318, 1907),
in the Peirce Edition Project (ed), *The Essential Peirce: Selected Philosophical Writings, vol. 2:
Selected Philosophical Writings (1893-1913)* (Bloomington, IN: Indiana University Press, 1998),
pp. 400–401).

describe Scriptural Reasoning as a form of "hearth to hearth" engagement. In this symbol, the hearth represents a place of life-sustaining warmth (where individuals can seek help in times of extreme need) that also holds a potential for life-threatening danger (since the fire that warms the hearth can, if badly tended, break out and kill). For some Abrahamic religious groups, texts of sacred scripture are hearths around which everyday religious life is nurtured and, in times of severe crisis, around which sources of renewal can be found and shared so that ruptured religious lives can be healed or redemptively transformed. Textual Reasoning groups might gather in that way to help uncover sources for repairing binarism or schism within a given sub-tradition. Scriptural Reasoning groups might gather in that way when the greatest challenge comes from interreligious tension. In that case, the success of Scriptural Reasoning may derive from an unexpected source. As noted earlier, the style of Scriptural Reasoning may tempt participants (often unawares) to reveal to members of other faiths some of the warmth and ingenuousness they display in intimate settings of scripture study among coreligionists at home. This hearth-to-hearth sharing may open participants, gradually, to compare notes on ways that, in times of terrible change, their traditions disclose unanticipated resources for renewal.

Conclusion: Scriptural Reasoning, Receptive Ecumenism, and Comparative Theology

After this volume's profound review and comparison of Scriptural Reasoning, Receptive Ecumenism, and Comparative Theology, I believe the most important question is not "what are their similarities and differences?", but "how will they best share a unity across difference, a division of labor, and complementary yet different modes of reparative reasoning?" I conclude by making note of the recommendations that move me most in each of the essays:

- Michael Barnes: *Ressourcement:* Here are three complementary paths for retrieving resources through which the divine spirit may renew and repair our work in the academy, in the religious houses, and in our overlapping societies. For each path, "Tradition and scripture together form a single sacred deposit of the word of God".
- Kevin L. Hughes: *A Theology of the Fourfold Sense* "is thus as much a spirituality as a hermeneutical rule". Here are three complementary paths to understanding the place of the Word in each of our religious traditions, "drawing scriptures closer to the center" of our lives and expanding scriptures' semantic fields.
- David Dault: *Healing a Broken Word:* If Scriptural Reasoning detects and responds to wounds across the scriptural traditions, and if Receptive Ecumenism detects and responds to wounds across the church, shall we

not also attend comparably to wounds within each House?! Here is a call to remember Textual Reasoning (in this case, "Catholic Reasoning") as a prerequisite for Scriptural Reasoning (or Receptive Ecumenism).

- Anna Bonta Moreland: *Analogical Reading:* "Reason corresponds no longer to a set of beliefs that must be accepted by all before conversation begins. Rather, *'rationality* will then show itself in practices which can be followed and understood by persons operating in similar fashion from different grounding convictions' " (citing David Burrell). A rule for all three paths.
- Paul D. Murray: *Postliberal, pragmatic strategies* "for taking seriously and living fruitfully the fact of diversely traditioned particularity without collapsing into a closed, conflictual tribalism or reverting to a universalising common core theory of religious traditions". A strategy for all three paths in their different ways.
- David F. Ford: *Gaudium et Spes*: "Its inter-faith significance lies in its address to all humanity, its vision of the church in the service of the common good of all humanity, its recognition of the scale and profundity of the changes the world has been going through in recent centuries, and its clear commitment to conversation and collaboration with all who work for peace and human flourishing." The service of reparative reasoning for all three paths.
- Mike Higton: If Christian doctrinal discourse functions to discipline ongoing scriptural reading (not simply to codify and express its results) then the real substance of Christian doctrinal deliberation can be present in interreligious scriptural dialogues. From Comparative Theology (reading carefully in interiority) to Textual Reasoning/Receptive Ecumenism (Christian doctrinal reasoning) to Doctrinal Reasoning in Scriptural Reasoning!
- Tracy Sayuki Tiemeier: *Interlacing* "preserves difference, valuing the inherent beauty of each strand, yet noting the ongoing richness of bringing together the sacred and the beautiful". The interlacing of Comparative Theology as resource also for the braidings undertaken in Receptive Ecumenism and Scriptural Reasoning.
- Nicholas Adams: *Small Scale Inquiries and Long-Term Disagreement*: When pursuit of the same is put aside, the microscope uncovers all of creation in a drop of water. So many elements and atoms to discover differently.

INDEX

Modern Theology 29:4 October 2013
ISSN 0266-7177 (Print)
ISSN 1468-0025 (Online)

DOI: 10.1111/moth.12075

CONTRIBUTORS BIOS

David F. Ford OBE is Regius Professor of Divinity at the University of Cambridge, a Fellow of Selwyn College, and Director of the Cambridge Inter-faith Programme. He co-founded the Scriptural Reasoning movement and holds the Sternberg Foundation Gold Medal for Inter-faith Relations (2008) and the Coventry International Prize for Peace and Reconciliation (2012). His recent publications include: *The Future of Christian Theology* (Wiley-Blackwell, 2011); *Christian Wisdom: Desiring God and Learning in Love* (Cambridge University Press, 2007); *Shaping Theology: Engagements in a Religious and Secular World* (Blackwell, 2007); *The Promise of Scriptural Reasoning*, ed. with C. C. Pecknold (Blackwell, 2006).

Michael Barnes SJ is professor of interreligious relations at Heythrop College in the University of London, where he is also Dean of Research Students. He is the author of six books, including *Theology and the Dialogue of Religions* (Cambridge University Press, 2002) and, most recently, *Interreligious Learning* (Cambridge University Press, 2012).

Kevin L. Hughes is an associate professor at Villanova University, jointly appointed in the department of Theology & Religious Studies and in the department of Humanities, where he currently serves as chair. His recent published work has focused on scholastic theology, especially St. Bonaventure, and on Henri de Lubac and the *ressourcement* movement. He lives in Media, Pennsylvania with his wife and three daughters.

David Dault was assistant professor of Catholic Studies at Christian Brothers University from 2009–2013. He is currently the President of the Chicago Sunday Evening Club, a religious nonprofit with a rich history of more than a century of ecumenical service in ministry and broadcasting. He is also the executive producer and host of the radio show *Things Not Seen: Conversations about Culture and Faith* (thingsnotseenradio.com). David is a trustee of the recently formed Society for Comparative Research in Iconic and Performative

Texts (SCRIPT), and has worked extensively in North America as a practitioner of Scriptural Reasoning. His first book, *The Covert Magisterium: Theology, Textuality, and the Question of Scripture*, is forthcoming from Fortress Academic Press.

Anna Bonta Moreland is an Associate Professor in the Department of Humanities at Villanova University. She received her Ph.D. in Systematic Theology from Boston College (2006). Her areas of research include faith and reason, medieval theology with an emphasis on Thomas Aquinas, and the theology of religious pluralism. She has written *Known by Nature: Thomas Aquinas on Natural Knowledge of God* (Crossroad Herder, 2010) and co-edited *New Voices in Catholic Theology* (Crossroad Herder, 2012).

Paul D. Murray is Professor of Systematic Theology within the Department of Theology and Religion at Durham University, where he is also Dean and Director of the Centre for Catholic Studies. He serves on the third phase of work of the Anglican-Roman Catholic International Commission (ARCIC III) and from 2012–2014 as the President of the Catholic Theological Association of Great Britain. His first monograph was *Reason, Truth and Theology in Pragmatist Perspective* (2004). He is editor of *Receptive Ecumenism and the Call to Catholic Learning: Exploring a Way for Contemporary Ecumenism* (2008), and co-editor of *Ressourcement: A Movement for Renewal in Twentieth Century Catholic Theology* (2012). He has also contributed many well-received essays to various leading journals and scholarly collections.

Mike Higton has recently become Professor of Theology and Ministry at Durham University, having previously worked at the Cambridge Inter-faith Programme and in the Department of Theology and Religion at the University of Exeter. His publications include *Christ, Providence and History: Hans W. Frei's Public Theology* (2004), *Difficult Gospel: The Theology of Rowan Williams* (2004), *Christian Doctrine* (2008), *A Theology of Higher Education* (2012) and, with Rachel Muers, *The Text in Play: Experiments in Reading Scripture* (2012).

Tracy Sayuki Tiemeier is Associate Professor of Theological Studies at Loyola Marymount University (Los Angeles) and Co-Chair of the Los Angeles Hindu-Catholic Dialogue. She teaches and researches in the areas of Hindu-Christian studies, comparative theology, interreligious dialogue, feminist theology, and Asian and Asian American theology. Her current work examines classical Tamil articulations of female virtue as a way to problematize Catholic teachings on gender complementarity.

Nicholas Adams is Senior Lecturer in Theology and Ethics at the University of Edinburgh. He is the author of *Habermas and Theology* (Cambridge

University Press. 2006) and *Eclipse of Grace: Divine and Human Action in Hegel* (Wiley-Blackwell 2013).

Francis X. Clooney, S.J., joined the Harvard Divinity School faculty in 2005. He is Parkman Professor of Divinity and Professor of Comparative Theology and, since 2010, Director of the Center for the Study of World Religions. After earning his doctorate in South Asian languages and civilizations (University of Chicago, 1984), he taught at Boston College for 21 years before coming to Harvard. His primary areas of scholarship are theological commentarial writings in the Sanskrit and Tamil traditions of Hindu India, and the developing field of comparative theology, a discipline distinguished by attentiveness to the dynamics of theological learning deepened through the study of traditions other than one's own. He has also written on the Jesuit missionary tradition, particularly in India, and the dynamics of dialogue in the contemporary world. Clooney is the author of numerous articles and books, including *Beyond Compare: St. Francis de Sales and Sri Vedanta Desika on Loving Surrender to God* (Georgetown University Press, 2008), *The Truth, the Way, the Life: Christian Commentary on the Three Holy Mantras of the Srivaisnava Hindus* (Peeters Publishing, 2008), and *Comparative Theology: Deep Learning across Religious Borders* (Wiley-Blackwell, 2010). He recently edited *The New Comparative Theology: Voices from the Next Generation* (Continuum, 2010). His latest book, *His Hiding Place Is Darkness: A Hindu-Catholic Theopoetics of Divine Absence* (Stanford University Press, 2013), is an exercise in dramatic theology, exploring the absence of God in accord with the biblical *Song of Songs* and the Hindu *Holy Word of Mouth* (*Tiruvaymoli*). He is a Roman Catholic priest and a member of the Society of Jesus. In July 2010 he was elected a Fellow of the British Academy.

Maria Massi Dakake holds a B.A. from Cornell University (1990) and an M.A. (1998) and Ph.D. (2000) in Near Eastern Studies from Princeton University. She is currently Associate Professor of Religious Studies at George Mason University in Fairfax, Virginia, where she has recently been elected Chair of the Religious Studies Department (term to begin in Fall 2013), and is a founding member and director of the interdisciplinary Islamic Studies program. Her research interests and publications lie in the fields of Islamic intellectual history, with a particular interest in Shi'ite and Sufi traditions, Quran and commentary, and in women's religious experience. Her book, *The Charismatic Community: Shi'ite Identity in Early Islam*, was published by SUNY Press in 2008. She has just completed work on a collaborative project to produce the *Harper Collins Study Quran*, which includes verse-by-verse annotation and extensive commentary on the Quranic text, to be published in Spring 2014.

Peter Ochs is Edgar Bronfman Professor of Modern Judaic Studies at the University of Virginia. Co-founder of the Society for Textual Reasoning and the Society for Scriptural Reasoning. Among his book publications are *Another Reformation: Postliberal Christianity and the Jews* (2011); *The Free Church and Israel's Covenant* (2010); *Crisis, Call and Leadership in the Abrahamic Traditions,* (ed. with Stacy Johnson, 2009); *Peirce, Pragmatism, and the Logic of Scripture* (1998).

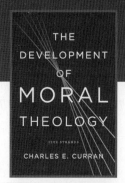

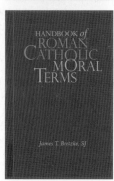